Leave The Gallows Hungry

First Fleet to Australia

GW00482343

Leave The Gallows Hungry

First Fleet to Australia

Stanley Wilson

LEAVE THE GALLOWS HUNGRY
First Fleet to Australia

First published in 2010 by JSW Books
7 Osgodby Close,
Scarborough,
North Yorkshire

A CIP catalogue record for this book is available
from the British Library

ISBN 978-1-4457-3735-5

Also by Stanley Wilson:

The Way of the Sea and Other Stories
JSW Books 1992
The Way of the Sea and Other Stories
Ulverscroft 1999

Cover picture:

From a watercolour possibly by George William Evans (1780-1852).

"An East View of part of Port Jackson from the West side of Sydney
Cove called Dawes's Point, New South Wales." [1809?]

INTRODUCTION

The first convict fleet to New South Wales, 'The First Fleet', sailed from Portsmouth on Sunday, 13th May 1787, and, after a voyage of 15,000 miles, dropped anchor in Sydney Cove on 26th January 1788.

LEAVE THE GALLOWS HUNGRY tells the story of the desperate injustices before the fleet's departure and the privations, the misery, the love affairs, the conflicts and the courage displayed during a terrible voyage and the early days of the convicts' new lives in a hostile country, thousands of miles from home.

Historical characters are featured extensively but the author's portrayal of their personality, actions and conversations is wholly imaginary. All other characters are entirely fictitious.

To Michael, Anne and Andy
whose help was invaluable

Chapter 1

Once more she smoothed the white basque jacket, once more straightened the fichu of Turkish belladine. Then, careful not to disturb auburn ringlets, she tied the ribbons of her bonnet.

In front of the mirror, Margaret Dunne turned this way and that.

"Splendid, Bridget," she murmured.

The maid, smiling in self-satisfaction, dropped a faint curtsey.

"Proud of you, Miss Margaret."

Margaret raised the hem of the emerald green skirt for brief inspection of her shoes then reached for a cape.

"Scarce need for capes this morning, Miss Margaret. But perhaps it completes the picture for your visitor."

Margaret frowned.

"Visitor?"

"Mr McQuaid."

Margaret stole a further glance at herself in the mirror.

"Oh, I'd forgotten. But it's father he'll want."

"He asked for you."

Margaret raised both hands, and fingers wide apart, shook them.

"No, no. I couldn't. Tell him you can't find me."

She glanced urgently out of the window. In the September sun the glittering waters of the Thames were seductive, beckoning.

"Tell him - tell him I must have been called away suddenly. Show him to the river-room with a bottle - two bottles - best Madeira. Father'll be here in a few minutes."

"Madeira at nine in the morning, Miss Margaret?"

"Do as I say. But first unlock me the door into Burr Street."

The irritating reminder about the visitor had brought a faint flush to Margaret's cheeks. Bridget eyed her appraisingly.

"Even lovelier than your mother was. - An extremely fortunate young gentleman waiting?"

* * * * *

His shoe buckles were of silver, his shirt fine cambric, the breeches soft doeskin. There was scarcely another apprentice anywhere in London garbed so splendidly as Jonathan Pettifer that morning in the year 1786.

He flicked an imaginary speck of dust from the high collar of his embroidered coat and, as he bent to smooth away the non-existent crease in the breeches, a shaft of sunlight seized upon a silver buckle, momentarily dazzling him. His smile was proud. He could not have the faintest inkling that, before long, base metal would usurp the silver.

With eager anticipation he peered through the latticed window of the house in Sea Coal Lane. In the welcome and warmth of September sun it seemed the whole of London was rejoicing with him.

Matthew Gross, Ludgate apothecary whose reputation straddled the seven seas, no longer would take him to task for failing to reduce coarse crystals to a fine pollen, no longer stand at his elbow to ensure nightly study of Nicholas Culpeper.

Today, Jonathan Pettifer was twenty. His apprenticeship to Gross had crept to its end with a reluctant "If you'd had parents, Pettifer, they might well have been pleased with you. That doesn't, of course, entitle you to be pleased with yourself."

But Matthew Gross's smile, a rare indulgence, expressed admiration enough.

Setting the wide-brimmed beaver hat at a jauntier angle, Jonathan stepped into the Sunday bustle of Sea Coal Lane. Close by the Tower Margaret could already be waiting.

"Apothecary!"

Jonathan was bowled back into the house by a mountain of a man who stumbled after him then lay sprawled at his feet. Hands thrust under the stranger's armpits, Jonathan dragged him, struggling and groaning, to a sofa in the back room.

"Mr Gross, can you come?"

Night-cap awry, nightgown crumpled, Matthew Gross padded barefoot down the stairs. Without so much as a word, he took the sick man's head in his hands and directed the sweating face towards the window. Peering into the man's eyes, he pressed his thumbs deep into the cold and moist palms.

"Hm," Gross murmured. He turned to Jonathan. "Diagnose."

Jonathan's eyes narrowed.

"The ague, sir?"

"Explain."

"Shivering, sweating, teeth chattering, eyes bloodshot. Wild as a mad bull then quiet as a mouse. The ague, yes, sir."

Gross nodded.

"Seafaring?" he said to the stranger.

"Forty years," the man growled, dragging his hands away from the apothecary.

"A slaver?"

"What's that to you?"

Gross's expression, hitherto vaguely benign, hardened.

"Patients answering well are treated well." He glanced towards Jonathan. "Slaver's affliction," he said quietly. "It's often more than black gold they snatch in the jungles of Africa."

The seaman groaned.

"The remedy? You know it?"

Gross nodded.

"Well enough. Possession's a different matter. Take yourself to Andrew Dean in St Catherine's Walk. He'll prepare a tincture of Peruvian bark."

Battling to raise himself from the sofa, the man flung out a hand to seek Gross's support but another attack of the shivers seized him and, like a sack of corn suddenly emptied, he collapsed on the floor.

Together Jonathan and Gross lifted the man back to the sofa.

"I - I couldn't...." the seaman gasped. Fumbling inside his jerkin he dragged out a leather bag. Golden guineas, glittering in a shaft of sunlight, cascaded to the floor. "T-take all you need - then more."

Gross's expression was flint-like.

"Slaver's gold. I'll touch none of it. Let him crawl on his belly every inch of the way to St. Catherine's," he said, turning towards the staircase.

Jonathan eyed the pile of guineas.

"I'll go to Mr Dean, sir," he said to his erstwhile mentor now already halfway up the stairs.

Gross paused, turned and shrugged.

"If you were still my apprentice I'd..."

The sick man groaned.

"I - beg you. Please..."

Jonathan scooped up a handful of guineas.

"Back in an hour, Mr Gross."

In spite of the heat of the sun and the discomfort of new shoes, Jonathan ran, without once pausing for breath, down Sea Coal Lane, up Ludgate Hill, past St. Paul's and on to Eastcheap. At length he came to Tower Hill.

Margaret was waiting. She too had been in frantic haste. Her cheeks were again flushed, this time, however for more welcome reason. Wisps of auburn hair struggled free of her bonnet. Shapely breasts, urged high by the tight bodice, urgently rose and fell as she struggled to recover breath.

"Freedom?" she whispered, when at length their lips parted.

"Tomorrow, strictly. But Matthew Gross never insisted on Sunday labours," Jonathan said, all thought for the seaman and his Peruvian bark suddenly gone.

Margaret smiled.

Then gaily, "Tomorrow for us then."

Jonathan seized both her hands and swiftly bent to kiss partially revealed breasts.

"Why not now?" he murmured without raising his head.

Margaret laughed.

"The whole of London looking on?"

It was barely ten o' clock but the morning sun had beguiled so many Londoners into forsaking their beds that there was scarcely space for one more stroller on Tower Hill that September morning.

"Then where tomorrow, my sweet?" There was a frantic urgency in his tone.

Margaret gasped over the intensity of his embrace, then the gasp soared to a piercing shriek.

Half a dozen pairs of hands had seized hold of Jonathan. A length of filthy rag, dragged across his open mouth, was knotted swiftly and with savagery at the back of his neck.

Other pairs of hands seized hold of Margaret. Kicking and screaming, she was dragged, helpless, over the grass of Tower Hill but not one of the Sunday morning strollers raised so much as a murmur in protest.

Jonathan, frantic, battling to free himself of the gag, plunged forward, pitching two of his captors into the midst of the gaping onlookers. He lunged with both elbows. There was a groan. The gag slackened. Then some heavy instrument thudded to his jaw and, blood seeping from his mouth, he collapsed.

Two men dressed in shabby military uniform seized him by the ankles and he was dragged, feet first, up Tower Hill.

Chapter 2

S tench of stale tobacco smoke and sour ale. Jonathan put a tentative hand to his jaw. The toe of a dirty black shoe slid under his neck to raise his head from the noisome earth floor.

"Up. Up pretty boy."

The shoe lifted Jonathan's head further inches.

"Tck, tck, not all that pretty. You was - once, though."

Jonathan at once seized an ankle and its owner, cursing, stumbled.

"Scum."

A well-aimed pewter tankard thudded against Jonathan's temple. He was dragged to his feet and pursued by a hail of fists he stumbled through a doorway in the direction of a man in naval officer's uniform seated at a table.

"Closer," the man rasped.

Jonathan, dazed, shuffled forward.

"Head down."

The flat of a cutlass across his ear and cheek sent him spinning into a corner. He was at once hauled to his feet and thrust back to the table.

"Injured one of my men," the naval man said. "You'll pay, by God's teeth, you'll pay."

Jonathan gazed dully at the man, shaking his head. The cutlass had slashed deep, an upper front tooth was missing, the cambric white shirt was drenched with blood.

"P-pay? Pay?" he muttered.

The naval officer jerked his head in the direction of a door.

"King's parlour. Next!"

The butt of a musket thudded to the base of Jonathan's skull and a voice spat in his ear, "Attention. Bow to the lieutenant."

Then he was hustled down stone steps towards a heavily studded door guarded by two sentries.

"One more guest for His Majesty," the ruffian who had propelled Jonathan down the steps said, dragging the palm of his hand across the young apothecary's cheek. "Bursting with good red blood, see?"

One of the sentries directed the muzzle of his musket at the doorway while his companion drove back the bolts and kicked the door open. A boot at Jonathan's backside sent him sprawling into a blackness of stale sweat and foul breath. Floundering over a confusion of arms and legs he was brought to an abrupt halt by a wall. He collapsed face-down on the muddy floor.

Long-nailed fingers at once seized him by the ankle and he drew back his leg to lunge at the unseen assailant. His heel struck home. There was a scream of agony but the shoe with its silver buckle had already gone. His thinly-stockinged foot touched the chill mud of the prison floor. He winced. Then oblivion came.

The thud of a musket butt jerked Jonathan back to consciousness. Struggling to his feet in the overcrowded cell, he gingerly put a hand to his mouth and traced the cutlass wound, a gash which extended from the corner of his mouth to his ear. Frantic to stem the flow of blood, he contrived to wedge the wound between forefinger and thumb, at the same clamping the inside flesh of his cheek with his teeth.

The faint glimmer of daylight from a crack in the brickwork of the opposite wall picked out a dwarf-like creature sitting knees hunched to chin. Jonathan stretched out a hand to touch a shoulder no thicker than two of his knuckles. His lips battled to shape "Why?" and he drew in a sharp breath as his wound opened again. "Why - all - this?"

"Hell-spawn Askew."

"Askew?"

"Lieutenant Askew. Press gang man. His Majesty's chief body snatcher."

For the briefest of moments Jonathan relaxed the clamp over his wound allowing it to gape wide, giving the hitherto dark, handsome features a leering, manic appearance. Blood seeping into his mouth brought on a paroxysm of coughing.

"B-body snatcher?"

Jonathan's new-found companion chuckled.

"No haunting graveyards, no dragging from the gallows. Askew gets paid for live bodies, not rotting corpses - except for the lobscouse he unearths when live bodies are scarce."

"Wh-what's that?"

"Meat from the cess-pits. The food his gracious Majesty grants to all gallant sailormen of the lower deck."

Jonathan's grasp on the puny shoulder tightened.

"How d'you know?"

The dwarf man wriggled to free himself of Jonathan's hold.

"Cease the bone-crushing and I'll tell you... Ah, that's better. Falling into the clutches of the press gang runs in the family."

"What family?"

"Stocksbridge of Deptford. We never learn." The man thrust out a hand, bony and tiny as his shoulder. "Daniel Stocksbridge."

"Jonathan Pettifer."

"Well, don't look so miserable, Jonathan Pettifer."

"But pressed men never see freedom again."

"Some do. I had a brother snatched and home in twelve months."

On haunches, back to the wall, Jonathan shifted position to face Stocksbridge.

"Go on."

"Aboard a man-o'-war at anchor off an island in the Indies. A bumboat load of blackamoor women clambered aboard selling rum and fruit. He changed clothes with one of them."

"And got ashore?"

"Not only ashore but home in nine weeks and paid for his trouble. A merchantman, short of crew, gave him three golden guineas to work his passage to Plymouth."

Jonathan sat back.

"Glad we met, Stocksbridge."

* * * * *

"Help! Please, please, help!"

Margaret Dunne's frantic cries went unanswered. She was dragged away, screaming and struggling, by one of the scores of ruffians who day and night infested Tower Hill in search of easy pickings, from solitary women or from pockets.

Elsewhere on the hill, agog at the sight of a naval search party in action, a jeering mob was swiftly gathering. Clacking tongues had it that seamen from the man-o'-war

Sirius, lying at Greenwich, had landed to capture a deserter, that tall dark stripling in fancy embroidered coat, doeskin breeches and silver-buckled shoes.

Since none of their own kind wore white cambric shirts and scarce any had ever managed to escape from a man-o'-war, it was wholly unjust that a mere youth could not only wriggle free of the King's clutches but even flaunt his success by a carefree stroll about Tower Hill, a bedizened wench on his arm.

"Ten thousand lashes."

"The flesh off his backbone."

"Let's see his eyes bulge. Swing him from the yardarm."

Then rumour's tongue had second thoughts. To the more knowing of the mob, suddenly it seemed less than likely that a naval party would row upriver all the way from Greenwich pursuing a single deserter when scores of replacement seamen idling on Greenwich waterfront were there for the snatching.

As the jeering men and women closed in on the spectacle of Jonathan's losing battle with his assailants, a man leapt from the crowd and yelled, "To your homes - fast."

"Out of the way!"

"Bloody fools. Naval party, my arse. Press gang!"

The mob stopped dead in its tracks. The ways of the navy's press gang were known only too well. Many who were in that Sunday morning crowd lived close by Tower Hill, in Crutched Fryers and Pepys Street and Coopers Row. There was scarce a woman among them who did not pine for a husband or a son or a lover condemned for the rest of his life, as a rule mercifully brief, to the stinking orlop deck of a British man-o'-war.

Cursing, they turned as one and swept up Tower Hill in the wake of Margaret and her captor.

Three times, by dint of frantic struggle, Margaret had managed to shake herself free of the ruffian's grasp and three times he had succeeded in grabbing her ankles and dragging her to the ground again. But, at her fourth attempt she scrambled into a deep clump of bushes and this time the man failed to follow.

Still thirsting for blood, the mob of Tower Hill had laid excited hands on him. Cheated out of the spectacle of a dandy getting his deserts, it required little to convince them that the man who had snatched Margaret was a member of the press gang and in the vicinity of the Tower a press man on his own was a rare and delectable sight.

Press gang men, it was rumoured, possessed hearts of stone, the blood in their veins coal black. There was no better time than this sunny Sunday morning to prove or disprove the rumours.

The quarry in their midst, already stripped naked, bleeding and shrieking as dozens of hands clawed in frantic effort to wreak some private vengeance, the men and women surged back down the Hill.

Margaret, panting and sobbing, lay in the bushes until the shrieking of the mob had died away, then she crept into the open. Her basque jacket was missing, her emerald green skirt hung in tatters, bonnet lost, and her bodice, ripped from yoke to waist, revealed breasts savaged and bleeding. Gasping and sobbing, she gathered the ragged clothes about her and, the hem of her skirt trailing in the mud, limped and stumbled to her home in St. Catherine's.

Jeremiah Dunne, ship's chandler, was checking sacks of rice and maize as his mud-bespattered, dishevelled daughter appeared at the entrance of his warehouse.

He glanced up and frowned.

"Away, woman, or I call the thief-taker."

"Father."

"Margaret. Good God."

An arm firmly around her waist, Dunne gently led his daughter up an open wooden staircase, through the office of his warehouse and into the living quarters beyond.

"I'll call Bridget."

"Please, father....."

"She'll prepare a bath and lay out a fresh gown. - We'll talk later."

"That could be too late. Listen, please."

Arms crossed tight about her, Margaret sank into a chair and, between sobs, recounted the events of that autumn morning on Tower Hill.

"Foolish, foolish." Dunne slowly shook his head. "Surely you knew. Tower Hill and its rich Sunday pickings for the press gang."

"Please, please, father, rescue Jonathan."

Dunne pursed his lips.

"Rescue? What, precisely could I do, King George so desperate for sailors?"

"You often send supplies to men-o'-war."

"Not often enough. And now just as the Navy Commissioners seem likely to improve my trade in rice I'd be crazy to interfere with their trade in recruits."

Margaret bounced from her chair.

"Jonathan's a human being, not a sack of rice. Father, please......."

Dunne steered his daughter back to her chair and he stood in front of her, arms akimbo, feet apart.

"I cannot - I will not - interfere and jeopardise trade."

Dunne was a solid, muscular man of middle height yet Margaret, leaping from her chair once more, sent him reeling, "Leave Jonathan to die?"

"Nonsense, child," Dunne said, attempting an arm round Margaret's shoulder. "He'll be back some day."

"Some day?" Margaret spurned the arm. "Pressed men never, never come back."

Dunne's smile was indulgent.

"There'll be many another waiting for you, even as you are now, like some ragamuffin from Wapping Way. Go bathe and change your gown. I'm expecting Turnbull McQuaid this afternoon. Play hostess with my best brandy."

Margaret's eyes widened.

"Mr McQuaid? Hasn't he lots of influence with the Admiralty?"

"If he hadn't, d'you imagine I'd suggest best brandy?"

"So you see some way of freeing Jonathan?"

"More likely a way to pay for more expensive gowns. Go get ready to greet Mr McQuaid."

Chapter 3

The rear entrance to Dunne's premises in St. Catherine's lay in Burr Street and was rarely used. After lengthy tussles with bolts and keys Margaret emerged, glancing swiftly to left and to right. Burr Street was deserted. Now bathed, perfumed and cosseted by her maid Bridget, fresh gown concealed beneath a hooded black cloak, Margaret hastened up Red Cross Street and along Butcher Row, her aim to visit every tavern in the vicinity of Tower Hill.

There was little doubt, however, that the first inn she came to, the Two Dutch Skippers, was the place she sought. At its entrance a pair of guards with muskets and cutlasses were lounging while, close by, were huddled small groups of women, whispering to each other and occasionally bursting into tears.

Margaret made her way between the huddles of women and, with a heavily bejewelled hand, flung back her hood to free a cascade of auburn hair.

"The lieutenant wishes to see me," she said to one of the guards.

The look in the soldier's eyes was lascivious.

"Why, doxy?"

Margaret spoke softly.

"Are you a man?"

The soldier's response was to drive a hand deep between her thighs. Margaret, gasping, winced and recoiled at the man's savagery.

"Then - then you'll know what the lieutenant wants."

"But if he doesn't?"

"There could be others."

The soldier poked his head inside the doorway of the tavern.

"Visitor for Lieutenant Askew."

A man in an apron, the innkeeper, heavy-eyed, swaying, stumbled into the sunshine.

"Lieutenant's busy," he mumbled.

"Not too busy for this," the guard said, roughly fondling Margaret's buttocks as he propelled her towards the arms of the drunken innkeeper.

Margaret swiftly sidestepped another lascivious hand and slipped past the man into the tavern.

In a room at the end of the inn's central passage, facing the open doorway was a man in naval officer's uniform. Lieutenant Askew lolled over a table, his head surrounded by an array of empty goblets.

"May I come in?"

Askew jerked up his head. A hand flopped on the table and a dozen goblets bounced to the floor. His eyes fought and failed to focus on his visitor.

"Indeed, indeed, yes, madam."

Askew surged up from his chair and, with tipsy gallantry, offered it to Margaret.

"Admiral....." she said, then, ignoring the proffered chair, she paused.

Askew's smile was inane but the flattery had by no means escaped him.

"Lieutenant. Only a lieutenant. Lieutenant Askew, madam."

The salute was clumsy, exaggerated.

"I - I seek a favour, lieutenant."

Askew grasped the table edge in a desperate effort to remain upright. His gaze staggered from fair-skinned features to roundness of bosom to line of thigh precisely outlined beneath the skirt. He licked his lips as he slid an arm around Margaret's waist.

"You're the one with all the favours, madam."

Margaret gasped. The hold on her waist was brutal.

"What favour could an elderly lieutenant possibly offer?"

Margaret removed one of her diamond rings.

"The release of a prisoner."

Mouth wide open, Askew kissed her. She cringed, she shuddered at the foulness of his breath.

With considerable effort Askew straightened up.

"And have me court-martialled?"

"Court-martialled? For simply opening and closing a cellar door?"

Margaret surreptitiously wiped her mouth with a perfumed handkerchief.

"'No keeping cellar to be opened except in the presence of an officer and two armed guards' - Admiral's orders," Askew intoned.

Margaret raised a hand and, even in the gloomy back room of the Two Dutch Skippers, the array of rings with their precious stones shone like beacons as she artfully bent her fingers.

"I've never met a guard who could resist diamonds and gold," she said softly.

Askew, swaying tipsily, eyes closed, shook his head.

"There was never a common soldier who wouldn't swear in court an officer had commanded him to ignore regulations."

Seizing Askew's podgy hand Margaret squeezed it. Her voice was almost inaudible.

"You have keys, lieutenant?"

Askew's free hand patted his substantial waist and nodded.

"Then when the tavern closes tonight we could unlock the cellar."

Askew's frown was tipsy.

"T-two men on guard all night. Two men."

"Who've been on guard all day?"

Askew hiccupped.

"Yes."

"So they could be very sleepy."

Margaret removed a second ring.

"Enough ale to keep two men drunk for twelve months."

Margaret would have released Askew's hand but his grip tightened.

"T-talk of bribery here is - is madness. But in my chamber" Askew pointed to the ceiling "we could be private."

Before Margaret was able to reply Askew dragged her to him. His mouth frantically sought hers, her ears, her neck and finally, like a leech ravenous for blood, the gap between her breasts.

She thrust a heavily bejewelled hand between her bosom and the slavering mouth. He recoiled, hand clamped over lips savaged by the diamonds.

"Vixen."

"Treat me like some Tower Hill whore. The privacy of your bedchamber, maybe, but not the stinking tap room of a common ale house."

Feeling for the table edge, Askew took an uncertain backward step.

He belched.

"Oh, I do beg your pardon."

Askew was a man in his late fifties, of less than average height, paunchy. His ill-fitting uniform bore the stains of years of roistering, the over-thick thighs threatened to burst the seams of his grimy breeches.

"Yes, yes, the bedchamber," he went on, the smile coarse, lustful.

His attempt to embrace Margaret was clumsy. He stumbled and, nimbly sidestepping, Margaret thrust him to a chair.

"Order brandy." she said, standing inches beyond Askew's reach.

Askew's reply was a further attempt to seize hold of her but once more she eluded him. Arms flailing, he lost balance and toppled from the chair. His head struck the edge of the table. The iron-grey wig slid to the floor, revealing a pale and bald scalp. Margaret, grimacing, hauled him back to his chair and with a lace handkerchief made half-hearted attempt to staunch the flow of blood from a gash on his forehead.

She caught sight of the table top, the circles left by countless brandy goblets, each, doubtless, marking celebration of yet another successful snatch on Tower Hill. Grimacing, she tossed aside the sodden handkerchief and eyed the blood now beginning to trickle down the lieutenant's cheek.

"Lieutenant."

Askew, eyes closed, grunted.

"Call the innkeeper, lieutenant."

Saliva creeping from a corner of Askew's mouth mingled with blood from the gash on his head.

"Wh- a - a - t ?"

"The innkeeper. Order brandy for your bedchamber."

Taking Askew's hands Margaret hauled him to his feet, thrust the wig over his bald head and steered him along the passage to the newel post at the foot of the staircase.

Her tone was peremptory.

"Order the brandy."

Askew frowned tipsily.

"Pascoe, Pascoe," he mouthed as he began to stumble up the stairs.

On the narrow landing Margaret eased her way past and opened a door. Askew blundered into the room, tripped and fell.

"On your feet, lieutenant. Don't let the innkeeper find you like this."

Pascoe crawled across the floor and scrambled to the bed where he collapsed on his back, legs dangling over the edge.

There was a gentle knock on the door. Seizing Askew's hands, Margaret dragged him upright and rammed the wig firmly on the bald pate.

"The innkeeper's there."

Askew stiffened. His tone was instantly sober.

"Enter."

Bearing a tray with two goblets and a brandy bottle Pascoe came into the room. He bowed with deference to Askew and placed the tray on the window sill. He winked obscenely in Margaret's direction, gave Askew a second bow and was about to leave when Margaret said,

"Lieutenant Askew orders you to serve the duty guards with a bottle of rum."

In spite of his tipsy condition Askew was vehement.

"No such thing."

"But lieutenant," Margaret said, "those wretched fellows at the door of the keeping cellar, there since daybreak and now all night."

Pascoe glanced uncertainly from one to the other.

"No, no," Askew roared.

Margaret turned to Pascoe.

"If the lieutenant can't afford rum then....."

"I'll pay for ale," Askew rasped.

"Ale?" Margaret's tone was patronising."Cold, cold ale in dank cellar passages. For chilled bones it has to be rum. Rum, Mr Tavernkeeper."

Margaret bundled Pascoe to the landing, thrust coins into his hand and motioned him down the stairs.

Back in the room she closed the door then kissed Askew lightly on the cheek.

"You make a fool of me, wench."

"A wise and generous fool, lieutenant."

Askew attempted to return the kiss but Margaret had already moved to the window where she began to pour brandy. Before she could hand the goblet to him he came upon her, one hand seeking her breasts, the other thrusting up her skirts, ruthless fingers plunging deep inside her.

The half-filled glass splintered against the wall and Margaret's scream of protest was stifled to a moan as Askew hurled her, face to the bed, wrenching and tearing skirt and underwear until she lay naked from the waist down.

"Oh, my God, no! Please."

Askew seized her by the ankles, flung her on to her back and struggled frantically to remove his bursting breeches.

"Please, please, no...."

Eyes wide and wild, Askew responded with an animal-like grunt and his yellowed tongue, pointed almost like that of a serpent, darted in and out over brown-stained teeth. Thick and powerful hands forced her knees apart. Eyes tight closed, teeth clenched, she turned her face into the bedding and raised her tightly clenched fists in hopeless attempt to avert the horror of forced penetration by the drunken Askew.

"Oh, God," she shrieked.

The cry was so loud that she failed to hear the grunt from Askew, a grunt that faded to a gasp then to a faint whimper. Brutal hands had ceased to savage her knees. Askew, silent, was suddenly still. With caution Margaret opened her eyes. Askew now on his feet, began to sway. No longer restrained by breeches that hung over his knees, his belly was expansive and pendulous. The swaying was short-lived. Margaret rolled aside in time to avoid being crushed by the press-gang officer's vast bulk. He slumped, face down on the bed. His frame jerked briefly then lay still.

At once, Margaret slid to the floor and straightened as best she could her ripped and disarrayed clothing.

Grimacing, she contrived to drag up Askew's breeches to conceal his naked buttocks. Then by tugging to and fro at the bedclothes she managed to turn him on his back, his breathing heavy, stertorous. When she wrenched the bunch of keys from the belt of his breeches his sole response was a faint grunt.

Margaret tiptoed across the room and, after a backward glance at the silent, motionless Askew, she inched the door ajar. No sound came from the darkened landing. She closed the door behind her and hurried down the stairs. There was a babel of voices, punctuated by outbursts of ribaldry, as she crept past closed doors and into the room where she had first met Askew, her objective the keeping cellar, temporary prison for Jonathan and the other pressed men.

The door on the far side creaked as she opened it. She stood and waited. Silence. She slipped through the doorway and, by the flickering light of a lantern hanging high on the wall, she glimpsed a stone stairway twisting down to pit-like darkness. Gathering her skirts about her, the stench of stagnant water heavy in her nostrils, she began to descend.

At the foot of the steps lay a passage where puddles reflected light from another lantern. At each side of a heavily studded door an armed sentry lolled, head back to the wall, eyes closed. At the sentries' feet lay a collection of empty bottles.

Margaret fingered Askew's keys, pondered for a moment, selected the largest of them and worked her way along the wall. Neither of the sentries stirred.

From the other side of the studded door came muffled voices and an occasional moan. Crouched low, she circled one of the soldiers and slid the key into the lock. Then a pair of hands seized her by the throat and she was dragged along the passage, up the stone steps and into a room where she was thrust into a chair. Pascoe, the innkeeper, holding high a lantern leered closely at her face. As she shrank from the ale-sodden breath he struck her across the cheek.

"No, no, no," she screamed.

Again Pascoe struck, more brutally this time.

"What d'you mean, 'No, no no'? I don't want your body, you filthy whore. The rings. Lucky for you it wasn't the sentries. They'd've had rings and thighs as well."

Margaret pressed her hands to her face.

"Let me go - please, please."

Pascoe wrenched away her hands from her face and tore off one ring but another he was unable to drag free. He rammed the lantern on the table and drew a knife from his belt.

"Take off or I chop off."

Margaret quivering, sobbing, removed the rest of her rings and thrust them all into the innkeeper's spatulate outstretched hand.

"Now, please let me go."

"Go?" Pascoe said, then, with more emphasis, "Go?"

"You've taken all my rings, I've got no money. What more....?"

"Wreck my trade and imagine a few paltry rings enough?"

"Wreck trade?"

"Not ale, not brandy. The official trade."

"I don't understand."

"You understand all right. For years my tavern the rondy for the press gang, then a strumpet like you wrecks its good name."

"I - I ruin the name of a common ale-house?"

"Overnight."

"I still can't understand."

"Tower Hill whore. Inflame Lieutenant Askew so he takes a fit. Then snatch his keys to free King George's new sailormen. And more. Grab the lieutenant's purse. The Lords of the Admiralty could well move future custom to the Riverside Mariner."

Margaret was almost incoherent.

"How dare..... ? I swear...."

"Time enough for swearing - in front of the magistrates."

Pascoe's tone was cold, venomous. "See." He thrust a hand under his filthy apron, drew out a leather purse and shook it upside down over the table. "The lieutenant's purse - empty."

"Oh, no, no...."

"Oh, yes, yes. I saw you and the lieutenant in his bedchamber, getting him drunk. Then I discover him there, unconscious and on his own."

"You know I didn't...."

The corpulent Pascoe, slow and tipsy, was in no way prepared for the swift attack. Margaret deftly overturned the table. Its edge struck the innkeeper in his substantial belly. He lost balance and before he could manage to stumble to his feet Margaret had escaped along the passage and out to the darkness of deserted Tower Hill.

Panting, sobbing, she paused for a moment. Beyond an occasional burst of ribald laughter and snatches of song escaping from the Two Dutch Skippers as a door opened and closed there was silence.

Chapter 4

Heavy bolts dragged back, door kicked wide open, the flickering light of a lantern revealed the press gang's harvest, men sprawled over the rough earth floor or leaning disconsolately against the slimy walls of the cellar.

"Keep clear, scum."

A figure filling the doorway momentarily blotted out the light from the lantern then it stumbled over the sprawl of bodies to land with a thud at Jonathan's feet.

The newcomer was a negro, in waisted cutaway coat, frogged, embroidered and gold-buttoned, white breeches, white stockings, buckled shoes. He lay motionless, groaning.

Jonathan dragged the man to a sitting position.

"Who are you?"

The negro continued to groan.

Jonathan seized the huge frame by its shoulders.

"Your name?"

"V-Vincent, sah. Master flog Vincent. Vincent get no eat."

"Unlikely."

"M-master. Chair. T-Tower Hill," the negro whispered.

Jonathan nudged Stocksbridge.

"What's he mean?"

"Master probably a wealthy city merchant out for an airing in his sedan. Left it for a few minutes' stroll and - well, one of his blackbirds snatched. Both blackbirds maybe. Where Joseph, Vincent?"

"Joseph, sah?"

"Your blackamoor friend."

"Hezekiah?"

"Yes. Where Hezekiah?"

Vincent's head inclined towards his shoulder and shook.

"Hezekiah kill."

"Press man? When the gang jumped on you?"

Vincent began to tremble.

"Y - yes, sah."

"Where Hezekiah now? I'd like to thank him."

Vincent's reply was to point a finger into his mouth.

Daniel shook his head and turned to Jonathan.

"Hezekiah'll be floating face down in the Thames," Daniel said. "Blackie showed you. They rammed a flintlock in the poor devil's mouth. Blew his brains out."

"Surely they.....?"

"Very, very illegal, resisting press gang. Better that way though than over the bulwarks, limbs blown off, later."

The giant negro suddenly burst into tears.

"Give him some hope, Stocksbridge."

Daniel Stocksbridge inched nearer.

"For simple souls like him, there ain't any. I've told you, the only release for the likes of him's overboard when the surgeon's too incompetent or too drunk to treat the wounds."

At once Vincent lurched to his feet. Jonathan followed suit. Jonathan was tall but the negro towered twelve inches above him.

"I go. My master."

He brushed Jonathan aside and stumbled towards the door.

Daniel bounced to his feet.

"Bide your time or you'll be black burgoo by morning."

But already the door had swung open and the butts of two muskets lunged at Vincent. He coughed, staggered and collapsed on the floor. Picking his way over prostrate bodies Jonathan seized the negro by his velvet collar and dragged him to the wall.

"Let me have a look at him," Daniel said.

"What good can you do?" Jonathan said.

"Three years assistant to a surgeon at Spitalfields."

Jonathan eyed Stocksbridge with suspicion.

"Which surgeon?"

"John Turnpenny."

Jonathan remained suspicious.

"The man who always swears by purple loosestrife for wounds?"

"Liar, am I? You could be speaking of David Deas." Daniel was smiling, confident. "Turnpenny made his name, remember, with asarum europoeum."

Jonathan's suspicions were not entirely allayed.

"For pleurisies?"

"Somewhat higher in the body."

"Go on," Jonathan said. "Go on."

"As a cephalic."

Jonathan burst into laughter and slapped Daniel on the back with a force that sent the little man sprawling.

"I believe you," he said, baring Vincent's chest for Daniel's inspection.

Daniel's delicate fingers pressed and probed and explored.

"Severe bruising, that's all. Rib cage like steel. He'll live." Daniel buttoned Vincent's shirt. "Now, what about your story, Pettifer?"

"Little to it, really. Apprenticed to a Ludgate apothecary."

"Matthew Gross?"

"You guessed?"

"Only one apothecary in Ludgate. Nobody attempts competition with Gross. Fortunate in your apprenticeship?"

"Very."

"You could be a liar, Pettifer."

Jonathan's hand pressed firmly to the wound on his cheek. Blood had begun to ooze afresh.

"Liar?"

"Prove what you say."

"How?"

"Back in Sea Coal Lane which of Gross's specifics would you turn to for that wound?"

"This time of year - late summer leaves of hare's ear."

"What would Gross call it?"

"Dupleurum rotundifolium."

Daniel Stocksbridge nodded his head.

"Not quite such a liar as I imagined, Pettifer. Nowhere near as big a liar as me. It was me the press gang snatched, not a brother. It was my escape in the Indies."

"Only to be snatched again?"

Stocksbridge gave a confident nod.

"I'll escape. You as well."

"How?"

Daniel tapped the side of his nose and beckoned Jonathan to come closer.

"When the press gang lieutenant says 'Occupation?'", Daniel whispered into Jonathan's ear, "tell him 'surgeon'. He'll demand papers. 'Lost', say. But he'll see you'll get a loblolly boy's job."

"Loblolly boy?"

"Fetch and carry for the ship's surgeon. Scrape maggots out of wounds. Saw off injured arms and legs. Stack the wounded in the orlop deck. Roll the badly wounded and dead overboard."

"I could never....."

"If it's survival, you do anything. Anything. The sick aboard a man-o'-war get garlic and rice and sugar. And the loblolly boys grab their share."

"Rob the sick?"

"And the dead. Never overboard with a corpse till the stench makes you want to vomit. Meantime collect corpse's rations."

Vincent, hitherto quiet, stirred and groaned.

"Master waiting."

Daniel leaned forward to lay a gentle hand on the negro's shoulder. The crack high in the opposite wall admitted now only the faintest glimmer of light.

"Sleep, blackamoor. Tomorrow a lot less comfortable than today. Keep up your strength."

At the first suggestion of daylight from the crack in the wall the cellar door moved grudging inches and a musket barrel thrust through the opening.

"Up, up."

Cursing, groaning, coughing, the prisoners struggled to their feet.

"Hand on heads, face the wall. Now, sideways, slowly to the door. One at a time."

Daniel Stocksbridge was first to leap through the doorway into the passage. The butt of a musket propelled him up stone steps and into a room where, flanked by guards, Lieutenant Askew sat at a table.

"Name?

"Daniel Stocksbridge, sir."

"Age?"

"Twenty three, sir."

"Occupation?"

"Surgeon, sir."

"Indentures?"

"Stolen, sir."

Face devoid of expression, Askew gave a minimal jerk of his head and Daniel was frog-marched to the kitchen of the tavern where his wrists were roped behind his back and his ankles fettered.

"Turn to the wall. Squat," a guard barked.

Vincent similarly roped and fettered was hurled to the floor alongside Daniel.

"On your feet."

The guard thrust a rope through the bonded wrists of each prisoner. One end of it he looped over a hook in the wall and the other he swung so that it cracked like a whip.

"Beads in the devil's necklace," he said as he repeatedly lashed the legs of each pressed man. "First navy lesson. Learn to dance. Learn the horn-pipe, whore-spawn."

By mid-morning, the necklace of twenty-five men was complete, Jonathan, bound and ironed like the rest, the final bead.

The keeping cellar, stinking and empty, was ready for the next cull of Tower Hill.

Paler even than usual, Lieutenant Askew, swaying tipsily, appeared in the doorway of the tavern kitchen. He flung a brief glance at the captives, strung along three walls and he barked, "Move."

Muskets goaded the prisoners out of the tavern and shuffling, stumbling, they were driven down a cobbled path of Tower Hill to the Thames.

Jonathan, last man on the chain, tripped and fell.

Through the crowd gathered to battle for a glimpse of the captives Margaret had wormed her breathless, desperate way.

"Jonathan."

As those ahead on the rope trudged on, hauling Jonathan behind them, she flung herself at him to plant a kiss on the wounded cheek.

"Wait, oh, wait for me, my darling," he whispered hoarsely as he was dragged, crawling and staggering in turn, along the path.

"I'll wait and wait and wait, I promise, my love."

A guard spat in Margaret's face.

"Ay, wait for him. He'll be back - in a shark's belly," he rasped seizing her by the hair and hurling her aside.

But, in an instant, Margaret had jabbed sharply manicured fingernails into his eyes then just as swiftly disappeared into the depths of the crowd on Tower Hill.

Chapter 5

Harried by musket butt and flat of cutlass, the pressed men clambered from press tender to receiving ship where, wrists still tied behind them, they were forced to run the gauntlet of the ship's company armed with knotted ropes.

Jonathan stumbled once and fell, his mouth temptingly close to a sailor's ankle. He bit deep, severing the man's Achilles tendon and, clear above the howls of the pressed men as the nettles laced with wire struck home, he heard his victim's screech of agony. In spite of the hail of blows he struggled to his feet and burst into laughter. One tormentor at least would never again be capable of standing up to wield a taunter's weapon.

Daniel's gentle hand traced lightly over Jonathan's shoulders as they sat together in the gaol below decks.

"Badly hurt?"

Jonathan shrugged yet, at the same time, winced. Even Daniel's sensitive palm created fresh agony.

"Should've warned you," Daniel went on. "One of the few pleasures granted a man-o'-war's company, nettling the pressed men."

"Banning water another pleasure?" Jonathan said.

At once Daniel put a finger to his lips.

"Pressed men never ask for water."

Barely had Daniel uttered his words when a reedy, cracked voice called, "Water, water."

"Who wants water?"

Every one of the prisoners looked up to the seaman standing on the wooden grating overhead.

"Me, me."

"All of us."

"Share this, then," the seaman bellowed and he tipped a barrel of water through the grating, drenching all who waited anxiously below.

Their backs close to the bulwark, Jonathan and Daniel escaped much of the deluge but Jonathan's face was splashed.

"Salt - salt water," he said, licking his lips.

Daniel's laugh was swift, mirthless.

"With added flavours." Daniel's tongue gingerly tasted his own lips. "London Town's necessary houses."

Immediate horror spread over Jonathan's face.

"Necessary houses?"

"My very words."

"Feeding us on the plague."

"Apothecary, you know a little too much."

"But surely...."

"Discipline first, health second. If pressed men survive London sewage they survive the filth of the orlop deck. And if they don't - plenty more pickings on Tower Hill."

The seaman re-appeared at the grating.

"Tide's on the ebb, shipmates. Another barrel before it all runs out to sea?"

The man did not wait for a reply and those who were slow to skip aside suffered a further drenching in the foul water from the river Thames.

* * * * *

The door in Burr Street was still unbolted when Margaret returned home. She crept unnoticed to her room and found Bridget there.

"Mistress Margaret, the master's been seeking you everywhere."

"Help me out of these and burn them," Margaret said, dragging off her filthy tattered clothes.

"But the taffeta...."

"Burn it, burn it," Margaret screamed." Get me hot water - and every drop of perfume you can lay hands on."

An hour later, bathed and perfumed and freshly gowned, paler than usual but all signs of her ordeal on Tower Hill well concealed, Margaret walked sedately into the drawing room where her father sat in earnest conversation with a visitor, Turnbull McQuaid.

McQuaid leapt to his feet and bowed.

Turnbull McQuaid was in his early forties, six feet tall with a hint of floridness in his otherwise fair complexion suggesting a luxurious way of life, more than amply borne out by the excellence of his silk shirt, the fit of his tunic and pink satin breeches. His long artistic fingers carried with ease a profusion of diamond rings, the buckles of his shoes were substantial and of gold.

"My daughter, Margaret," Dunne said with pride.

Margaret dropped a faint curtsey to the visitor.

The latter bowed a second time and took Margaret's proffered hand.

"Apologies for not greeting you yesterday, Mr McQuaid."

"A pleasure enhanced by the waiting."

"From now on we'll be seeing Mr McQuaid quite often," Dunne said. "Exploring certain projects together."

Margaret looked to McQuaid. She made no effort to conceal the anxiety of her tone.

"Could - could it be with the Lords of the Admiralty?"

McQuaid nodded.

"And others just as important."

"Not before time," Dunne said. "Mr McQuaid's business has suffered badly from government policy."

Margaret glanced at McQuaid's heavily-bejewelled fingers, at the diamond and sapphire fob hanging from his waist.

"Badly?" she said.

McQuaid frowned.

"Extremely badly, Mistress Dunne."

"Now that we are on the brink of - er - partnership, Turnbull, you must start calling her 'Margaret'."

"I and my father before me," McQuaid said, ignoring Dunne, "enjoyed a steady trade victualling convict transports to America. Then what? The colonial rabble seized independence - and wanted no more convicts."

"Nor did we," Dunne said.

"Nor do we," McQuaid said. "So the government's launched fresh plans for emptying Newgate and the other gaols...."

"Leaving the gallows hungry," Dunne said.

"...by sending our worst felons to establish a colony at Botany Bay," McQuaid continued.

"Botany Bay, Mr McQuaid?"

"Far side of the globe. With your father's help I supply the victuals."

Margaret glanced from one to the other. There was solid self-satisfaction evident on both faces.

"Profit from the miseries of other people, father?"

Dunne sneered.

"People? Ruffians, horse-thieves, pickpockets, whores, pimps. Each and every one of 'em gallows-meat. Now they're going to get a chance to work for King George and themselves. A benevolent government presents them with free food and passage to a land of milk and honey. Profit from others' misery? Doesn't the butcher profit from hungers, the apothecary from stomach gripes and fevers? Mr McQuaid and I are performing almost an act of charity. The occasion calls for best madeira. Entertain Mr McQuaid until his carriage arrives."

Dunne shook McQuaid's hand then went on, "I look forward to the Victualling Commissioners' contract," he said with a wink. "Forgive me if I leave you now. An East Indiaman at Cold Harbour grows restive for its salt pork."

Chapter 6

"Stocksbridge, we've got to get out of this," Jonathan said.

"Cannons have ears. Carry on talking like that and you'll get us blown to kingdom come."

Jonathan, leaning against the bulwark, dropped to his haunches.

"What hope?" he whispered.

"Next few days, a little. Then, for a month, practically none. Give me your shoe."

Jonathan kicked off his remaining shoe. Daniel, wrists roped tight behind him, eased forward to retrieve it. In spite of the watchful eye of the gunner manning the culverin, he shuffled to an iron ring embedded in the planking. It was the work of a moment to wedge the shoe buckle between timber and ring then wrench it free of the leather.

His back now to the iron ring, Daniel Stocksbridge began to rock slowly to and fro, rubbing the buckle against the iron to give the former a sharp edge. His actions continued to be unnoticed by the guard and, as he went on preparing the makeshift knife, the culverin was dragged away and the overhead wooden grating rammed into place.

Smiling, triumphant, Daniel wriggled his way to Jonathan.

"Back to back," he hissed. "If my knife slips, not so much as a murmur or we'll get trampled to death in the scuffle for it. When your wrists are free, pretend they're still tied, then take the buckle and cut my ropes."

Soon, Daniel and Jonathan were sitting, backs to the bulwark, freed hands firmly behind them. Jonathan raised a hand to his wounded cheek. The bleeding had ceased and, when his fingers explored the savage gash, he was no longer inclined to flinch.

"If you could find a needle and thread I'd invite you to stitch my face, surgeon," he said, nudging Daniel.

A pair of dark-skinned hands, roped at the wrist, jabbed Jonathan's ribs. The voice was hoarse.

"Knife."

Jonathan turned. Vincent now bore not the faintest resemblance to the periwigged flunkey of the previous day. His tunic and shirt hung in tatters, his wig had gone, revealing a closely-shaven scalp, his legs had lost the white stockings and both buckled shoes were missing.

"You've been keeping very quiet," Daniel said. "Did they flog you?"

Vincent grunted and twisted round to reveal his naked back. The flesh resembled raw liver.

"I'll free your wrists," Daniel said. "Till I give the word, keep your hands behind you. We could soon be needing those splendid biceps of yours."

Vincent was scarcely free of his bonds when the hatch grating was dragged aside and a ladder lowered into the midst of the pressed men. Outlined black against the evening sky, a master-at-arms stood on the hatch coaming.

"Twenty of you,- up, up, up."

Fewer than a dozen men rose to their feet.

"Twenty, twenty."

More men, including Jonathan, Daniel and Vincent rose and shuffled towards the ladder. To Jonathan ahead and Vincent closely following, Daniel hissed, "Hands behind your back, grip the rope with your fingers."

Feeble from lack of food and water, stiff after so long in the cramped prison deck, most of the men found it impossible to mount the vertical ladder, wrists pinioned behind them.

The first to attempt the ascent got no farther than the fourth rung before toppling backwards. The man following fared no better.

Daniel elbowed Jonathan.

"Shoulders forward - and bring your feet together before taking the next rung."

He repeated the instructions to Vincent.

"Kill us?" the negro said.

"Not for a long, long time. Maybe now chance to get back to your master's sedan."

Alongside the master-at-arms on deck, the boatswain's mate was standing, lantern in one hand, cat-o'-nine-tails in the other.

"Next man to miss his footing wins a kiss from the King's cat."

Halfway up the ladder, Jonathan not only discovered the advantage of placing the ball of his foot instead of the instep on a rung but also, in spite of renewed agony from his wounded cheek, of pressing his chin on each rung as he climbed. As he eased his body over the hatch coaming the cat-o'-nine-tails flicked across his shoulders.

The master-at-arms sneered.

"A kiss, that's all. Gentle warning to the rest of the whore-spawn down there."

Bundled overside into a smaller craft, Jonathan, Daniel, Vincent and the rest were thrust below into a darkness so oppressive that it seemed a substance on its own. Everywhere the stench of stagnant water and urine and vomit assailed their nostrils.

Jonathan let out a gasp as teeth like needles bit deep into his bare foot. He thrust out a hand. The fur was smooth and warm to the touch. Again he gasped.

"Rats."

Another, and vaster, hand at once closed over Jonathan's. The squirming captive beneath squealed briefly. The enveloping hand relaxed and the creature, large as a cat, dropped limp to the decking.

Vincent gurgled with pleasure.

"Next time - man," he said.

Daniel's hand went exploring the darkness in search of the negro.

"Ever killed a man, blackamoor?"

"Three, sah."

"For baiting you?"

"For stealing Vincent's woman."

"How d'you kill?"

Vincent seized Daniel's hand. At once the little man was writhing, helpless, under the vice-like grip of no more than a forefinger and a thumb.

"Fingers, sah. Just fingers."

"Like the biceps, keep 'em in good trim, blackie," Daniel said, rubbing his hand. "We'll be needing 'em very soon."

* * * * *

"A splendid madeira."

McQuaid's eyes narrowed as they struggled to bring Margaret back into focus.

She had drunk sparingly, he excessively. There were two empty madeira bottles on the table and a third had now been broached.

McQuaid drained his goblet and slid it across the refectory table towards Margaret.

"You - you make a pleasing hostess."

"Thank you, Mr McQuaid."

She leaned over the table, close enough to her guest to detect the maze of tiny red veins in his cheeks, the odour of pomade on his wig and the madeira vapours heavy on his breath.

"You've friends in the Navy Board and the Admiralty?"

The pair's faces were almost touching and although McQuaid sought no further intimacy any earlier remoteness had now dissipated.

"I have, yes."

McQuaid's tongue pronounced the simple words with some difficulty.

Margaret replenished his already half-empty goblet.

"Would you help me, Mr McQuaid?"

Turnbull McQuaid's forehead set in a frown. In spite of the wine his tone was guarded.

"Help?"

"A young man snatched by the press gang. I - I want him free."

"What young man?"

Impulsively Margaret seized the hand as it relinquished the goblet.

"Please."

McQuaid, lips tight, shook his head.

"The Admiralty rarely, if ever, relents. But tell me about him."

"Dragged away on Sunday morning."

"His name?"

"Jonathan Pettifer."

"Describe him."

"An apothecary with - with a brilliant future."

"Describe, I said!"

"Dark hair, swarthy complexion, somewhat taller than you."

"Strong?"

"Immensely."

"Powerful shoulders, narrow hips, long muscular legs?"

"Well, yes."

Margaret got to her feet and stared at McQuaid, puzzled.

"You - you ask the sort of questions a woman might ask about a man."

Swaying uncertainly, McQuaid also got to his feet.

"I - I may be of some - some help." The voice was thick. He folded his arms and took a deep breath. "Much depends on your answer."

"Anything, Mr McQuaid. Anything."

"Marry me."

"Marry?"

"That's what I said."

Margaret shrank away.

"I - I couldn't."

Although McQuaid's look was thunderous his words were calm and measured.

"Then no help for your Pettifer."

"But I couldn't marry you. I'm in love with Jonathan."

McQuaid grasped the table edge.

"Who mentioned 'love'?" he said scathingly. "I'm seeking a business union."

"A stake in father's chandlery?"

"Partly my plan."

McQuaid seemed to be at once sober. He eyed Margaret carefully, slowly up and down.

"A woman handsome enough," he said, nodding his head. "And a handsome woman's a great help to wider circles."

"The sole reason for wanting to marry me?"

"I - have - no - need - of - women. But I implore you...."

Margaret stared in mounting disbelief at the handsome features.

"Implore me? I don't understand....."

McQuaid's face was impassive.

"Business, purely business. You could have your Pettifer. With discretion a dozen Pettifers for all I cared."

"You - you beg me to marry you, yet in the same breath happily pass me over to another man?"

McQuaid thumped the table with a ferocity that made his crystal goblet bounce then shatter.

"Ever since my youth I've been an outcast, a leper, battling to keep the secret." He jabbed a bejewelled finger at his forehead. "The taunts, the jibes of my schooldays go on torturing. "

Margaret eyed him with a mixture of puzzlement and fear.

"Your secret, what?"

"I'm different. You desire Pettifer as a lover. I, too, might well desire him."

Margaret's eyes opened wide.

"Oh, my God!"

McQuaid seized both her hands.

"Understand?"

Margaret struggled free of his grasp.

"Have - have you ever proposed marriage to any other woman?"

"Once."

"And the answer?"

McQuaid, suddenly looking much older than his years and considerably less debonair, shrugged.

"My reply's the same, Mr McQuaid. Never that sort of bargain. Never."

And as Margaret fled from the room she collided with her father.

Chapter 7

At first light the hatch cover was dragged aside and the foot of a ladder thudded to the prison deck.

"Exercise!" the master-at-arms bellowed.

Desperate for respite from the gut-wrenching stench of tightly packed human bodies and vomit, every one of the pressed men kicked and clawed in an effort to reach the ladder first.

Vincent, the negro, hurling his fellow prisoners to left and right, was the first there and he kept all contenders at bay to clear a passage for Jonathan and Daniel.

"Our chance, maybe," Daniel murmured as he began to clamber up the ladder, followed closely by Jonathan, Vincent and the rest of the prisoners.

"March! Single file - two paces apart - larboard to starboard to larboard. And mouths shut," the master-at-arms rasped when the pressed men had assembled on deck. He pointed towards the boatswain's mate standing by, swinging his cat-o'-nine-tails. "The cat's still screaming for a taste of good red blood."

The captives, hungry and thirsty, heads bowed, wrists still roped behind their backs, shuffled from gunwale to gunwale and back to gunwale on the holystoned deck of the receiving ship.

Daniel glanced covertly to left and to right. Two sentries with muskets guarded the ventilating scuttle of the prison deck, two guarded the forecastle, two guarded the poop and one stood at the door of the great cabin.

The boatswain's mate, alone now that the master-at-arms had gone below, to keep the pressed men on the move lightly flicked his cat-o'-nine tails at ankles as the men continued their forced march.

In spite of tightly bound strips torn from Jonathan's shirt, the blood continued to seep from Vincent's back, savaged the previous day by the seamen's nettles. The massive negro, head down, wrists pressed together as if still bound, trudged stolidly in line across the deck.

Throughout the enforced exercise there was always at least one captive momentarily concealed from the eyes of the boatswain's mate by the thick main mast.

"Kill?" Daniel whispered urgently to the back of the negro's head when the mast provided its brief cover.

Vincent nodded.

"Swim?" Daniel said at the next opportunity.

Again Vincent nodded.

And next time, "Inside great cabin. Hostage. Understand?"

Vincent shrugged and shook his head but it was not until they were hidden again that Daniel had opportunity to elaborate.

"Capture. But no garrotting - yet."

During the course of a score of circuits, Daniel was able to convey the complete escape plan to Vincent and Jonathan, directly following. The latter had already passed on the sharpened shoe buckle so that all the captives were able secretly to slash their bonds.

Suddenly, "Man overboard," Daniel yelled.

The sentries followed Daniel in his rush to larboard. One of them, however, remained on guard outside the great cabin but before the man had chance to raise his musket he was bowled over by the massive Vincent who, laying hold of him as a battering ram, burst into the cabin and floored the receiving-ship's commander, breakfasting there alone.

Pitching the unconscious sentry under the table, Vincent seized the man's cutlass and, ramming it, flat side, across the throat of the astonished commander, he drove his captive to the main deck. The poop was deserted. Those who had been guarding it were held captive by Jonathan, a musket at their heads.

Thuds and screams and outburst of raucous laughter surged through the open hatch of the press deck. Captured musket at the ready, Daniel knelt to peer into the gloom. A guard, musket muzzle rammed into his ear by one of the pressed men, was flogging the boatswain's mate with his own cat-o'-nine-tails.

Daniel jerked a thumb to starboard.

"Now."

Followed by Jonathan and two other pressed men, Daniel plunged overside, swam underwater, surfaced below the overhang of the poop deck and seized hold of the rudder.

Vincent, the ship's commander firmly wedged under his arm, broke water and hoisted his sodden, spluttering captive over the top of the rudder.

"Master commander not struggle," Vincent said, tugging playfully at the rope encircling the naval officer's neck.

"Not struggle or he have wet garrotting."

"You'll - you'll be shot...."

Daniel spat river water into the commander's wide open mouth.

"We'll swim together so close, my friend, that when musket bullets start flying we go to the bottom together."

"A flogging round the fleet, keel-hauled then hanging."

Daniel tugged on the neck rope.

"Before we all go to the bottom, or after, sir?" Daniel turned to the fugitives. "Now a swim of two hundred yards."

He pointed south to the river bank. "A cottage, see? A path to its left down-river. Strike out westwards. The tide'll take us. Anchors away."

Grasping the commander's rope, Vincent grabbed the man's feet and dragged him from his perch on the rudder. Then, the captive firmly wedged under one arm, he plunged off in pursuit of the others.

Daniel glanced over his shoulder as he swam.

"Close, close. So musket bullets can't tell the difference, pressed naval commanders and press-ganged men."

Not even a single musket volley, however, pursued the escapers with their hostage and there was no sign of any boat following by the time they reached and scrambled up the muddy river bank.

The cottage, possibly once the abode of a waterman but long since abandoned to the mud and the flotsam of Thames tides, offered a welcome respite and roof to the fugitives.

Groaning, retching and vomiting from a surfeit of river water, the naval commander sat hunched in a corner.

"Set him free?" Jonathan said to Daniel.

Stripped naked and shivering, Daniel was squeezing water from his clothes.

"Leave him or…" He gave a savage twist to his sodden shirt. "But nothing hasty."

The two other escapers, overhearing, leapt to their feet and made for the commander. Vincent hurled them both aside.

"Mine," he said, seizing the rope still knotted around the naval man's neck and drawing himself up to tower over the others. "Vincent master now."

Daniel, with a strength wholly belying his diminutive frame, grabbed Vincent's ankle and the huge negro, overbalancing, crashed to the earth floor.

"No killings till I give the word. And I'm giving none. Rope the sea-rat's wrists and let him go on spewing up in peace. Time we were off."

By mid-morning the sun had almost dried the clothes of the fugitives but they were now weak from lack of food and the struggle against the seemingly endless marshes.

Earlier the two other escapers had decided to strike out to the east. Jonathan, Daniel and Vincent, intent upon putting as great a distance as possible between themselves and the river Thames trudged southwards. It was early afternoon when they came to Woolwich Common and there, on a rise beside a clump of bushes, they slumped gratefully to the warm and dry grass.

Jonathan put an exploratory hand to his injured cheek. The rawness of the wound, in spite of the lack of skilled attention, was almost gone. He smiled, then immediately winced as muscles dragged at healing flesh.

Daniel had been watching closely.

"Smiles and at last something to smile about."

Jonathan nodded and glanced in the direction of the river.

"Why no search party, I wonder?"

"Got as far as the commander and decided to consign us to hell and the mud," Daniel said, outstretched on his back, hands behind his head. "Tower Hill's always ready with fresh pickings. Maybe an arrangement with the receiving ship."

"Arrangement?"

"Askew and the ship's commander. Let escapers go and fill the gaps next Sunday morning. The gallant lieutenant gets a fee for every pressed man - then a share-out with the commander."

"Unlikely to search for us then."

"Very unlikely. Where's Vincent?"

Daniel scrambled to his feet and was greeted by a loud snore coming from deep inside the bushes.

"Vincent."

The negro emerged, yawning and stretching.

"Now, listen, both of you, "Daniel went on, "we're naval deserters now. Your reward two hundred and fifty lashes. Not the gentle lashes of a rich master, Vincent. Few men survive one hundred from the cat. So we all have new past lives."

"New lives?" Vincent said.

"You, blackamoor, came ashore from your ship at Wapping. You got drunk, your drinking companions stole your purse and by the time you got back to Wapping your ship had sailed."

Daniel turned to Jonathan.

"You hail from Deptford. Your parents are dead. Your father was a tanner and you were apprenticed to him. But did you go on tanning? Not likely. The raw hide of cows causes smallpox, they say, so when your mother and father died from it a fortnight ago you fled from Deptford."

"What about you?" Jonathan said.

Daniel closed one eye for a moment's contemplation.

"A dealer in teeth."

"What?"

"From our soldiers killed in the colonies. Shipped back by the barrel-load to Limehouse Dock."

"Out of dead soldiers' mouths?"

"The dead no longer eat, Pettifer."

"Who buys the teeth?"

"The quality of London's best drawing-rooms."

"A trade picked up from your father, I suppose?"

"Couldn't follow father's calling. He was a pardons vendor. Quarrelled with his priestly contact and committed suicide."

"Look," Jonathan said.

In the distance on the road skirting the rise where they had been resting a coach was heading west.

Quickly Jonathan bound his shoeless foot again in strips of doeskin ripped from the waist of his breeches. Tripping and stumbling, he made for the bottom of the hill.

Arms frantically waving, he took up a stance in the middle of the road.

"Stop, stop!"

Chapter 8

Jeremiah Dunne seized Margaret by the arm as she attempted to squeeze past on the narrow landing.

"What exactly was this bargain you could never, never strike with Turnbull McQuaid? Don't you dare upset him."

Dunne's words were loud enough to be audible in the sittingroom,

Margaret struggled to free herself.

"I - I can't explain… Let me go! I feel …. "

Before Margaret could continue, McQuaid appeared in the doorway, swaying, one hand seeking the jamb for support.

"By no means upsetting me. By no means. Charming, charming hostess, Dunne."

He belched and swiftly put a hand to his mouth.

"I - I do beg your pardon. I - I think, indeed, I feel sure we can - can come to some arrangement. In due course… In due course."

"Never, never."

Margaret, now free of her father's grasp, fled along the landing to her bedroom. Hurling herself inside she locked the door.

Jeremiah's expression was thunderous.

"A good brandy is called for, Turnbull," he said, steering McQuaid to a chair in the sittingroom.

From the bottom shelf of a cupboard he dragged out a jeroboam and, taking McQuaid's goblet, he filled it to the brim. McQuaid, steady now that he was comfortably seated, savoured the liquor.

"A trifle fiery," he said, brows in knitted, exaggerated concentration. "But a future of some interest."

"Rather like my daughter, hm?"

"Precisely, precisely."

McQuaid, downing the contents of his goblet in a single gulp, thrust the glass across the table to be filled a second time.

"The best that ever by-passed the revenue men's gauging rods," Dunne said, winking. "Forgive the suggestion, Turnbull, but your palate, after the madeira, could be somewhat - shall we say - jaded. Why didn't you first sip then discard?"

Dunne filled his mouth with the spirit, rolled it briefly around his tongue then spat into the fireplace. Blue flames leapt from the burning coals.

"I owe Margaret an apology," McQuaid said, voice thick, words halting and slurred.

"Surely it's Margaret who ought to apologise."

"My - my request was premature."

"Request?"

"Premature, premature."

"What request, Turnbull?"

McQuaid once more tendered his empty goblet.

"She - she refused, Dunne. Refused."

A sob escaped McQuaid's sagging mouth as he slumped face down on the table. Dunne carried and dragged his unconscious guest to a sofa and covered him with a sheepskin rug.

"Sleep you well, partner," he said softly and he hurried to Margaret's bedroom. The door was locked. The side of his clenched fist thudded the wood.

"Margaret."

There was no response.

"Open at once."

The lock clicked. The door moved grudging inches. He kicked it wide open and strode into the room.

"Explain."

Dunne was standing, his feet apart, in front of the fireplace.

Margaret had already retreated to sit on the edge of her bed.

"He asked me to marry him," she said wearily.

"And....?"

"I refused."

"Realise what that means?"

"To me?"

"To me as well."

"Selling me as part of a business deal, father?"

"I can think of more sensible ways of describing it. There's been many a worse marriage arrangement."

"I can't stand the sight of Turnbull McQuaid. It's not simply disliking the man, I detest him. He revolts me."

"But can't you understand? No husbandly demands. Become his hostess, provide an air of respectability. And, the rest of the time, follow your own inclinations."

"If I marry, I'll marry for love. I'll want children. I fancy no life bribing shipowners and navy people to buy Mr McQuaid's salt pork and rum and sugar and sail canvas. Can - you - not - understand?"

Jeremiah Dunne stepped to the window that overlooked St Catherine's with its view of a barquentine loading cargo at Crow's Nest Wharf and, on the other side of the Thames, a brig discharging at St Saviour's Dock.

Dunne was deeply thoughtful.

"With McQuaid I'd have a monopoly over this stretch of the river. A complete monopoly." He turned to Margaret. His voice was soft. "I'd never, never attempt to force you into the marriage - or should we term it a 'partnership'? - but I beg you to give the idea more thought."

"More thought? But I've already......"

"Since your mother died I've struggled to give you every luxury within, and sometimes beyond, my means. This has become your way of life. With McQuaid you'd fare even better." Dunne paused. "But marry your struggling and penniless apothecary and you'd find selling pills and potions would do little more than keep you in rags!"

"I - I don't care....."

"At the moment maybe not. But I suggest you start thinking. A very long time before pressed men get ashore - if ever."

McQuaid, snoring and in a stupor, was still lying on the sofa when Jeremiah Dunne returned to the sittingroom. He crossed to the table, filled a goblet with brandy and held it close to his visitor's nostrils.

"Turnbull," he whispered urgently into McQuaid's ear.

Mouth slack and half open, McQuaid continued to snore.

The voice was loud this time.

"Turnbull."

The snoring ceased. There was a grunt from the back of McQuaid's throat. The snoring resumed.

Brandy jeroboam under his arm, Dunne left the room and closed the door behind him. He hastened along the landing, through the chandlery office, down the staircase and into the warehouse stacked, roof-high, with sacks of rice and maize.

The tall double doors of the warehouse were closed. Dunne shook them to ensure that the locking bar was securely in place. Then he walked the stack, counting as he went the sacks in the base row. At the seventeenth sack he halted and, with remarkably little effort, he dragged away the sack from the third row immediately above, followed by the sack in the second row.

Carrying a lantern and the jeroboam Dunne wormed his way through the opening he had created into a short passage that led to a cavern, walls of sacks of rice and maize, its contents hundreds of ankers of brandy. With a valinche he drew off sufficient spirit from the nearest anker to fill the jeroboam then creeping out of his cavern of contraband he replaced the sacks to conceal the secret entrance once more.

Alone at the Two Dutch Skippers, Pascoe, the innkeeper, was polishing pewter tankards when Jeremiah Dunne arrived.

"You again? If it's information about ships and selling your wares, a waste of your time - and mine. Sailormen come here for wine and ale - not to be plied with questions."

Dunne regarded Pascoe with feigned surprise.

"Questions? A proposition."

Dunne placed the jeroboam on the table.

"Treat your palate to this, Mr Innkeeper."

Without grace, Pascoe hoisted the bottle to his mouth and filled it with the bland yet burning liquid. He rolled it briefly around his tongue before swallowing.

"Fair," he said.

"Is that all? Nothing better ever crossed the English Channel."

Dunne sipped at the jeroboam sparingly.

"Exquisite."

"Maybe - in time. At the moment too young, too fiery," Pascoe said. "A goodly stock?"

"Enough only for my best customers."

"Price?"

"Irresistible. Ten ankers at a time though."

Pascoe ceased polishing pewter to move closer.

"Ten? The exciseman's always sniffing around my cellars. One, maybe a couple, but ten....."

Dunne recharged Pascoe's goblet and poured sparingly for himself.

"What'll you pay for two ankers?" There was a faint suggestion of anxiety in Dunne's tone.

Pascoe smiled. He was well on the way to winning his usual skirmish with Jeremiah Dunne. Running contraband liquor entailed immediate outlay of money for Dunne. The mate of the ship, the crewmen who put the ankers overside, the boatman who rowed them to land, the man with the riverside cottage and secret cellars, they all demanded payment in advance. Pascoe was well aware of Dunne's need to recoup quickly and the nagging problem of concealing hundreds of ankers from the eyes of the revenue men.

"Barter?" Pascoe said.

"What's on offer?"

"This," Pascoe said holding aloft a diamond and sapphire ring. "And this." He produced a second ring set with a large solitaire diamond.

Dunne took both rings and crossed to the window for closer inspection. He frowned. There was deep suspicion in his tone.

"Where did you get them?"

"Do I enquire about the source of your brandy?"

"I must know, Pascoe."

The innkeeper winked.

"We've done business together long enough to accept and pay without question," he said, snatching back the rings.

Dunne seized him by the throat.

"Where - did - you - get - them?"

Gasping for breath, Pascoe wriggled free.

Dunne, suddenly pale, began to shake.

"S-sorry, Pascoe. Those - those rings belong to my daughter. I'd recognise them anywhere. The diamond and sapphire my late wife's. The solitaire I bought for my daughter's last birthday."

"Your daughter?" Pascoe, rubbing his reddened neck, spat. "The woman with those rings is a Tower Hill whore."

"What - what d'you mean? Tower Hill whore?"

"A popular whore at that, judging by the quality of her jewellery and silks and satins. Poxy blowse."

Again Dunne seized Pascoe by the throat and dragged him to the centre of the room.

"Poxy blowse? My daughter? Describe her."

The innkeeper struggled as ineffectively as a chicken about to have its neck pulled.

"Cease the choking and I'll tell you."

Dunne relaxed his hold.

"Auburn hair, ringlets to her shoulder," Pascoe said, gasping. "Fresh complexion, five feet six, hazel eyes, soft of voice....."

With a strength born of many years lifting heavy sacks and stowing wine and spirit casks, Jeremiah Dunne sent the innkeeper spinning across the room. He thudded against a table and collapsed. Rising at length on unsteady legs, Pascoe said softly, venomously, "And a pickpocket to boot, the Bow Street magistrates'll be pleased to learn."

"Pickpocket?"

"One naval officer left unconscious, purse empty. I found him. She tried bribing me, keeping me quiet with a couple of rings. Something else, Dunne. That officer was on the brink of death. So add 'attempted murder' to your list."

"My daughter would never, never...."

"Try convincing the magistrates, Jeremiah Dunne."

Chapter 9

"Stop, stop!"

Arms flailing Jonathan stumbled to the middle of the road, directly in the path of the oncoming coach.

He was no longer the dapper and newly-qualified apothecary emerging into the sunshine of Sea Coal Lane to meet Margaret Dunne but a grimy, ragged footpad, face deep-scarred, front tooth missing, holding up the Dover-to-London coach.

The coachman dragged on the reins and the coach swung wildly in the direction of the roadside ditch. The thong of the man's whip snaked so skilfully around Jonathan's neck that he was snatched off his feet, spun and pitched face down on the dusty road.

"Up, up."

The coach-guard, flintlock to Jonathan's temple, stirred him with the toe of his boot then dragged him upright. Three portly men, also armed with flintlocks, scrambled out of the coach to snatch a wary look at the Greenwich footpad. One less timid than the others inched forward to seize Jonathan by the hair and thrust the muzzle of his pistol into Jonathan's ear.

"Scum of the road. Do I blow your brains out?"

With clenched fist the man sent Jonathan spinning. Once more the coachman's whip curled around his neck.

"I - I beg you. I'm no footpad. Set upon and robbed." Jonathan was gasping for breath. "W-walked all the way from....."

"Lash him to the coach roof and be on our way."

From the safety of a dense clump of bushes, Daniel and Vincent looked on helplessly as the coach, Jonathan lashed face upwards on its roof, moved off on the last few miles to its London destination, the yard of the Swan With Two Nicks, no great distance from the Ludgate premises of the apothecary, Matthew Gross.

* * * * *

Jonathan sat hunched on damp, decaying straw in an atmosphere pervaded by the stench of sweat and ailing bodies and urine. In an effort to control an urge to vomit from a stomach starved for days of any sustenance Jonathan forced his forehead to his knees. In spite of manacled wrists, by leaning to one side, he succeeded in forcing his fingers into the pocket of his breeches where some of the guineas given to him by the ague-smitten mariner in Sea Coal Lane still lay. One of the coins he had already given to the chief gaoler, reward for not fastening an iron collar to his neck.

"Gaoler!" The voice was reedy and hoarse. "Gaoler!"

Kicking his way over recumbent bodies a turnkey appeared and thrust a piece of bread towards the mouth of one of the other prisoners, taking care to hold it no more than a hair's breadth beyond the wretched man's lips.

"Six and eightpence."

So far as the iron collar would permit, the prisoner, sallow and skeletal, raised his head.

"But I gave you six and eight this morning."

Withdrawing the bread, the turnkey laughed.

"Stay hungry?"

Jonathan held out a golden guinea.

"Bread and water for us both."

The turnkey snatched the coin, inspected it, cogitated for a moment then, sneering, he tore the piece of bread in half, gave a piece to Jonathan and the remainder to the other prisoner.

"And the water?" Jonathan said.

"Later," the man said and was gone.

Next morning, now fettered as well as manacled, Jonathan was dragged from the gaol to the magistrates' court in Bow Street.

The law was in exceptionally jovial mood. Jonathan had been fortunate, the presiding magistrate said, not to have been shot out of hand when he attempted to hold up the stage coach. In spite of severe provocation the mercy of good and true citizens had prevailed. And now that very same mercy would prevail among the magistrates. Not only mercy but charity as well.

"His Majesty's Government invites you to take a voyage to a land where baser instincts may be curbed but if not curbed then it will not greatly matter. Perish or prosper, suffer or enjoy. His Majesty is delighted to be rid of you." The presiding magistrate struck the desk with a gavel. "Transportation. Seven years."

Jonathan glanced uncomprehendingly from one magistrate to another.

"Understand?" one said.

Jonathan shook his head.

"When his Majesty can spare ships for you and other rogues and vagabonds, nightwalkers and murderers and draw-latches, you will set sail somewhere. Wherever it may be, there you can rob and kill to your heart's content. Have you ever sailed the ocean?"

Again Jonathan shook his head.

"Then we'll arrange a taste. Aboard a Greenwich prison hulk for your first taste of salt water."

A turnkey dragged Jonathan, stumbling, sprawling, out of the court room. With a score of other manacled and fettered prisoners he was bundled into a wagon. Chained to its sides so that each man faced outwards, hapless target for every street urchin's spittle and brickbat on the way, they were driven across Blackfriars Bridge to the Obelisk, onwards to the Dover Road and thence to the river Thames.

It was mid-evening when the cart lurched to a halt, pitching the captives forward like skittles.

"On your feet."

A turnkey from Newgate prison who had accompanied the waggon counted the men and withdrew the chain which linked them to each other. One at a time they were hauled from the tail of the cart by a pair of soldiers and forced to lie, face down, on the ground until the corporal of the guard gave orders for them to stand upright.

"Hands above your heads. Higher, higher. You, scarface." The corporal thudded his musket butt at Jonathan's chest, "Lead."

In the gathering dusk the file of prisoners came to a riverside jetty where they were driven aboard a ferry-boat, then rowed to a vessel, black against the evening sky, bobbing at anchor on the tide. Hastily assembled in the failing light on the deck of the anchored vessel they were counted by the turnkey.

"Happy sailings," he rasped as he clambered overside and disappeared. "May you turn yellow, green, then slowly rot."

Her timbers long since too spongy for further duties as a man-o'-war, the dismasted Industria had given over her decks to accommodate the overflow of convicts from Newgate and other gaols.

The new arrivals, still manacled and fettered, were urgently tumbled down a series of rickety ladders until they reached the lowest deck where bilge water sluiced to and fro as the hulk swayed and shuddered on the incoming tide.

Guards dragged up the ladder and closed the trapdoor to the deck above. A single lantern, swaying from the ceiling, emphasised rather than relieved the dank gloom of the Industria's orlop deck.

Stumbling over motionless bodies Jonathan reached out to a bulwark for support. The timbers squelched and collapsed under his hand. There was a gaping hole in the side of the hulk, only partially covered by tattered sail canvas that flapped disconsolately in the evening breeze. He was about to drag the canvas aside when a hand seized his manacled wrist.

"Fool," a voice hissed. "In irons you'll sink like a stone."

Jonathan jerked free but the hand grabbed once more.

"Sea Coal Lane."

In the breeze the canvas lifted long enough to admit sufficient light for Jonathan to recognise Daniel Stocksbridge.

Chapter 10

A series of thuds on the warehouse door dragged Jeremiah Dunne out of a fitful sleep.

"Open, open!"

Dunne thrust his feet into slippers and stumbled along the dark landing, through the office of his warehouse and down the wooden staircase.

"Open, open, open!"

Dunne calmly lit a pair of lanterns and began a detailed inspection of the stacked rice and maize bags to the accompaniment of thuds that grew louder and more frequent.

When satisfied that there was nothing to suggest concealed stocks of contraband spirits he went to the warehouse doors.

"Why this hell-begotten din? No supplies this time of night."

Thud followed thud. The heavy doors began to bulge.

"Easy, easy."

"Open!"

Dunne flung a final, searching glance at the precisely stacked rice and maize.

"Bloody revenue rats," he said, raising the bar of the warehouse doors.

Thrusting ahead of him with a long stave a man in cloak and tricorne hat bundled Dunne aside and followed by a dozen others he strode to the centre of the warehouse.

"Jeremiah Dunne?"

"Who the hell.....?"

"Are you Dunne?"

"Revenue men?"

"Thief-catchers. I said, 'Are you Jeremiah Dunne?'"

"Yes, why?"

"A daughter, Margaret Dunne?"

Jeremiah nodded.

"Where?"

"Like all good citizens at this hour - in bed."

"Well, there's a bed of straw for her at Newgate."

"Get out!"

The blow from the thief-catcher's stave sent Dunne spinning against the sacks of rice and maize.

"Fetch her."

"Why, why?"

"Theft and attempted murder."

"Never."

"That's what they all say."

All dozen men swarmed up the staircase and moving swiftly from room to room, Dunne stumbling after them, they at length found Margaret. One of the men dragged away the bedclothes.

Margaret screamed.

"Dress. Two minutes. Take money. A lot of money. Newgate's a costly hostelry."

"Help, father, help!"

The ruffian grabbed Margaret's hair and dragged her towards a pile of clothes.

"Put 'em on."

Margaret made an attempt to escape through the bedroom door but two other thief-catchers were there, barricading the opening with staves. Beyond, on the landing, Jeremiah Dunne stood helpless.

"Try not to worry, dear. We have friends, influential..."

Margaret was bundled along the landing, down the staircase and into the chill darkness of St Catherine's. When they reached the corner of Nightingale Lane a gust of wind seized her unfastened cloak. She made frantic but fruitless attempt to retrieve it but her captors bustled her onwards.

"Plenty warm enough in Newgate. Nearest place to hell on earth," one of them said, prodding her with his stave.

* * * * *

Breathless, frantic, Jeremiah Dunne hammered on the ornate oak door of a house at the corner of Well Close Square.

Nothing more than a cloak over his nightgown, bare feet in slippers, Dunne stood, shivering. Bolts thudded back, the door opened, a lantern swung inches away from his face and the muzzle of a flintlock pistol rammed into his chest.

"Help, Turnbull, for God's sake, help me."

McQuaid motioned Dunne inside then closed and bolted the door.

"Revenue men?" McQuaid said tersely.

Dunne shook his head.

McQuaid directed him to the sittingroom where he lit a candelabra.

"Sit down. Not revenue men?"

Dunne buried his face in his hands.

"No."

McQuaid filled two goblets.

"Here, drink."

"Who then?"

"Thief-catchers."

"For you?"

Dunne drained his goblet.

"Margaret! A dozen of them. Half an hour ago. Dragged her off to Newgate."

"Newgate?"

"Help her, Turnbull, for Christ's sweet sake."

McQuaid sat back, arms folded and gave a rueful smile.

"No keys to Newgate, Dunne. Why come to me?"

"Not many hours ago you were begging Margaret to be your wife. 'Why come to me?' you now say. You have friends in high places."

McQuaid gave a patronising nod of the head.

"Acquaintances, not friends."

Hands clasped, Dunne leaned forward.

"I'm desperate, Turnbull. You know what happens to a woman...."

McQuaid rose and placed a hand on Dunne's shoulder.

"There must be some mistake. They've got the wrong woman. At first light to Newgate yourself and pay up. In Newgate money talks more effectively than anywhere else in London."

The brandy had brought crimson to Dunne's cheeks. He rose to his feet, a pathetic creature in long black cloak, peruke awry.

"Mistake all right but evidence clear enough. Theft and attempted murder."

McQuaid's eyes narrowed.

"Attempted murder?"

"A naval officer."

"Clear evidence you say?"

"Crystal clear."

McQuaid replenished Dunne's goblet.

"Then, sorry. Nothing I can do."

"What's - what's wrong, Turnbull?" He seized McQuaid's hand. "Why can't you help? Two days ago asking, nay, begging Margaret to marry you now you abandon her to garrotting and burning and God knows what. Why, why, why?"

Dunne stumbled back to his chair and buried his face in his hands.

McQuaid took a deep draught of brandy and, seated on the edge of the table, one foot on the floor, the other swinging, he said, "A long story. I miss my bed. Come at mid-day and I'll tell you."

Dunne raised his head.

"Tell me now."

"You'll not like it."

"Tell me - please."

"Ever since I became aware I didn't look on women like other men but found pleasure in youths and other males I've suffered the tortures of the damned," McQuaid leaned towards Dunne, an agonised twitch briefly seizing his handsome features, "the damned."

"I know all this, Turnbull. I've known for years. It's never interfered with our association. I sympathise."

As if he had not heard Dunne's words McQuaid continued, "All my early business life I kept to the shadows, cajoling, begging, bribing every inch of the way. Then naval contracts began to arrive. At first very small, profits often less than the bribes. When boatmen refused to turn out at three o' clock on winter mornings and row stores to ships weighing anchor on the early tide, I used to take the oars myself."

"Yes, yes, I remember your early struggles, Turnbull."

"Slowly attitudes began to change. Those who'd never hesitated to empty chamber pots over my head as I sneaked along dark streets now keen to make my acquaintance. Soon, not only ships' chandlery but ships as well. Blackamoors from the coast of Africa for the planters in Virginia.

"The first time I saw sweating negroes chained below deck in one of my ships I vomited. I was responsible for their suffering. Then I told myself if I didn't supply the ships some competitor would jump in. The negroes suffered because they had black skins. But hadn't I suffered, a sort of woman in a man's body? Never again, I decided, was I going to vomit at the sight of chained-up blackamoors."

With no thought of lost sleep now, apparently, McQuaid paused to recharge both goblets.

"The government began to hand out contracts. My possessions grew. I bought all this." He pointed to the ornate ceiling, the paintings, the silver candelabra, the sumptuous arras, the ornate furniture. "Unassailable now, Jeremiah Dunne." McQuaid's eyes glistened in the light of the candles. "Power at last."

"But I've told you, I know all this, Turnbull. You've always been welcome under my roof. Always...."

"And until this moment you've been welcome under mine. But not any more. Our association's at an end, Dunne."

Jeremiah Dunne's voice was unnaturally high.

"Why, why?. Margaret in Newgate. Surely somebody you can contact.- I'll pay, I'll pay. Down to my very last penny."

McQuaid's response was to take Dunne by the elbow and steer him across the room to the door.

About to step into the hall Jeremiah Dunne turned, "You haven't told me your reasons yet."

"Think, man, just think. Your daughter robs and tries to murder a naval officer. The evidence, you tell me, beyond question."

"Yes."

"At the moment I'm negotiating with the naval authority over a charter. Swear secrecy?"

"Of course."

"If ever you betrayed me, y'know, the revenue men'd be turning your place upside down and inside out the very next morning."

McQuaid opened the outer door. Ill-clad Dunne shivered.

"I've told you. I swear."

"Well, the Navy Board's contractor says one of my brigs is suitable for transporting convicts to maybe Africa, maybe the New Hebrides. What's more, I'd be supplying clothing and victuals for crew, guards and convicts."

"So intercession could ruin your prospects with the Navy Board?"

"Precisely."

"And no compunction over profiting from misery?"

"Misery?"

Turnbull McQuaid's laughter echoed and re-echoed in the silence of Well Close Square.

"What possible misery could there be aboard a vessel named 'Friendship'?"

The carved oak door slammed and Jeremiah Dunne, cloak tight about him, scurried along deserted Nightingale Lane to his home in St. Catherine's.

Chapter 11

Jonathan tugged the matted red hair.

"How did you get here?"

"A man has to live," Daniel Stocksbridge said wryly, "even a fool like me. Of all the pockets to pick in London I had to choose a thief-taker's."

"Escape together then," Jonathan said, pointing towards the hole in the ship's side.

Daniel shook his head and nodded in the direction of the other prisoners.

"A dozen hands willing to help, oh, yes. Every one of them preferring your rations to your company. But thirty pounds of iron -" Stocksbridge rattled his manacles, "not much help to swimmers. Bide your time. Chances aren't many."

"There must be some."

"Not before Botany Bay."

"Where?"

"Didn't the kind magistrates enlighten you?"

"Something about transportation, that's all."

"I learned a little more. One was drunk, one was deaf, the third fast asleep. We're both booked for a passage and same destination without a doubt. The drunk mumbled something about oafs like me ungrateful for opportunities of a new life in a new land. I offered to change places and he wasn't very pleased. Remember the spikes round the convict box in the sessions house?"

"Yes," Jonathan said.

"Two turnkeys impaled the back of my breeches on them. I dangled in front of the magistrates like a gasping cod. The deaf one spent half an hour explaining I'd be better off as a fish swimming to Botany Bay than a passenger in a convict transport. Have you money?"

"A little."

"Use it to stay alive. Nobody survives longer than a month in the filth and bilge of an orlop. Buy air. Bribe a guard for a move to a higher deck. Beg him to sell you a blanket and a mat. They want you dead without the cost of the hangman. They'll work you till you drop. Rest whenever you can."

Long before any sign of daylight through the hole in the ship's side the overhead trapdoor was dragged aside and a ladder thrust into the orlop deck.

"Out, out!."

The convicts scrambled to their feet and shuffled towards the ladder, ankle fetters allowing paces no more than twelve inches. The ladder rungs were so spaced that climbing, except by repeatedly taking the whole weight of their bodies on their hands was almost impossible. In spite of vicious bites from the whips awaiting them at every deck level progress was sluggish. By the time the men made the top deck daylight had already arrived. The Thames was swathed in grey mist. Exhausted they collapsed on the wet planking.

"On your feet. Strip!"

Once more the whips flicked over backs and necks and faces. The guards roared with laughter at the antics of the manacled and fettered prisoners struggling to wriggle out of their clothes.

A few, including Jonathan and Daniel, had been held only a short time in gaol before trial so their clothes at worst were no more than grimy and torn. Most, however had lain in Newgate and elsewhere for months, years, before sentence. One wore a leather jerkin back to front as breeches, his legs in the sleeves. Two had no shirts but wore women's bodices. Another was clothed in nothing but a canvas apron, stretching from his armpits to his ankles and roped around the waist. Few had stockings, almost all hobbled on feet bound in rags.

"If they won't come off, rip 'em off," a guard bellowed and, with the tip of his cutlass he sliced a man's ragged breeches from waist to crotch.

Naked and barefoot the twenty men stood hunched and shivering in the dank morning air.

"Wash."

A bucket of river water was allocated to every two men and those slow to use it were promptly seized by a guard and rammed head first into the bucket.

"Dry yourselves."

The men dried their shivering bodies as best they could with their discarded garments and then to each was flung a coarse shirt, a shapeless grey jacket and wide cotton breeches.

"Attention."

The convicts were cudgelled into line for a cursory inspection by the captain of the hulk.

"Work hard," he barked, "and your only fear'll be the man next to you in the night. Worse fates, remember, than garrotting. Good behaviour earns shorter sentences, lighter leg-irons. Attempts to escape are bound to fail. My men are forbidden to drag you from the Thames either gasping or already a bloated water-sodden corpse. That's all."

Pannikins of watery porridge, salt and small beer were then brought to the convicts from the galley.

"Ten minutes - then it's work, work, work."

For most of the time submerged to the neck in the river, the prisoners spent all morning dragging timbers round the end of a jetty to replace its rotting piles. By mid-day many of them, weakened by months of Newgate starvation and brutality, had scrambled to the river bank and there, despite being harried by the guards' whips, gratefully collapsed in the soft mud.

Many of the timber piles were so heavily waterlogged that they refused to float and the convicts were driven to dragging and thrusting the clumsy timbers below water. As one of the piles was being nudged round the tip of the jetty a prisoner flung both arms over it for momentary respite. The thong of a whip snaked around the man's neck hoisting him clear of the water.

His fingers frantically clawing at the air, the prisoner, squealing in terror and agony, disappeared into the murky waters of the Thames.

Jonathan snatched a gulp of air and plunged deep. The rescue attempt was fruitless. When, gasping and spitting out foul water, he surfaced alone and flung his arms over the timber for a brief rest, a guard's whip snatched his waist. Before the man could drag at the wire-tipped thong, Jonathan seized and wrenched. The guard, standing on the edge of the jetty, teetered briefly before plunging headlong into the river.

There was no shortage of pairs of hands desperate to hold the guard beneath the partially submerged timber. It was a corpse that, in due course, Jonathan dragged to the river bank.

No sooner had the men finished their supper of oxhead gristle, black bread and thin ale than their stomachs, already overburdened with noxious river water, were in revolt. As the hulk rolled and pitched and shivered on the incoming tide every morsel of food for which they had so frantically craved since morning was vomited to the deck.

Like the rest, Jonathan lay prostrate, heaving. His years as a pressed man standing him now in good stead, Daniel went on eating gristle and congealed fat with relish.

The thong of a whip flicked Jonathan's ankle. Although the touch was light it drew blood from skin softened by many hours immersed in river water.

"You tried to rescue one of our men this morning."

Jonathan glanced up, puzzled, at the guard with the whip.

"As brave attempt at rescue as I've seen, sir," Daniel said quickly, wiping greasy lips. "Only seconds too late to save the gentleman's life, sir."

The whip curled around Daniel's waist.

"Shut up, you." The guard turned to Jonathan. "From tomorrow a lamp-man. Up before first light, collect your lantern, rouse your deck. Blankets and mats stowed, every man on the top deck inside fifteen minutes - or we look for another lamp-man."

Daniel's toe secretly touched Jonathan's shin.

"Yes, sir. Thank you."

"And you can show how good a lamp-man you are by getting a mob together now and swabbing the deck free of vomit before you go below."

The moment the guard was out of earshot Daniel whispered, "Show willing. Your life - and mine - depend on it. A lamp-man earns more food, lighter irons."

"Why pick a convict?"

Daniel tapped the side of his nose.

"Imagine the fate of a guard with a lantern in the orlop deck. Eyes gouged out for a start. It could happen to a prisoner, of course. But you helped drown a guard this morning. Prisoners don't forget. You're a hero to both sides now."

Chapter 12

Half-naked, caked in gaol-house filth, the girl, no more than a child, pointed urgent fingers to her mouth. Margaret made to take the emaciated forearm but, eyes wide with terror, the child squealed and shrank away.

"Hungry?" Margaret said.

The child again pointed to its mouth.

A scrawny, parchment-faced woman, leaning against the wall of the cell, shook her head.

"Hungry all the time, that 'un. Tackles every newcomer. Got rid of her once to the masters' side." The woman's cackle was obscene. "Soon back to the common side. Didn't much fancy gentry using her."

"Using?"

"You're a woman. You ought to know."

Margaret gave an involuntary shiver. She still had a little bread. It was stale, part of the twopenny ration flung at each prisoner most days in Newgate. She offered some to the child who leapt forward to seize and devour it.

"Who are you?"

The small girl grunted.

"She's no idea," the parchment-faced woman said. "And if she had she couldn't tell you."

"Couldn't.....?"

"Nobody taught her, see?"

Margaret glanced at the emaciated child.

"How old?"

The woman shrugged.

"Ten, eleven. Who knows? Born in that corner, they say. She was around when they dumped me here five years ago. I remember her mother."

Margaret edged close to her informant but quickly recoiled at the stench of a body unwashed for years.

"You, five years of this? For what?"

"Giving a crust to a convict on his way to the colonies."

"What was your sentence?"

The woman regarded Margaret with a faintly quizzical air.

"Sentence? Hardly a soul here with a sentence. They're all just waiting, waiting."

"My God. And that child?"

"The mother left her. Had to. They garrotte and burn mothers and grandmothers, never children. The turnkeys gave the child a real treat. If you ask me, the first she ever had. After the hangman had garrotted the mother with a chain they lifted the child to the platform so's she could watch her sizzle to a cinder."

"In God's name, where?"

"At the gates. The child was delighted. Clapped its hands, they say. Never ever seen a fire or felt so warm."

Margaret held out the remainder of the bread. The child snatched and at once devoured it. Margaret's hand crept to the skinny shoulders. Resistance was token and brief. Tiny, timid, claw-like hands began to fondle the fabric of Margaret's velvet gown. They slid to the firm rounded breasts, struggling to part the fabric and the matted, lice-ridden head, lips wide, went in pursuit of a bared nipple.

Rocking with laughter, the scrawny woman cuffed the child so that it went spinning to the wall.

"Its mother always let it. Never anything to suck at though." She put a hand to her own bosom, flat as the cell wall. "Never, never anything," she said, half to herself.

The child crept back to Margaret who, her bodice now tight-laced, covered her breasts firmly with crossed arms.

"How can I get her some food?" she said to the crone.

"Pay the turnkey a golden guinea for a move to the masters' side. A woman like you'd make a score of guineas before sundown," the woman said, nodding and winking towards Margaret's bosom.

"Any other way?"

"For a guinea any turnkey'll get you beef, bread and ale."

Margaret, a tempting coin between her fingers, beckoned a bluff-faced ruffian, a bundle of keys at his belt, who was lolling in the archway that connected the two cells. At once the turnkey lunged his way through the groups of prisoners. He appraised Margaret from head to toe.

"Clean, pretty, young," he said, one huge hand taking her waist, the other fondling her buttocks.

Trembling, Margaret thrust away the invading hands.

"And how did my pretty one come by a whole golden guinea?"the man added archly, again fondling her buttocks.

The old crone cackled.

"I can tell you."

"Shut up, you."

The turnkey squeezed her breasts with such savagery that Margaret screamed loud in protest. Thick, hungry lips clamped ruthlessly over hers silencing her at once.

"I'll tell you where she gets her golden guineas. In a whorehouse. Know why she's here? If you was a London gentleman and some lady presented you with the gleets you'd get her thrown into Newgate somehow, wouldn't you?"

The turnkey ceased his savagery and turned.

"Gleets?"

"The gleets, the pox. Be told by an old woman - don't so much as touch her. Find yourself some clean and wholesome wench."

The turnkey slapped Margaret's face. She fell. Scrambling quickly to her feet, the guinea still in her hand, she thrust it at him.

"Get me beef and bread and good wine. And don't be afraid." Margaret flung a covert glance at the woman and gave an almost imperceptible wink. "You may not have the gleets. But if ever....then I can help. Ladies in my profession have knowledge of certain and sure cures. Now the bread, beef, wine, quickly."

The food and wine were good and plentiful. The old woman, head slumped, soon lay in a drunken stupor. Margaret settled down to doze and the child, who had never eaten so well in all her life, crept to Margaret's lap and there drifted off to sleep.

The faintest glimmer of daybreak was creeping through the bars of the tiny window high in the wall of the cell when the turnkey arrived.

"Me?" the old woman said, eyes open in an instant, struggling to her feet.

"No, not you, old sow. You."

The turnkey grabbed Margaret and hauled her upright, thrusting the little girl aside. Still half asleep, the child kicked and fought to bite the gaoler. The man's fist sent her crashing to the floor where she lay awkward-limbed and whimpering briefly.

Margaret tore free of the turnkey's grasp and dropped to her knees beside the emaciated child.

"Killed her, killed her."

The turnkey slid a foot under the child and turned her over. The whimpers resumed.

"Still alive, see? Brats like that never die," he said grabbing Margaret by the hair. "Take good care of her, promise me," Margaret whispered urgently to the old woman and, as the turnkey was dragging her to the door, she threw a guinea.

"I promise if you'll tell me," the woman called, catching the coin.

Margaret struggled against the savage hands of the gaoler.

"Tell you what?"

"What influence? Here only a day or two then a trial. I wait and wait and wait."

Margaret's reply was lost as the heavy door thudded behind her. The little girl scrambled to her feet.

"Ma - mam-ma!" she screamed, beating the timbers of the door with puny fists.

For the first time in five years the old woman glimpsed tears in the eyes of the little girl. And some perceptive onlooker might have detected a rare moisture in her own.

* * * * *

The walls of Margaret's condemned hold were lined in planking studded with broadheaded nails, the solitary window was small and high and double grated. Crouching close-ironed to a ring in the centre of the floor, Margaret struggled to raise her head as the door was kicked open.

"A visitor," the turnkey barked.

Turnbull McQuaid's gold-topped, ivory walking-stick urged the man to one side then pointed towards the door.

"Leave us," he said thrusting a bottle into the gaoler's eager hands. "And don't come back till it's empty."

McQuaid minced his way between puddles of water and, removing the beaver hat with a flourish, gave Margaret an extravagant bow.

Margaret, wincing at the bite of the chains, neck awry as she strove to look up at McQuaid, frowned.

"You? How?"

Mcquaid's smile was confident.

"A quart of even the most modest brandy opens many a door."

"I wish you'd go."

"I've come to..."

"To gloat?"

McQuaid's tone was earnest. It sounded honest as well.

"To explain," he said.

He folded his arms and, face devoid of expression, surveyed in silence the woman whom he had begged so recently to become his wife.

Margaret rattled the chains.

"How can explanations help?"

"I've used every possible influence."

Margaret's finger pointed to the blackened timbers of the walls and the puddles of noisome water.

"Every possible influence didn't get me very far."

"And how d'you imagine you had such an early trial? Most prisoners pitched into Newgate never come to trial. They're left there to rot. I saved you from that kind of fate."

"All you've done is bring the stake nearer," Margaret was now screaming her words. "Know what the magistrates said? 'Woman, you won't have to hang'. And why not? Because hanging a woman's indelicate. Too indelicate, the hangman seizing the woman's legs as she swings on the rope and slowly and agonisingly chokes. So - so some filthy drunken turnkey drags me down from the gallows and half garrottes me - then I'm chained to the stake and burned."

A flicker of acute distaste crossed his face as McQuaid placed a hand on Margaret's matted auburn hair.

"You'll not hang, nor be garrotted nor burn. I have a plan."

Margaret shook her head.

"No possible escape."

"There is indeed."

"You can get me free?"

"Direct contact with the Navy Board. If I'm prepared to trim my charges, keep certain unnamed gentlemen in brandy and geneva then....."

"Then I can go free?"

"Well, not exactly. The contracts are for ships and victualling them to the far side of the earth. You'll sail in one of them."

"Sail?"

"Instead of being burned at the stake outside Newgate prison."

"I - I don't understand..."

"I've done my best. Soon you'll be setting sail from Portsmouth or Plymouth - aboard a convict ship bound for Botany Bay."

Chapter 13

Lantern held high, Jonathan struggled to count the convicts, huddled, two men to a mat, in the orlop deck of the prison hulk Industria.

Forward of the overhead trapdoor, other prisoners brought aboard late the previous evening lay on bare and sodden planking, so callously jammed together that, in the feeble light of the lantern, Jonathan had difficulty in counting them. Over-anxious to avoid stepping on bodies he stumbled and a powerful hand seized his ankle. He lowered the lantern to see a hand chocolate-brown. The face of Vincent, the negro broke into a broad smile. Jonathan gave the wide-nostrilled nose a gentle tweak.

"A convict?"

"Footpad," Vincent said in a burst of laughter.

Overhead a whip cracked.

"Upper deck, lamp-man. Every one of 'em."

The new arrivals, closest to the trapdoor, were first up the ladder. On the ice-encrusted upper deck they were bludgeoned into rows for inspection by a corporal of the guard.

"Strip! Wash."

Grey prison garb was flung at each wet, shivering prisoner.

"Dress! Now the rest of the scum, lamp-man."

Jonathan clambered below to lead on deck the remaining prisoners.

Breakfast of porridge, bread washed down with beef and barley gruel was substantially more generous than usual.

"Lamp-man."

A gentle fist dug into Jonathan's back. He turned.

Daniel Stocksbridge winked.

"Things afoot," he said.

"What?"

"No man ever went to the gallows clean clothed, full bellied. Food like this says hard work on the way."

Daniel was silenced by a pair of shoes flung in his face.

Jonathan spun round to be met by the sting of a whip.

"Hand out shoes, lamp-man, and lead the men overside."

In the river barge, bumping the side of the Industria, two blacksmiths, their anvils amidships, awaited the prisoners to chain them together in groups of ten. When the barge became so overladen that water began to seep over the gunwales, Jonathan and another lamp-man were ordered to paddle the craft to a riverside jetty.

Ashore, heavily guarded, the groups of prisoners took to the road in single file. With brief intervals for rest, they trudged until dark then a guard fired a musket into the air.

"Halt! Sleep."

The convicts collapsed on the hard-frozen grass at the roadside.

* * * * *

Four weeks later, still in irons, the prisoners who had managed to survive the march reached Plymouth gaol.

They had trudged and stumbled, scrambled and often crawled, along ice-bound roads and deep-rutted cart tracks, their clothing in tatters. Their shoes long since worn out they had completed the last fifty miles of the journey on feet bound in straw and rags.

In the freezing fog which enveloped the streets of Plymouth that evening the prisoners' arrival passed almost unnoticed by the townsfolk. For once the men were spared the shower of brickbats, curses and spitting which had been their usual greeting in every village and town through which they had plodded on their way from the Thames prison hulk Industria.

The convicts were admitted through a narrow wicket gate in the main doors of the gaol. When a turnkey had given a receipt for each man to the guards, the convicts were lined up and propelled forward to an anvil where a smith struck off their manacles.

When it came to Vincent's turn the smith paused. Summoning a turnkey he pointed to the massive wrists of the negro. Made for a slighter man, Vincent's manacles had bitten deep, the flesh ravaged and suppurating.

The blacksmith slowly shook his head.

"Could be a bit painful," he said with a wry smile.

The turnkey flung a disinterested glance at Vincent's savaged wrists and his lips curled.

"Instructions," he said.

The smith shrugged. He struck hard.

There was a howl of anguish then a roar from Vincent.

The wrist still bearing its iron shackle thudded like a sledge hammer into the skull of the blacksmith. The scream from the smith echoed and re-echoed round the courtyard of the gaol. Flinging up both arms he collapsed, blood spurting from nose and mouth while a grey jelly-like substance oozed slowly from his shattered skull to the cobble stones.

A musket cracked and Vincent spun a complete circle. His knees crumpled. A second shot pitched him face down, silent and motionless, alongside the dead blacksmith. And he lay there until a pair of turnkeys seized his ankles to drag his bloody, splendid body to the gaol furnace.

Chapter 14

Long before reaching the Obelisk, the convict women found it safer to crouch below the waist-high rail of the waggon, the more readily to dodge the hail of rotten apples and stones accompanied by the torrents of abuse. The gaol cart came to a halt only once. At the junction of Kennington Lane and Canterbury Row a pair of thief-takers, lantern held high, jabbed the tips of their staves at the driver but seeing the chained convict women they spat and ordered the waggoner to drive on.

Margaret's cloak was of thick wool and, lined with black fustian, more than adequate protection from the chill and the damp of the winter night. The garment had been flung over her shoulders by the smith sent to unrivet her from the floor shackles in Newgate's condemned hold.

"A gift from a friend," the man had whispered, at the same time thrusting coins into her hand. "And more gifts from him."

Ankles still fettered Margaret had staggered through the cell door, a turnkey's club harrying her, to join other women beside the gaoler's waggon in Newgate courtyard. Hoisted aboard the vehicle and chained in groups of three, the convicts were manacled to the uprights so that they lined each side and left the centre of the cart free.

The woman standing beside Margaret dug her in the ribs.

"What you done?"

Margaret eased back the hood of her cloak.

"Nothing," she said.

Margaret's questioner was a dark-haired, delicately-featured woman, more reminiscent of some elegant drawingroom than a noisome Newgate cell.

"We all say that."

Margaret shrugged and was about to cover her head with the hood once more when the woman's hand, warm and gentle, touched Margaret's cheek.

"You could be right," she said. "We're not all made the same."

"Are we not?" Margaret said with lacklustre interest, firmly replacing her hood.

"But if you should ever need a pardon ...."

"A what?"

"With a Martha Kerwin pardon you walk past St Peter with a confident smile any day or night."

"Pardons don't seem to have helped you very much."

"A sewer-rat of a priest. Demanded his share - and a lot else. Ever had a priest? Anxious, clumsy, all over too soon." Martha gave Margaret a wink. "No quicker way into Newgate than saying 'No' to a priest. Unless it's saying 'no' to a prime minister. Quite sure you're not guilty? Not even the littlest sin against His Divine and Glorious Majesty?"

Margaret shook her head with vigour.

"But I saw you. Staggering out of the condemned hold. Kind to the blacksmith, were you?"

"No, no, no."

"Tck, tck, tck. I was just asking. We women do right to offer favours for favours. See that one?" Martha indicated with the jerk of a thumb the third member of their chain group. There was no reaction from the hooded prisoner. "I mentioned prime minister, didn't I? She refused to be kind to Mr Pitt. Mr William Pitt, believe it or not." Martha again jerked her thumb. "Then finds herself in Newgate. Why? Attempted assault on Mr William Pitt, Prime Minister. Here, take a good look at her."

Martha's hand drew back the woman's hood to reveal pale, delicate features.

"No, no, please - please leave me alone."

Elegant fingers quickly pulled the hood over the agonised face.

"Scratched the great man's poxy face when he struggled to force her thighs apart. And no magistrate panting for a knighthood could fail to impose a sentence of less than fourteen years on such a brutal woman, could he?"

Martha tapped the girl on her shoulder.

"Silly lass. Should've let Mr Pitt have his gentleman's way with you. Better getting rolled by a prime minister in Westminster clean linen sheets than in Newgate's rotting straw by some stinking, sweating turnkey."

Sobbing, the girl turned away.

"Here, drink this, dear." Martha tone was kindly. She thrust a horn goblet into the hood. "Keep the cold out, the spirits up."

The hooded head shook.

Martha Kerwin shrugged and offered the goblet to Margaret.

"No thank you."

Putting the goblet to her own lips Martha drained its contents in a gulp.

"Lifeblood," she said licking her lips. "Pardons save our souls from hell and damnation. Rum saves us from worse in Newgate."

"You - you found rum in Newgate?" Margaret said.

"On the masters' side they wash their feet in it."

"But how did you.....?"

"In exchange for papal pardons. Even the turnkeys. Garrotting and eye-gouging and rape every day, in sore need of pardons. I sold more in Newgate than they sell in Paternoster Row."

The convict waggon rattled and jerked to a halt in the cobbled yard of an inn. The women, many sleeping fitfully, were pitched forward screaming as chains dragged on freezing flesh.

A pair of guards with muskets had been sitting with the waggoner and one of them now clambered over the tail of the vehicle to check the convicts.

"We stay for an hour. Heads down - or suffer," he said with a significant nod in the direction of the tavern door from which repeated bursts of raucous laughter were escaping. "Many a man in there this time o' the night who'd never notice the stench of Newgate on you."

If the women had been listening to the warning they paid scant attention to it. The moment that guards and driver had disappeared into the inn, the night air was sharp with women's chatter. Two men reeled out of the doorway, heard the voices, paused for a moment and then stumbled towards the waggon. One collided with the side and a firm round hand promptly darted between the wooden bars before the man collapsed on the cobblestones. His companion, still upright, hauled him to his feet and the pair staggered off into the night.

"The only sort of man I've ever loved," Martha Kerwin whispered gleefully to Margaret.

There was a moon, visible occasionally between scudding clouds and in one of the brief moon-lit moments Margaret glimpsed something in Martha's grasp.

"His purse?"

"Mine now," Martha said thrusting it between her breasts.

The next pair of men were less drunk and more purposeful.

The girl who, with finger nails, had once successfully fought off the attention of a prime minister was standing closest to the waggon's tail. The men leapt on to the cart.

One of them ripped her skirt from waist to hem and, although she was shackled to Margaret and Martha, his companion made determined effort to mount her.

One moment the man's mouth was smothering the girl's screams and the next he was jerking away from her unyielding body, his sudden howl of deep-throated agony turning to a choking gasp. With fettered feet Margaret and Martha kicked the would-be rapist off the cart and he lay, moaning, gasping on the cobblestones.

The whimpering girl slowly adjusted her torn skirt. She coughed and spat. Martha wiped her lips and showed her the blood on the rag, black in the moonlight.

"Did he bite?"

"No," the girl replied softly.

"No?"

"I did. The blood's his."

"His?"

"His tongue. I bit it. Right through."

"Pity no chance for biting something else!" Martha said and her arms, encircling the weeping girl's head, clasped it to her bosom.

The freezing fog of Plymouth was the only greeting for the women convicts as their waggon jolted to a final halt outside a tall building, blind of windows.

"On your feet."

The guards marched the length of the convict waggon, prodding their captives with muskets. But after their lengthy journey trailing through rain and wind and frost the women were all far beyond response to any ruthlessness now. They went on huddling together as closely as their fetters allowed.

"Up, up."

The guard unlocked the chains that fastened the women to the sides of the waggon then again jabbed them, clothes stiff with frost, bared heads powdered with rime.

"Move, move. Nowt for your bellies till you're beyond those doors."

All except one, grasping the rails with frost-bitten fingers, struggled to their feet. The girl who had resisted William Pitt remained hunched and still on the waggon floor. Chained to her, Martha and Margaret struggled to rouse the girl. The head was lolling, the eyes, barely open were unblinking.

"Guard, please."

A musket muzzle lifted the sagging jaw.

"A stiff," the man called to his companion.

The second guard glanced briefly at the lolling head.

"Get a receipt for it. Let 'em find out inside." He jerked a thumb in the direction of the gaolhouse door. "And keep your mouth shut." He pointed to Margaret and Martha. "That goes for you and you as well. Or I'll see you both get charged with murder."

In haste both guards prodded each woman yet again, this time to make sure that each was still alive, then they dragged the captives, chained in threes, out of the waggon and into line on the frost-covered cobbles outside the prison.

Without enthusiasm and at arm's length to avoid the lingering stench of Newgate, a turnkey briefly inspected each prisoner.

"Over there for unshackling."

Supporting the dead girl, Margaret and Martha limped and stumbled to the blacksmith and his anvil. As the chain link parted the girl's body slumped to the ground.

The smith, shrugging, thrust a hand between the breasts of the girl and drew forth a leather bag. His grin was lewd, confident.

"That's where they always hide it." He winked at Martha and Margaret."I'll be coming for yours soon, maybe." He motioned to a turnkey then the body. "All yours."

Ushered into a long, low-ceilinged room where wooden troughs lined one wall the women were ordered to strip and wash. In an adjacent cell, its walls newly-whitewashed, they were given a breakfast of porridge, soup and bread.

Chapter 15

For several years a vessel on the stocks in the early stages of construction, little more than keel and ribs, had lain untouched, virtually forgotten in a Scarborough shipyard. The owners of the skeleton ship had paid generously for information about the government's secret plans to empty England's gaols and prison hulks by sending their convicts to the Gambia. In eager anticipation of handsome and early profits the owners laid the keel. The information, however, proved unreliable so the embryo ship, ribs now warped and blackened, lay neglected until the arrival of a ship's chandler from Wapping.

Anxious to extend his business activities to embrace the newly developing ports of England's north-east coast, Turnbull McQuaid undertook the long and arduous journey by road from the Thames to Scarborough and Whitby. In Tindall's shipyard on Scarborough's Sandside he caught sight of the skeletal vessel originally intended for service as a convict transport to Africa.

The design of the vessel impressed McQuaid. Narrow-beamed and deep, such a ship would attract the minimum in harbour dues for the maximum quantity of possible cargo. He wasted no time in tracing the disillusioned owners who accepted with alacrity McQuaid's impudently trifling offer.

And Tindall, the shipbuilder, happy at the prospect of freeing the stocks on which the craft had been standing for so long, proved no match for McQuaid's ruthless style of bargaining.

Within six months the hull of the vessel was completed. In a further six months the ship was fitted out, rigged as a brig and, in the spring of the year 1784, she sailed south to a berth in St. Saviour's Dock at Redriff, on the south bank of the River Thames.

Because his covert gifts to friends in government circles were more generous than those given by the Scarborough shipowner, McQuaid was supplied with more reliable and wider information. In deference to those who had revealed to him the government's secret plans he named the vessel 'Friendship'.

For the time being she would carry cargoes of wines and spirits, silks and cottons and woollens but only on short hauls from continental ports thus being rarely absent for more than a fortnight at a time from her regular berth at St. Saviour's. Prompt availability and ease of access, friends in the Navy Board constantly whispered, was essential.

In August 1786 Friendship, with other selected vessels, was chosen by the Admiralty to transport convicts to New Holland. Turnbull McQuaid's judicious outlay at an obscure and small port on the north-east coast of England had served his purpose well.

Flat-bottomed and flatsided, Friendship was only 103 feet in length, her beam 24 feet but her shape and exceptional depth, as McQuaid at the outset had immediately recognised, meant that, if comfort be utterly disregarded, she could carry one hundred convicts to the other side of the earth.

The space for the officers and the officials in Friendship's cuddy was only marginally more generous than the six square feet allocated below decks to each convict. The brig had been moored at the quay in Plymouth's Dead Man's Bay for no more than a week yet tempers among officers and the rest of the complement were already frayed in the cramped conditions aboard the convict transport.

Crouched over the narrow table in the cuddy, Thomas Arndell, Friendship's surgeon, and Henry Bellamy, captain-lieutenant of marines, were playing chess.

Arndell moved his queen.

"Check."

Tipsily, for he had been drinking wine steadily since early morning and it was now evening, Henry Bellamy picked up his king and pointed it successively at various vacant squares.

Then, "Shit," he growled.

Sweeping the board clear of pieces he surged to his feet with such vigour that his head struck the low ceiling of the cuddy. He felt his scalp. There was blood.

William Faddy, marine lieutenant, clapped a hand over his mouth to conceal his mirth and turned away. Francis Walton, master of Friendship, laughed openly.

"Stick to your muskets and cutlasses, Bellamy. Forget about pawns and rooks."

Bellamy's attempts to stem the flow of blood were tipsy, ineffective.

"Go to hell."

"Sit down, Henry," Arndell said, bending to collect the scattered chessmen. "When you forget to lose your temper you'll remember, for a change, how to win. Let me see that injured pate."

Bellamy lay sprawled across the bulkhead bench and, as Arndell leaned over to inspect the cut, the marine's flailing arms sent the surgeon crashing between bench and table to the cuddy floor.

"To hell with the cut. When - when I need a surgeon, I'll summon one, not an apprentice butcher."

Arndell, nowhere near as drunk as Bellamy, grasped the table edge and eased himself to a chair.

"I'll have you know, soldier boy......"

"And I'll have Walton and Faddy here know about a man in Goswell Street. Both - both legs stiff as tree stumps after your butchery. And the - the woman of Puddledock Hill never again to suckle a child.... "

Eyes blazing, Arndell seized Bellamy by the throat.

"Surgeons' Hall know well enough my qualifications."

Bellamy was a tall and burly man. He hurled Arndell aside as if he were no more than a bundle of straw.

"Maybe. But nothing of your failures." Bellamy seized his empty goblet. "More wine, Walton."

The ship's master shook his head.

"You've drunk us dry, Henry."

"Open up the stores then."

"The contractors stipulate no broaching main stores till we set sail."

Careful now about the low ceiling Bellamy rose slowly to his feet.

His tone was scathing.

"Till we set sail. Hm. We won't be slipping moorings this side of Easter. A month at least. Maybe two. The main stores, Walton. And if there's trouble with padlocks I'm handy with a musket."

At this, Henry Bellamy keeled over but before he could hit the floor Faddy and Arndell had grabbed him and laid him, facing the bulkhead, on the bench.

"There is more wine," Walton said quietly, producing a bottle and charging three goblets. He drained one before going on. "Was Henry right about the man's legs, Thomas?"

"Yes."

"Is that why you signed on with me? To escape?"

Thomas Arndell contemplated his untouched goblet.

"The Goswell Street man came to me long past aid from anybody on earth, expecting a miracle. The woman as well." Arndell gulped his wine. "Bad news travels fast. Nobody hears about sight restored to a man in Spitalfields. They all forget about the child I sat with for seven nights till it could breathe properly again."

"I'm still surprised the Commissioners of Sick and Wounded agreed you're capable of tending the ship's company and a hundred convicts," Walton said acidly.

"Paying as they do, the Commissioners are in no position to enquire into achievement or failure. I suggest you reserve judgment till Botany Bay."

Walton reached the door of the cuddy then turned.

"Sooner than that. First batch of prisoners arrives in the morning."

Faddy nodded briefly to Arndell, threw a glance at his superior officer snoring on the couch then followed Walton up the companionway. Arndell reached for the wine bottle and contemplated it for a moment. Then, ramming home the cork, he thrust it into the locker.

Chapter 16

The convicted men were roused from sleep at three o' clock in the morning, given breakfast of porridge, bread and honey, then herded into the exercise yard of Playhouse Gaol.

A dusting of snow on the cobblestones showed sickly yellow in the flickering light of the lanterns. The men, shivering in such clothes as had survived the march across southern England from the Thames prison hulk, were bullied into single file, ironed once more and threaded on chains in groups of ten.

Daniel flinched as the ice-encrusted manacles were clamped over his wrists. Ironed immediately ahead of him, Jonathan gave him a playful nudge as he stepped away from the anvil.

"Hold on hard," he whispered.

The self-styled vendor of soldiers' teeth stared blankly ahead.

"Can't much longer."

"You've got to."

"More marching? Impossible. Look."

Daniel pointed, with hands close manacled, to his feet bound in rags.

"But you made 250 miles from London."

Daniel's reply was lost in the clatter of heavy chains on the cobbles. As soon as the last man was ironed the convicts were driven through the narrow wicket gate into the sleeping Plymouth street.

Although Deadman's Quay was little more than a mile distant the prison governor had insisted that the convicts be marched so that they reached the quay before dawn lest townsfolk be perturbed by the presence in their midst of an army of pickpockets, horse-thieves, drawlatches and the like.

* * * * *

It was past midnight when Henry Bellamy stirred. He was stiff and chilled from lying on the cuddy bench but the only effect of his earlier and excessive drinking was tetchiness. The moment his eyes opened they had turned to the table where a number of empty goblets, but no full wine bottles, were standing.

"Hell and damnation to you, Walton. Damnation."

Bellamy lurched to his feet and made for the companionway.

As he emerged on deck an icy blast sweeping up the Channel snatched away his breath. He dragged the tricorne hat more firmly over his ears and stormed down the gangplank. He was not long in finding a tavern which welcomed customers even at that hour of the night.

The only other occupants, two women and a man, dug each other in the ribs when Bellamy staggered in and ordered a bottle of rum. Customers who ordered and paid for a full bottle of spirits were a rarity in Plymouth's Marrow Bone Walk.

One of the women, blonde, buxom, somewhat sallow and vaguely raddled, picked up her empty beaker and sidled up to Bellamy. Her appraisal of the marine officer's uniform was immediate, saucy, blatant.

"Welcome to the Cat and Fiddle, sir. It's not all that often a real gentleman comes this way."

Until that moment scarcely conscious of the presence of other customers, Bellamy screwed up his eyes to peer at the woman. He motioned to a chair on the other side of the table.

His voice was thick, the words slurred, "Hm? Sit."

He poured a generous glass of rum and gulped avidly.

"Influence, sir?"

Bellamy regarded the woman without interest.

"What d'you mean?"

"That rum, sir, it's very special. For important customers, nobody else."

Bellamy let out a tipsy guffaw.

"Important? Me? I'm not important. Begging a drink?"

The smile that crept across the woman's face, assiduously practised in front of a mirror daily for many a year, was now becoming increasingly ineffective. But in the soft light of a pair of lanterns, the puckered lips, the crinkled eyes were at once powerful magnets to the drunken Bellamy. With one hand he poured rum into the woman's beaker, oblivious of the fact that much of the spirit was escaping to the table. The other hand went to fondle the amplitude of naked breast escaping from the woman's overtight bodice.

Sipping daintily, the woman made not the slightest effort to restrain the kneading hand. Her erstwhile companions on the far side of the room nodded, winked knowingly then swiftly left. Apart from a serving wench in the background idly picking her nails, Bellamy and the woman were alone.

"Very, very few gentlemen we see here, sir," the woman whispered. She drained her goblet. At once Bellamy re-filled it. "In Plymouth for long?"

"Long as necessary," Bellamy said. Powerful spatulate fingers continued to knead bare flesh.

Bellamy rose to uncertain feet and, swaying, his head struck a low beam. The impact, however, unlike its predecessor in the Friendship's cuddy, was cushioned by tricorne hat and wig. The woman bounced from her chair and although she stood no higher than Bellamy's chin she thrust an arm over his shoulder, seized and hid the rum bottle in the folds of her skirt and steered the tipsy Bellamy towards the door. Beyond was a staircase.

All of a sudden it seemed that Henry Bellamy ceased to be fuddled by the alcohol. He lifted the woman, one arm under her shoulders, the other up her skirts to encircle her thighs and he charged to the top of the staircase where a lantern revealed an open door and beyond that a bed.

He flung the woman across the bed and wrenched aside her skirt, underskirt and drawers. Her thighs forced wide apart, she responded by struggling to open the front flap of Bellamy's breeches.

Frantic, the marines officer thrust away the woman's hands and dragged aside the interfering buckskin. While his tongue performed wild gyrations with her tongue his fingers, now inside her bodice, were savagely squeezing her nipples.

He thrust deep into her.

"Oh, my God, wonderful," she breathed.

Suddenly, and all too soon for the Plymouth woman, Bellamy now limp, withdrew. Still desperate for him she thrust both hands down between his body and her own but in spite of frenetic attempts to rouse him again, he remained flaccid and inert. Panting, she wriggled determinedly to one side and clamped her legs ferociously round a thick, muscular thigh. She moaned softly. A gasp escaped her lips. Then her whole body went limp. Slowly, reluctantly she eased herself free of Bellamy who, snoring, lay now in a deep and tipsy asleep.

In spite of his considerable bulk the woman managed to turn the marines officer on to his back. Henry Bellamy's only response was a momentary hiatus in his snoring.

By the light from the lantern which she took from the landing she contemplated for a moment the strong lean face before planting a kiss on the slightly parted lips.

"Handsome - but no great lover," she said softly and, with a skill clearly born of long practice, she rifled his pockets and then tore away the buttons of his tunic.

"Keepsakes." she said, kissing the sleeping Bellamy once more. "Not often a real live captain comes my way. Sad you came to me so tipsy, sir."

Outstretched on the rime-covered cobbles of Marrow Bone Walk, Henry Bellamy awoke, stiff and shivering, an empty rum bottle cradled in his arms. His tunic was wide open, his breeches lay about his knees. He lurched to his feet and, one hand to the wall of the Cat and Fiddle for support, he succeeded, after several attempts, to drag up and fasten his breeches although similar attempts with the buttonless tunic proved a dismal failure.

"Poxy harlot," he bellowed to the silent Marrow Bone Walk.

He put the empty rum bottle to his lips.

"Poxy, poxy harlot."

The empty bottle crashed through the window of the Cat and Fiddle.

It was four o' clock in the morning when Henry Bellamy staggered along the quiet quay of Deadman's Bay. Both sentries at the foot of Friendship's gangplank, foreheads in their hands resting on their musket muzzles, were asleep.

Bellamy kicked each musket butt, sending the men sprawling.

"Scum. - See me aboard."

The sentries scrambled to their feet and, one ahead of the captain-lieutenant, the other bringing up the rear, they escorted him on deck.

About to escort him to his cabin, the men were knocked aside and Bellamy stumbled down the companionway to the cuddy. The goblets, empty, were still on the table but there were no bottles. He lunged at the door of the locker. It was padlocked. He thumped the panels with his fists.

"Hell-spawn Walton."

Swaying perilously he dragged off the buttonless tunic, folded it to form a pillow, flung himself on the bench and at once fell asleep.

Chapter 17

Since first light, and it was now past noon, the convicts had stood waiting and shivering in driving sleet on the quay at Deadman's Bay.

Francis Walton, master of the convict transport Friendship, also was waiting. The prisoners could not be taken to their gaol in the 'tween decks of the vessel until they had been inspected by Captain-lieutenant of Marines Henry Bellamy and so far there was no sign of Bellamy. For an hour, with mounting impatience, Walton had paced Friendship's deck. At length he paused at the head of the gangplank.

"Get Captain Bellamy," he said to the sentry.

"Gangplank never to be left. Captain's orders."

"Why?"

"Escapers."

"What escapers?"

"Convicts."

"But they're all on the quay, you fool."

"Captain's orders," the sentry said dully.

"Give me that musket. Now get the captain."

Minutes later, unshaven and without tunic, Bellamy emerged from the companionway.

"What in hell.....?"

Unsteady, eyes no more than slits, Bellamy paused at the head of the gangplank.

"Look, the naval agent over there kicking his heels. And your convicts ready for inspection," Walton rasped.

"Inspect 'em then."

"It's you. You inspect. And give receipts to the agent and the Plymouth turnkey."

"No - you do it."

"Bloody baboon. The receipt's from you, life-and-death merchant aboard my ship. I'm only the master. I just pull on the bloody oars."

Walton, thrusting Bellamy to one side, summoned a guard.

"Get 'em lined up," he barked, pointing to the shivering, restive convicts and he followed, counting, as the marine thrust them into line. He snatched a sheet of paper from the turnkey and rammed it into Bellamy's unsteady hand.

"Here. Sign. Seventy-six prisoners."

Blood-shot eyes battling against feeble winter sunshine, Bellamy peered briefly at the line of ragged men and then at the paper.

"Seventeen, was it?"

"Hell's teeth." Walton beckoned to the waiting naval agent. "Come aboard. By tonight there's a chance he'll be able sign without tripping over the quill." He turned to the guard. "See the convicts on deck. Tell the galley to give 'em hot stew, bread and ale."

On deck the prisoners were freed from their linking chains but the manacles and fetters remained. They were fed generously and then, one by one, they were to be taken to the ship's cuddy for medical examination.

Although the convicts had washed daily during their sojourn in Plymouth Gaol the clothes they wore were those supplied on departure from the Thames hulk. The tattered garments were now so filthy and evil-smelling that, in spite of the icy winds raging up the English

Channel, Thomas Arndell had wedged the cuddy door wide open. Even then he strove to keep his distance.

Daniel Stocksbridge was the first convict to be examined.

"Name?"

"Daniel Stocksbridge, sir."

"Occupation?"

"Vendor of teeth from dead soldiers, sir."

Arndell glanced up from the list of convicts.

"Is - er - is there a steady demand?"

"London gentry - enormous, sir."

"What if no battles?"

"No dead soldiers, sir."

"And no teeth for the gentry."

"Nor food for me, sir."

Arndell glanced at emaciated features, sunken eyes, lips as pale as the cheeks, and, finally, a pair of bony hands.

"Very few battles of late?"

"I've been on holiday, sir."

"You can cease calling me 'sir'."

"Thank you, sir."

"Where was the holiday?"

"A Thames hulk."

"Why?"

"Waiting for battles. A man's got to eat. There was a stagecoach."

"Highwayman, hm?"

"Highwaymen have horses, they're rich. No, only a footpad."

"Daniel drew the ragged tunic more tightly about him.

"Go now, sir?"

Arndell rose to close the door.

"A few more questions. Consumption, the gleets.....?"

"Nor costiveness, nor convulsions," Daniel said tartly. "Two maladies only. Aversions to bitter cold and an empty belly."

Arndell gave a wry smile.

"Could selling teeth be no more than a hobby?"

"I'm an opportunist, sir."

"And not lacking common sense."

"Very, very little."

"Enough to heed a warning?"

"A warning, sir?"

"I detect signs of a 'tween decks lawyer."

"What d'you mean, sir?"

"Stirring up trouble, urging prisoners 'Stand up for your rights'. Remember this - convicts have no rights. Every officer, every guard, even a snotty-nosed apprentice can have you flogged, close-ironed, hanged, kicked overboard."

"But wouldn't the contractors suffer, sir?"

"That's what I mean, 'tween-decks lawyer. Knowing a little but not enough. The contractor's part of the bargain was taking you aboard - not pushing you ashore in New Holland.

"Spread the news in the 'tween-decks. Friendship's no slaver carrying negroes for profit. No buyers of powerful backs waiting on New Holland beaches. The government's sole aim is to get rid of you and the rest of you." Arndell rose. "Any questions?"

"Yes, sir. Are you really a surgeon?"

Arndell's jaw set hard. A pinkness suffused the side of his neck.

"Guard!"

A musketeer slammed to attention at the open door of the cuddy. "Back on deck."

Daniel stepped briskly into the alleyway, paused, then turned. .

"No insolence intended, sir. May I go on?"

"No!"

"You invited questions, sir."

Arndell raised a restraining hand to the guard.

"Well?"

"Please, are you really a surgeon?"

"Yes, but why?"

"A friend on the deck sorely wounded, sir." Daniel pointed to his cheek. "It might call for oak bark decoction or spirit of turpentine."

"What do you know of such things?"

"Very little, sir. But I lived in the country once and listened to countrymen talking. If you think oak bark or turpentine too astringent, you might consider an ointment of herb-robert with hog's lard."

Arndell's expression had already softened.

"And you still claim a business in soldiers' teeth?"

"I do, indeed, sir."

"You're a liar, convict. But I'll treat your friend. Name?"

"Jonathan Pettifer."

"Guard, remove this man. Next convict, Jonathan Pettifer."

The marine hustled Daniel up the companionway and returned alone.

"The convicts are in special order." The man pointed to the list of names on the table. There was undisguised insolence in his tone. "Pettifer has to take his turn."

"Pettifer is to be next," Arndell said.

"He's well down the list. Lieutenant Faddy says 'No.'" Arndell, arms folded, sat back and said very slowly, "Tell the lieutenant suspected plague can be a most unpleasant shipmate."

"Y - yes, sir."

Within minutes, keeping his distance, the marine was leading Jonathan into the cuddy. He hurried away at once, slamming the door behind him.

Across the table in silence Arndell surveyed the tall dark youth, gaunt and unsmiling. The smell of unclean clothes lay heavy on the air. Arndell grimaced.

"Strip to the waist," he said and opening the cuddy door he handed Jonathan's shirt to the guard, "The galley fire!".

Seated again at the table he said to Jonathan, half-naked and shivering, "Does this fit?"

Jonathan donned a military officer's tunic, stripped of buttons.

He smiled wanly.

"Fits, yes. But an officer's. I'd get flogged."

Arndell took the garment and turned it inside out.

"Try it now."

The tunic which had served Bellamy as a pillow overnight in the cuddy fitted Jonathan tolerably well.

Arndell laughed.

"Convict to captain in a trice. Now that wound."

The surgeon examined carefully the gash which swept from the corner of Jonathan's mouth to the lobe of his ear. It showed signs of healing but, in parts, the scab was suppurating, here and there were flecks of fresh blood.

"Treatment so far?"

Jonathan shook his head.

"How did you come by it?"

"A battle with the revenue men. I had to lie low. The wound was neglected. Lost a tooth as well."

Arndell's smile was not unsympathetic.

"Neither adds to your beauty. Captured?"

"No, no."

"Convicted though."

"For begging!"

"Seven years for begging?!"

"Begging a ride in a stagecoach with a brace of magistrates."

"Oh, oh. Nothing I can do about the sentence. The wound's different."

From a bulkhead locker Arndell brought out a jar.

"We'll try this."

"What?"

"Would you understand?"

"Maybe - maybe not."

"Then why ask?"

"Well as it's my wound it'd be good to know."

"You'll not be treating yourself."

"No."

"Little point then telling you anything."

Jonathan leaned forward to decipher the words on the jar's label.

"Oak bark decoction," he said quietly. "Hm."

"You can read? Any minute now you'll be saying the decoction's not suitable"

"There could be better preparations."

"Indeed?"

"Oak bark tends to be astringent."

"And how would a convicted felon from a Thames hulk know such a thing?"

"I - I used to be a tanner's apprentice. We had oak bark for treating cow hides. The local apothecary often called for supplies."

"So how might your apothecary treat a scab?"

"A decoction of birch leaves, maybe."

Arndell smiled broadly.

"And how d'you come to know about birch leaves?!"

"Birch grew in the tanner's garden. The apothecary was always asking for the leaves."

One hand cupping his chin, elbow on the table, the other hand resting on his knee. Arndell surveyed Jonathan through narrowed eyes.

"More accomplished telling lies than tanning hides, I'll wager, convict. You and Stocksbridge make a pair. When I've chosen the decoction I'll see you again."

Then, as the surgeon opened the door to summon a guard, he winked at Jonathan and whispered, "Birch leaves, yes, I think I agree."

The upper deck of Friendship was divided by a high wooden barricade, topped with iron spikes, stretching from larboard to starboard amidships, a narrow door at each end, guarded by a sentry.

When each of the convicts had been examined by the ship's surgeon, they were divided into gangs of six and driven through a barricade door and down a hatchway ladder.

Their new prison was the 'tween decks of Friendship with a ceiling of four feet. Separated by alleyways eighteen inches apart were rows of crudely fashioned two-tier bunks, so short that even the diminutive Daniel Stocksbridge found it impossible to stretch out full length and with a width of sixteen inches so narrow as to compel the men to lie not on their backs but on their sides.

Hunched, foetus-like, in a bunk across the alleyway, Jonathan bellowed above the hubbub of groans and curses and the clatter of irons, "Same as the slave ships."

Daniel, battling for a more comfortable position on the thin palliasse of straw, flinched as a splinter of rough-hewn timber drove deep behind a finger-nail.

"Worse. A hell of a lot worse," he shouted. "Blackbirds were given enough room to lie down in comfort. Space like this for about forty of 'em. We must be nearly double that."

Chapter 18

The women's respite in Plymouth Gaol was brief. Ten days after their arrival they were roused at midnight and given bread and cheese and small beer. They were hustled into the chill prison-courtyard where they were manacled and fettered once more.

Bellamy's interest in the shivering, disconsolate new arrivals on the quayside of Deadman's Bay was no greater than his enthusiasm for the men already battened down in Friendship's 'tween decks.

At the end of the line of twenty-two women, Francis Walton paused and turned to Bellamy.

"All yours, Henry. Any comment?"

"A poxy-looking lot," Bellamy said." Let 'em aboard. I'll sign."

At the head of the gangplank Arndell stood aside as Walton stepped on deck.

"By the look of 'em, you'll need all the surgery you ever learnt, Arndell," Walton said with a sneer.

Together they watched in silence as the women scrambled off the gangplank and were hastily lined up along the deck barricade by marines. Most of the prisoners, gaunt and pallid, dejected and shivering, were weeping.

Arndell's gaze moved, not unkindly, along the row of convict women.

"I'll need the cuddy again, Francis."

"Why?"

"The examinations."

"Oh, no you don't, leech-man. Once is enough. The place still reeks of Greenwich hulks and now you want to add the stench of Newgate. Examine 'em on deck. Under the awning aft."

"In the bitter cold?"

"Tween decks then."

"Too dark. In any case the women want privacy."

"Privacy? After Newgate it's a luxury they'd never appreciate."

The tip of Arndell's tongue touched his lower lip. The side of his neck was turning pink.

"Then - then I can't sign the medical certificates for the Navy Board."

Francis Walton was a man of no more than average height but he towered over the slightly-built young surgeon.

"A refusal?"

"N-no."

"What the hell is it then? Inability?"

"Yes."

"What?"

"I can't perform my duties without privacy and regard for the feelings of the wretched women."

Walton's laugh was without mirth.

"Women's feelings? These aren't women. They're convicted felons. The examination's not for their good. It's for the benefit of the ship's company. I want no gaolhouse plagues or fevers aboard any vessel I command."

"Then the sooner they're examined the better."

"In the 'tween decks."

"No."

"Upper deck then."

"Look at 'em, Francis. Look. Hunched, terrified, shivering, not well enough clad for a summer's day never mind freezing March."

"I've told you, Arndell. Not my cuddy for a mob of stinking, poxy, thieving sows....."

Without waiting to hear more Arndell strode over to the huddled women.

"Why're you here?" he said to one woman, sad-eyed, grey-haired, grey-faced.

"Collecting firewood, sir."

"To sell?"

"To keep my sick husband warm."

"Where is he now?"

The woman burst into tears.

"Dead, I suppose. Still sitting over the empty grate where I left him six months ago."

Arndell looked to her companion, in contrast younger, buxom and pretty.

"And you?"

"I refused a man."

Arndell smiled in disbelief.

"No woman's convicted for that, surely?"

"Unless the man happens to be a magistrate."

Arndell went back to Walton and drew him beyond earshot of the women.

"One of 'em a felon because she went collecting firewood to keep a sick husband warm, the other refused her body to a Bow Street magistrate. Stinking, poxy, thieving sows? Yes?"

Walton's grunt was non-committal.

"Their country never gave 'em a chance, Francis," Arndell went on, "nor, seemingly, will you. I need a chance as well. But cooped up with you and Bellamy I see little hope. I suggest a signal to the Commissioners. Tell them my cabin will be ready for my successor - if they can find one - inside ten minutes."

Thomas Arndell was packing his few possessions when Walton appeared at the open door of the surgeon's cabin, a windowless room that was little more than a narrow cupboard.

"One leech-man's as good as the next, I suppose," the ship's master said gruffly. "Use the cuddy."

Arndell continued his packing.

"Sure?" he said without looking up.

"Yeh."

"I'll stay on one condition - apart from the cuddy, of course."

"Go on." Walton rasped.

"Send all those pathetic creatures below. Give 'em tea laced with rum."

Walton's grunt was non-committal.

"Does that mean, 'yes'?"

Walton grunted a second time and Arndell began to unpack.

One by one throughout the day in the cuddy, Arndell painstakingly examined the women. Only one of them, elderly with ulcerated legs and elbows thick as ripe vegetable marrows, he judged unfit for what threatened to be a lengthy and arduous voyage to the other side of the world.

Meantime, so far as their ankle fetters allowed, the women shuffled disconsolately up and down the narrow alleyways between the tiers of bunks, their gaol separated from the men's gaol by a stout barricade floor to ceiling, larboard to starboard.

Not all, by any means, of the women had been convicted for such a trivial offence as gathering firewood, Arndell learned. Some were confidence tricksters, some were whores who skilfully picked pockets during the very act of hiring out their bodies.

In the short time between leaving the 'tween decks and presenting herself in the cuddy, Martha Kerwin had not only temporarily sold herself but also three eternal pardons to members of Friendship's crew. Early in the day, the surgeon's knife had disappeared from the cuddy table into the folds of a skirt and, when Arndell leaned over a woman for a closer examination of a rheumy eye, his gold watch slid into her bodice and remained there.

Margaret Dunne was the last of the women.

"Sit," Arndell said.

Arndell raised his head.

For silent moments, Arndell stared at Margaret, the auburn hair, the high cheekbones. the hazel eyes, the delicately shaped lips. Throughout her sojourn in Plymouth Gaol there had been warmth, food, soap and hot water so that Margaret's face no longer bore trace of Newgate pallor or indications of her days of agony in the condemned hold. The young surgeon, with patent effort, moved his gaze from her to papers on the table.

"You - you are...?" Arndell was struggling for words.

He did not look up.

"Margaret Dunne."

"What - er - what brings you here, Miss – er - Miss Dunne?"

"What brings.......?"

Diffidence, confusion, nervousness were all present on Arndell's face.

"You - er - you committed some crime?"

"No."

"Surely?"

"No point in explaining."

The captivated Arndell glanced around the cuddy. His lips began to move but at first no sound emerged.

"Would you - could you talk?"

"Ask what you must and let me go."

The pleading in Arndell's tone was all too evident.

"I beg you, please ....."

"You beg me. Beg me for what? Don't waste your time, surgeon. I have no phthisis, no cholera or dropsy, no ringworm, no spasms...."

Arndell rose to his feet.

"Please. My aim's to help you - and the rest of the convicts - er - women." He paused for a moment again to drink in the delicate features and the expressive eyes. "Fortunately, the horrors of Newgate seem to have left few, if any, physical scars."

Margaret's eyes blazed. The flat of her hand thudded down on the cuddy table.

"Few scars? Few scars, you say, surgeon?"

She raised the hem of her tattered skirt to reveal the irons that shackled her ankles. Gingerly she lifted the fetters. A gasp of agony escaped from her lips. The skin of one ankle was raw and flecked with blood. Part of the bone of her other ankle was totally bare of flesh.

"Oh, Christ," Arndell muttered. "Dear Christ."

Chapter 19

"Hear what I hear?"

Daniel lay in the alleyway between the bunks, an ear pressed hard to the bulkhead.

Jonathan scrambled out of his bunk and also listened.

"Women."

"A lot of 'em."

Jonathan, puzzled, shook his head.

"Women to Botany Bay? Surely not."

"Newgate has enough and to spare, they say."

"They'll never survive."

Again Daniel pressed an ear to the bulkhead.

"By the sound of 'em they're surviving well enough so far," he said with a chuckle.

The overhead trapdoor was flung back and a marine bellowed into the 'tween decks, "Pettifer, the convict Pettifer."

With a swift glance of uncertainty towards Daniel, Jonathan scrambled to his feet and stumbled to the ladder over the bodies of the other men sprawling in the alleyway.

Crawling from the hatch, Jonathan paused to gulp the chill, fresh air but the muzzle of a musket at once goaded him towards the barricade, down the companionway and then into the cuddy.

Seated at the cuddy table, facing an array of glass jars, Arndell glanced up.

"Birch leaf decoction," he said with a smile, handing one of the bottles to Jonathan.

"Thank you. Thank you very much. Just one question."

"Well?"

"How best to apply it."

Jonathan placed both hands, palms uppermost, on the table.

"No decoction mixed with filth can be a cure for scabs. Some muslin would be useful."

"Another solution - wash." Arndell said with impatience.

"Wash, sir? The only wash for me's the sputum from the consumptive I'm forced to lie cheek by jowl with in your gaol- deck."

"Not - not my gaol deck," Arndell snapped. "But I'll try to arrange ways of getting washed. If there'd been somewhere hereabouts for that consumptive he'd've been put ashore at once. But Plymouth's even less welcoming than Friendship. I rejected one convict, an elderly woman. The marines put her on the quay - a frozen corpse next morning."

"Fortunate woman," Jonathan said. "Why couldn't they leave us in the hulks to die? I can't see anybody surviving for long in those 'tween decks."

Arndell fingered his lips.

"I'll do everything possible....."

"To prolong the misery? The humane way would be a decoction of monk's hood with laudanum."

Arndell shook his head vigorously.

"I'll battle night and day for their survival. And you can help."

Jonathan regarded the surgeon with some surprise.

"I?"

"For a mere tanner's apprentice you show a remarkably lively mind - and knowledge. I could make good use of you."

Jonathan clanked the manacles.

"Free me of these?"

"No authority but you'd spend just your nights in the 'tween decks."

Jonathan shook his head.

"With them - but not of them? No, Mr Surgeon. Free man or shackled convict, nothing in between. In any case you underestimate my fellow felons. They'd regard me as a spy..."

"And you underestimate the rigours of a year voyaging to New Holland."

"Worse than a Thames hulk? The cold, the foul river water, the stench of rotting corpses?" Jonathan paused. "I remember a screaming fifteen year old boy, dragged out of his sleep to lie upside down with some brute frantic for a woman. Scarce chance for much screaming though. At the same time another fiend thrusting deep down the child's throat!"

Arndell's lips curled in horror.

"You suggesting some depraved beast going to seize you for -for some nefarious practice?"

"Maybe not. But sleeping men are easy targets. Like this."

Jonathan flung his hands over Arndell's head, the manacles threatening to garrotte the surgeon. Arndell let out a strangled cry and Jonathan released the hold.

The surgeon's hitherto pale features were now crimson.

"How - how dare you, convict? You'll hang for this."

"I was simply adding force to my point."

Arndell fondled his neck.

"Hang, hang."

"Mr Surgeon, in the past few months I've been flogged and flogged for no reason whatsoever. Forced to exist in filth, in stench, cold, wet. I've been dragged from my home, friends and profession. I've been shackled and starved. Now I'm threatened with the gallows. The rope for me and the rest of us in your gaol deck would be a blessing. So, for God's sake get on with it, man."

Arndell's crimson was now suffusing to a pale pink. He took a deep breath.

"We - we'd better talk. I was, maybe, thoughtless."

"Thoughtless? Thoughtless because you've never had the chance to think. The Sick and Hurt Commissioners should've made you spend a month in the orlop deck of a prison hulk, should've arranged tuition in the condemned hold of Newgate gaol. Then you'd see a simple, swift hanging as a blessing direct from heaven."

Jonathan began to pace the narrow cuddy.

Arndell motioned to a chair.

"You suggest I know nothing of my job?" he said calmly.

Jonathan took the chair, turned it round so that his elbows rested on its back and his legs straddled the seat.

"No, Mr Surgeon. All I say is you haven't the measure of convicts. For years. cowering under the shadow of the gallows - but no swift and simple hanging. More likely swing, gasping for breath, until tongues protrude and turn blue. Then cut down for castration, belly-slashing and ......"

Arndell thumped the table.

"I - I want to know no more. There are......"

It was Jonathan's turn to thump the table.

"But you have to know more, Arndell. You have to appreciate you're party to a brutality unequalled since the days of the Roman galley slaves."

With a sudden calmness, Arndell contemplated the once-handsome features, marred now by the scar that swept from a corner of the mouth to the lobe of an ear.

"So far as it lies in my power - and the longer the voyage the more powerful a ship's surgeon becomes - Friendship'll never be a floating Newgate. But I'll need help. You, Pettifer, as I've already told you, can supply it."

Jonathan regarded Thomas Arndell askance.

"How could a tanner's apprentice possibly help a man passed by Surgeons Hall?"

"Very little."

"Then why......?"

"Because you're no tanner's apprentice. A surgeon, once failed, like me?"

Jonathan evaded the question and raised high his manacled wrists.

"I said earlier, rid me of these. Not only me but Daniel Stocksbridge. And night and day freedom aboard for us both."

"Impossible."

"Discuss with the ship's master and the marines captain."

"I know their reply."

"Then you know mine, Mr Surgeon."

Chapter 20

Throughout the March night a searching east wind had swept torrential rain and sleet up the English Channel. Water had dripped incessantly from joins in the badly caulked planking of the upper deck, chilling and soaking the convict women below.

When a marine opened the trapdoor in the hatch-cover he was greeted by shrieks and cat-calls and a torrent of oaths.

"Grab 'im."

Promptly letting the ladder drop, the man stepped back and lunged with the butt of his musket at long-nailed fingers.

Bellamy, standing with Arndell at a discreet distance, jerked a thumb in the direction of the fingers clawing over the edge of the trapdoor.

"Changed your mind?"

"No," Arndell said quietly. "No reason to."

Shrieks and oaths from the women's gaol-deck continued unabated.

"By the sound of it, twenty two bloody good reasons. You'll be torn apart. Look." The fingers went on clawing, the oaths plombed new and blacker depths. "Still determined?"

Arndell's face was without expression.

"Yes."

"Idiot."

As Arndell made to step forward Bellamy clamped a hand on his shoulder.

"Wait for some of the stench to clear. I'll order a couple of musket volleys over their heads. Then my men'll give cover."

Arndell shook himself free of Bellamy's grasp and swiftly scrambled into the 'tween decks. He was at once assailed by the shrieking, cursing women. There was a sound of tearing fabric followed by a slap and a scream then a thud. One of the women lay outstretched on the floor.

"Act like wild cats and I treat you like wild cats. I'm here for your good not my own. On your feet, you."

The woman whose face the surgeon had slapped scrambled to her feet. It was Martha Kerwin, pardons vendor, her otherwise sallow cheek a deep crimson. Statuesque, raven-haired, face not without beauty in spite of months of privations in Newgate Gaol, she surveyed Arndell from head to toe with undisguised disdain.

Subconsciously, Arndell glanced towards the trapdoor above. Martha's eyes followed. She sneered.

"Soldier-boys with guns to protect him."

Arndell swallowed hard. To the marines with muskets at the ready he waved a dismissive hand.

"Away. At once."

He thrust himself into the midst of the women.

"A seamstress anywhere?"

Gently but firmly he pushed back the crowding women and raised the hem of his jerkin to show where it had been torn by Martha Kerwin.

His eyes ranged over the sullen-faced women until they settled on Margaret.

"You a seamstress?"

"And if not?"

"The sight of me every day in a torn tunic."

"Get me needle and thread."

"You sew well?"

"Passably."

Martha Kerwin pushed forward.

"The finest seam in London," she said.

"Splendid. Now, ladies," Arndell paused "ladies, your health is my responsibility....."

Martha elbowed the surgeon and winked at the other women.

"Rid us of these," Martha clanked her fetters. "Then warm, dry clothes."

"I'm afraid....."

"And good food, plenty of fresh air."

Arndell wiped his forehead with the palm of his hand.

"Shortcomings, I know. This is a ship, ladies, paid for by a government not exactly concerned about comfort. It looks on you all as less than useless." Arndell began to climb the ladder. He paused and turned. "But I'll go on reminding myself you're the opposite. Help me, please, to help you. Ready, Mistress Seamstress?"

Martha Kerwin, close behind Margaret, whispered, "Do what ever he asks, let him have what ever he wants. I mean that, what ever he wants - for all our sakes."

Arndell, now on the upper deck, strode ahead. Hampered by her fetters, Margaret struggled to follow across a clutter of ropes and tools and water casks and and provisions, all being assembled for stowage below. As Arndell stepped aside for her to shuffle through the doorway in the barricade, one of the sentries winked at his companion.

"Cleaned up and perfumed, I'd bed her myself."

The words were loud enough for Arndell to hear. With calculated gesture he held Margaret by the arm and escorted her to the companionway then, lifting her bodily, he carried her down the steps to the cuddy where he gently placed her on a chair. From the bulkhead locker he took an earthenware jar and a piece of muslin which he tore into strips.

"Smear your ankles with this and I'll bandage them. I can't take the fetters off but I can certainly relieve the pain."

He left the cuddy briefly to return with needle and thread. Margaret applied the ointment and with strips of muslin Arndell gently bandaged the savaged flesh.

"The rest of the ointment and bandage for the others," he said, rolling up the remainder of the muslin and handing it to her with the jar. "Now, if you please, the sewing."

He took off his jerkin and, glancing at the sleeve of his spotless linen shirt then Margaret's filthy ragged bodice, he frowned.

"Fresh clothing on its way," he said quickly. "First to the Portsmouth ships then here."

"Portsmouth? Where are we?"

"Plymouth. But the whole fleet assembles at Portsmouth."

"When?"

"When all the ships are provisioned, when Newgate and the Thames hulks cease sending - er - supplies."

"Oh."

Margaret threaded a needle.

"You don't seem very interested," Arndell said, watching the long and elegant fingers. "A fresh start, a new life."

Head down, unresponsive, Margaret began to sew.

"I -er - I could help," Arndell added.

"Help?"

She flung the half-mended jerkin in his face and lurched to her feet. Agony distorted her pallid features as the fetters twisted and bit deep into the muslin bandage. "No real reason to bring me here for a trifling repair like this. It could've easily been done in the gaol deck. But what ever your motives....."

"Motives?"

"If the would-be seamstress had been Sarah Garodby......"

"Who?"

"Pock-marked Sarah, the woman with the dropsy. You'd never've invited Mistress Sarah here."

"I make no distinctions...."

"If you've got designs on my body, well it's neither for barter nor for sale."

Arndell left his chair and, donning the jerkin, he pointed to the door of the cuddy. In silence he followed Margaret, awkward and slow because of the fetters, up the companionway. He went ahead to lead her along the cluttered deck and when they reached the prison hatch he said softly, "No more attempts 'to barter or buy' - "the words, the inflections were Margaret's own" - I swear. Oh, God, woman, I'm going frantic for...."

The rest of Arndell's words were lost as a marine slammed down the trapdoor and rammed home the bolts.

Henry Bellamy was alone in the cuddy, drinking, when Arndell returned.

"Brandy?"

Arndell slid forward a goblet. Tipsy Bellamy overfilled and liquor dribbled across the table to drip on to the cuddy floor. The surgeon drained the goblet in a single gulp. He pointed to the brandy slowly soaking into the planking.

"Like the floor in the 'tween decks."

Bellamy belched.

"Where your women have been pissing?"

"Sea water. Where they'll very soon be rotting if we don't do something right away."

More brandy sluiced into a goblet and more ran across the table to the cuddy floor.

"But you've already done something," Bellamy said thickly.

"An inspection of the quarters, that's all."

"Hindquarters?"

"A brief look at conditions."

"And rescued a wench for a tumble in the cuddy?"

"What d'you mean?"

"I saw. Coming down the companionway I saw you fondling the woman's leg. I didn't stay for more. Dammit, an officer and a gentleman doesn't...."

"I was simply binding the poor woman's ankles. Her leg-irons had caused the most horrendous wounds."

"What a mistake I made. Why ever didn't I think of becoming a back-alley barber and blood-letter? Oh, the opportunities....."

The palm of the young surgeon's hand left only trifling impression on the ruddy cheek of the burly marines officer.

Bellamy tried to retaliate but he was extremely drunk. With little effort Arndell was able to sidestep and dodge the clumsily aimed fist.

"You bloody leech," Bellamy mouthed.

Overbalancing, he collapsed on the cuddy floor.

Chapter 21

At the first mouthful of gruel, greasy with rancid butter, harsh from over-salted beef, Daniel Stocksbridge's stomach was in revolt.

For three days he had taken nothing more than a few tentative sips of water, brackish from standing undisturbed in casks for weeks on the open deck. The fetters bit deep into thin flesh as he twisted this way and that in an effort to ease his sweating, pain-wracked body. Seated beside him Jonathan had ripped away part of his shirt, dipped it in water and for an hour gently bathed his friend's brow.

"Dammit, I can do more than this," Jonathan said suddenly, flinging aside the rag. He jerked to his feet and elbowed his way through the knot of prisoners cramming the narrow aisle between the bunks to the trapdoor. He hammered urgently on the timbers.

"Guard, guard!"

The trapdoor was slow to open and even then it admitted little more than a whisper of daylight.

"A flogging if you don't shurrup."

"Not before we're all corpses. Typhus, cholera. Get the surgeon, quick."

The trapdoor dropped with a crash leaving the prison deck once more in semi-darkness. But within minutes it was raised again, a ladder thrust down and Arndell was bending over the opening to peer into the gloom.

"Who cries typhus?"

"Me, surgeon."

Arndell pointed to the ladder.

"Up."

In sunshine he and Jonathan stood face to face on the upper deck. Arndell was careful to keep his distance.

"Well?" he said.

"Maybe not typhus or cholera," Jonathan said.

"Then why.....?"

"The only way of getting the guard to contact you."

"Don't make a fool of me, convict."

"My friend Stocksbridge is dangerously ill."

"But not typhus, not cholera."

"No."

Arndell's manner was curt, caustic.

"So what precise malady does your great knowledge help us to diagnose?"

"Seafarer's ague, maybe."

Arndell, eyes narrowing, inspected Jonathan's features.

"You and Stocksbridge are still mysteries. Do I assume all will be revealed by the time we drop anchor in Botany Bay?!"

"No mystery at all, sir."

"Questions," Arndell said then glanced over his shoulder.

Two marines were craning their necks in the hope of overhearing the conversation. The surgeon motioned Jonathan to the ship's rail.

Leaning there Jonathan momentarily closed his eyes. The early spring sun was warm to shoulders bared after sacrificing the tattered shirt for Daniel Stocksbridge. High in Friendship's rigging a pair of gulls briefly tormented each other before flying away. In silence he watched the effortless flight.

"Envious?" Arndell said.

"Desperately."

"Short-lived freedom. December's hail and sleet'll be here again. They'll starve."

"And I won't?"

"Friendship'll be quite well provisioned. And they say Captain Cook was ecstatic about Botany Bay. Now, explain how a vendor of soldiers' teeth comes to be suffering from seaman's ague."

"Handling teeth from the Americas, could be."

"Almost as likely as suffering baldness after toothache. And how can a tanner's apprentice be so sure about such an affliction?"

"My master often had business with ships' captains. I've seen the sweating and shivering."

Arndell smiled.

"An answer for everything. You'll know the treatment, of course."

"I remember being sent to an apothecary for - would it be Peruvian bark?"

Arndell threw back his head and laughed.

"Back to your dungeon, tanner's apprentice. I'll see your accomplice gets his Peruvian bark. No doubt you'd prescribe it in decoction?"

* * * * *

Before Margaret's feet were free of the ladder she was assailed by the clamorous women.

"Was he forceful, dearie?" Martha Kerwin said, mouth close to Margaret's ear. "Or was he gentle - at first?"

Sarah Garodsby cackled obscenely.

"On top in his cabin? Or you on him?"

Margaret's lips curled in distaste. Martha bundled the rest of the women roughly aside.

"Make no mystery about it. Did he strip you? Was he stripped as well?"

"No."

"Well, what did you do for us?"

From inside her bodice, Margaret drew the jar of salve and a bundle of muslin strips.

"Treatment for sores," she said.

"The rum, the brandy?" Martha said.

"No."

"Then you made yourself too cheap." Martha spat with accuracy into a puddle on the floor. "What about us? What hopes for us older women when a young girl opens her thighs and gets rewarded with nothing but salve and a few scraps of muslin?"

"Maybe, maybe later..."

"Maybe? How much later? It's a long, long time to New Holland and already you've done your best to ruin us. I told you, didn't I, start high? Now Arndell, Bellamy, Walton, Faddy, every marine, every snotty-nosed sailor boy'll be offering no more than a dry biscuit before we get as far as Biscay Bay, never mind Botany Bay."

Margaret battled to escape from the jostling women.

"Leave me alone. Give me some peace."

Martha Kerwin, seizing Margaret's shoulder, shook her violently.

"Peace? There'll never be peace in this floating hellhole. We'll fight. Fight and fight, every minute, every inch of the way."

Margaret freed herself of the grasp..

"Fight? How? Against cannon, against twenty armed marines? They can starve us, iron us to the deck, feed us to the sharks. What sort of weapons have we got? None."

Charlotte Dudgeon, bright-eyed, buxom, fair, sidled up to Margaret.

"No weapons?" she said softly. "Next time that surgeon comes down we'll ......"

"No, no. Don't harm Thomas Arndell. He'll do all he can to help, I know."

"One at a time, I don't doubt," Martha Kerwin said, winking lewdly.

. A mischievous smile crept across Charlotte Dudgeon's face.

"Master Arndell'll get his chance. If he's so keen to help then he can stay down here with us. Held to ransom, hm? Not much to my taste. By the look of his breeches not enough thrust. But, as time goes by, some of the ladies," Charlotte's finger stabbed here and there "might be glad of even the gentlest tickle and tumble."

Chapter 22

Francis Walton thumped the cuddy table.

"Too dangerous. No convicts on deck yet. Escape into the Bay of Biscay, yes, but not at Deadman's Quay."

Arndell leaned forward to Walton and Henry Bellamy.

"How could they possibly escape? They can hardly put one foot in front of the other without tripping. The fetters see to that."

"I agree with Walton. No risks," Bellamy said.

Arndell sat back in his chair.

"One hundred manacled and fettered prisoners, feeble after months - some of them years - of gaol-house brutality and starvation, against twenty five marines with muskets, cutlasses, pistols, cannon - and you take 'no risks'. What exactly are the risks, Bellamy?"

"Many."

"Give me two."

"Apart from sneaking ashore, men and women coupling."

"But the deck barricade's iron-spiked and guarded enough to keep a whole army at bay. And all convicts needn't be on deck at the same time. If you've no confidence in muskets and iron spikes then - women abaft the barricade in the morning, men forrard in the afternoon."

Walton grimaced.

Arndell leaned forward once more.

"Listen, Francis. Beneath those hatches over one hundred pathetic creatures in damp and filth and stench that grow worse by the hour......"

"Brought it on themselves."

"Some, perhaps, but others in that stinking gaol-hold innocent as new-born babies. Remember, you're ship's master not gaoler, Francis Walton. The magistrates decided on punishment - transportation - but that wasn't intended to include twenty-four hours a day in a foetid gloom you can almost touch."

"I've already told you. I'll review when we've set sail, not before," Walton said.

"Too late. Unless those miserable wretches get fresh air and exercise you'll have more corpses than convicts in your 'tween decks. And I warn you, Francis, wooden hatch-covers never kept gaol fever at bay!"

Walton was immediately anxious.

"Gaol fever?"

"And worse. Everybody aboard's in danger. Everybody. Both prison decks are screaming out for drying out, brimstone fuming and lime wash."

A marine slammed to attention in the open doorway of the cuddy, "The convict with the plague, Dr Arndell."

The moment that Jonathan had murmured "Plague!", the convicts, terrified, had scrambled from their bunks and huddled together in a corner of the 'tween decks as far away from Daniel as possible. Jonathan was continuing to mop Daniel's brow when Arndell arrived.

"Quick, the lantern," the surgeon called to the marine hovering by the hatch cover and he dropped to his knees beside Daniel's bunk. He pressed an ear to the scrawny chest, at the same time his fingers sought

Daniel's pulse. He raised one of the sick man's drooping eyelids then slowly shook his head.

"Too late for his Peruvian bark - or any other decoction," he said softly.

In silence Jonathan closed the gaping mouth, the half-open eyes and, as he mopped the sweating brow, a sob escaped his quivering lips.

Arndell rejoined Bellamy and Walton in the cuddy.

"The first of many. You'll need my report for your log when I've finished it, Francis," he said and, dipping a quill into an ink horn, he wrote at considerable length in his pocket book while Bellamy and Walton watched silently the progress of the quill.

Before Arndell had time to sand the ink, Walton snatched the pocket book and, lips silently shaping each word, he slowly read the report then passed it to Bellamy.

After no more than a cursory glance, the marine captain pushed the book across the table to Arndell.

"The more corpses, the more victuals for the rest," Bellamy said. "Now there's an idea, Mr Blood-letter. With all your skills you could arrange a steady emptying of both stinking gaol-decks."

Arndell retrieved his book, tested the ink with a finger to ensure that it was dry then slid it into a tunic pocket.

"The insensitivity of the ship's master and the inhumanity of the captain of the guard should do the job quite effectively," he said to Bellamy. To Walton, about to remonstrate, he said, "At least you'll let the convicts on deck for the burial service."

Walton frowned

"Burial?"

"Burial, yes. A corpse, Francis, in your 'tween decks, the fever still on it. I suggest you have it brought on deck, firmly wrapped in winding sheet and canvas at once, and disposed of in Christian tradition."

"Waste of time," Bellamy growled.

"And a problem," Walton said. "While we're moored we can't pitch it overboard."

"No problem," Arndell said." Read the burial service then you and I will follow the corpse to Plymouth cemetery."

"Well, none of my marines'll be escorting a dead convict, that's certain," Bellamy rasped.

"No need for marines and muskets now. Corpses don't usually make a bolt for it."

"Damned nuisance in every way," Walton said.

"On the contrary, a blessing, Francis. While the convicts are on deck saying farewell to Daniel Stocksbridge your crew can burn brimstone in the men's prison-deck then limewash," Arndell said.

Arndell found most of the convicts still cowering in a corner of the 'tween decks. Daniel's body lay in its rags on a bunk, eyes closed, skinny hands across the chest.

"Can you lift him up the ladder?" Arndell said to Jonathan sitting beside the corpse.

Jonathan raised his manacles.

"Only with help," he said.

Arndell made his way to the huddled convicts.

"A volunteer to help move the body?"

The convicts were silent.

"Somebody to help. I promise he can stay on deck for the rest of the day. Warm sunshine up there - and fresh air," Arndell added.

At length one of the convicts extricated himself from the silent crowd and shuffled forward. The sunlight streaming through the open hatch revealed a pleasant-featured youth, tall, broad-shouldered. Arndell recoiled at the smell of the young prisoner.

"Name?"

"Richard," the youth said tonelessly.

"Richard what?"

The youth stared blankly.

"Richard."

Jonathan intervened. He put a finger to his lips.

"A dummy boy."

"Dummy?"

"Can hardly speak. An idiot. Gardener's assistant at Plymouth gaol. A hulk convict persuaded him to change places, promising him a sail in a big ship round the world."

Arndell turned to the boy.

"Thank you, Richard. On deck there'll be bread and honey and porter and sunshine for you." He turned to Jonathan.

"For you as well. The guards will call you shortly."

Chapter 23

Thomas Arndell peered into the gloom of the 'tween decks.

"Seamstress."

Martha Kerwin nudged Margaret.

"You again. Be kinder to him. Bring something tastier than ointment this time."

Pursued by a chorus of jeers and lewd jibes, Margaret hobbled across the planking to the opening overhead and laboriously climbed the ladder to the upper deck.

Arndell in embroidered jerkin, silk shirt, white buckskin breeches and silver buckled shoes contrasted sharply with convict Margaret in her shabby woollen cloak, grimy bodice and tattered skirt. The surgeon's black hair at the back was held by a bow of crimson velvet. Margaret's hand crept subconsciously to her own hair, escaping lank and dirty from her muslin cap.

Arndell gave a faint bow. The nearby sentries sniggered.

"Good day, seamstress. Another task. One not precisely to your taste but," Arndell lowered his voice, "it means brief liberty."

"What is it?"

"Ever had close content with a corpse, sewn its winding sheet, its canvas?"

Margaret shivered.

"No, no, I couldn't. I remember a Newgate woman and gaol fever. The turnkeys left the body with us three whole days and nights."

"No gaol fever, I swear. Poor wretch too weak to survive English Channel weather, nothing more." Arndell gave a smile of understanding. "Died barely an hour ago." He moved closer to prevent the guards' overhearing. "The rest of the day in fresh air and sunshine. I'll make arrangements for some good food."

The guards who had now moved to the ship's side were looking seawards. Arndell laid a hand on Margaret's shoulder.

"A ruse, that's all. I'll have cotton and canvas, needle and thread brought, then the body. It's on the other side." He pointed to the deck barricade. "It'll be taken away at once, I promise. A brief escape from the hell-hole for you."

"And what is it for you, surgeon?"

The side of Arndell's neck went pink. Turning on his heel he strode to the companionway and at once returned, accompanied by a young seaman.

"Fetch cotton sheets and canvas from the forrard hold, for one - no several - corpses." Arndell called to one of the marines idling at the rail. "He'll need help."

The guard response was a sneer.

"As you wish," Arndell went on. "There's a corpse in the 'tween decks and from what I recognise in the sickness the sooner it's covered up the better. There could be more by morning. Muskets and cutlasses won't be much protection."

Margaret, threading a needle, paused in alarm.

"Is - is there danger then?"

"None whatsoever. Creating fear, that's all," Arndell said, smiling." They've got their muskets, I've got my knowledge." The marine had already joined the seaman to collect the cotton and canvas. "See? Far more powerful than a bullet."

While the remaining sentry was still staring out to sea, Arndell passed a bottle of wine and a hunk of cheese to Margaret.

"Keep the other ladies quiet. Hide it ...

Arndell was cut short by the return of the seaman and the marine carrying bolts of canvas and cotton.

"Knife?" he said to the seaman.

The sailor produced a blade.

"Cut enough to wrap a body and give to the seamstress."

He turned to the marine, "Three convicts, one of them dead." He pointed to the door in the barricade. "I want them here. And keep your distance, particularly from the dead one."

After the seaman had cut pieces of cotton and canvas, struggling against a clutter of boxes and cages and ropes and water casks, Margaret managed to spread the fabric on the planking. She did not immediately see the pair of convicts carrying Daniel's body through the barricade doorway. Richard, dumb and half-witted, held the feet, Jonathan walking backwards, was holding Daniel's shoulders.

Suddenly, as they were passing through the doorway, Richard paused and lunged at the guard bringing up the rear. Daniel's heels thudded to the deck.

Within seconds, in spite of his shackles, the boy had made it to the ship's side. He hesitated briefly before plunging overboard.

Arndell reached the side in time to see the fugitive, manacled wrists high above his head, sink swiftly below the surface of the water.

Margaret scrambled to her feet. Jonathan, still grasping the shoulders of his dead friend, turned.

They stared at each other. Margaret pitifully gaunt, lank-haired, ragged: Jonathan emaciated, face grey as Daniel's and distorted by the scar that swept from an ear lobe to a corner of his mouth. Both struggled frantically for words that refused to come.

"Jonathan!"

"Margaret!"

Daniel's body slumped unheeded to the deck as Jonathan's manacled arms, slid over her shoulders, pathetically thin beneath the shabby cloak, and for the first time since that bright September morning on Tower Hill they were close once more. His mouth pressed deep and hungrily into the filthy auburn hair, then their lips came together.

"Oh, my God, what - what have they done to you, my beloved?"

He drew back briefly to scan the pallid features.

"I've waited, waited, my love. I promised, remember," she said.

Once more Jonathan drew her to him, once more their lips met and held.

The blow between Jonathan's shoulder blades sent them, locked in fevered embrace, sprawling on the deck.

Arndell made no effort to conceal his venom.

"A flogging for this, convict."

Jonathan tightened the embrace. This time the toe of Arndell's silver-buckled shoe drove into the small of his back.

"Up, up."

Jonathan struggled to his feet still frantically holding on to Margaret.

"Crazier than the idiot who plunged overboard. His agony was soon over. For you - three hundred lashes only the beginning," Arndell snarled.

Arndell's hands went to Margaret's waist to drag her away.

"No, no," she shrieked. "No."

At that moment two marines pushed through the barricade carrying the body of Richard.

"A second winding sheet, if you please, seamstress." Arndell beckoned the marines. "The convict Pettifer to the 'tween decks at once."

The butt of a musket thudded into Jonathan's back and he was thrust, bent almost double, through the barricade. He threw an anxious glance over his shoulder and glimpsed Arndell's attempt to embrace Margaret.

"God rot you."

Again the butt of a musket struck, sending him headlong down the hatchway to the gaol-deck.

The sun had disappeared behind a bank of grey cloud. Rain was now speckling the deck. Margaret dragged herself free of Arndell's fervent embrace.

"I want to go back!"

"Your ingratitude....!"

"Ingratitude?"

"Saved from that convict. Another minute and...."

"Saved? Mother of God!"

"Come, finish the sewing below," Arndell said, steering Margaret towards the companionway.

Rain was now falling steadily. Margaret covered her head with her hood and offered neither comment nor resistance.

"Do you seriously believe I didn't save you?" he said when they were seated in the cuddy. "Are you telling me you welcomed the savage embrace of that - that scar-face?"

"Yes."

"If you're so desperate for a male companion...."

"Desperate?"

"So it seems." Arndell seized Margaret's protesting hand. "Why not me?"

Margaret turned away her head.

"Let me go - please."

Arndell's grasp tightened.

"I - I beg you. Am I so loathsome?"

He fought to embrace her. In spite of the shackles she struggled free and stumbled towards the cuddy door.

"No, no, Dr.Arndell. Not loathsome."

"'Thomas', I beg you."

"No, no, Thomas."

"You still prefer that ragged stinking scoundrel to me?"

"Yes, yes, yes."

Chapter 24

Poring over a navigation chart on the table in the cuddy, Francis Walton gave Bellamy a covert wink as Thomas Arndell joined them.

"You get your wish, Thomas," Walton said. "Freedom for your convict friends from Newgate and the hulks."

Arndell's face lit up.

"When?"

"After we sail."

"Sailing, are we?"

"Tomorrow morning for Portsmouth and the Motherbank. We've decided the convicts can come on deck, the men forrard of the barricade in the mornings, the women aft of it in the afternoons."

"To your senses at last, Francis."

"Twelve men at a time, a chain through their manacles, for half an hour."

Arndell was incredulous.

"Twelve? Half an hour?"

"Enough," Bellamy said.

"You must be mad, both of you. Thirty minutes? It can take ten minutes for some of the poor devils to negotiate the ladder."

Walton laughed.

"The exercise'll do 'em good. I'll allow the women longer. Fewer of 'em so they can stay all afternoon - if you can get 'em to launder and repair linen for us."

Arndell stood up and folded his arms.

"I hope you're a better navigator than gaoler, Francis. Have you inspected the men's 'tween decks?"

"Yes."

"When?"

"Before they came aboard."

"Then take another look. Have you the faintest idea what it's like to fight for breath, to fight for existence, in barely six square feet of space, less than the area of this table?"

"You're an old hen, Arndell."

"Maybe, Francis. Take part in an experiment?" Arndell said, then glanced from Walton's no more than sturdy figure to Bellamy's substantial girth. "On second thoughts, Francis, not you but Henry. Up with you on the table, Henry."

Bellamy guffawed.

"Me? Why?"

"You telling me you're incapable?"

The table bolted to the planking in the centre of the cuddy was six feet long and two feet wide. With an agility that brought a gasp of admiration from Walton, the marines commander leapt up and sat on the table, cross-legged like a tailor.

"So far, so good," Arndell said." Now lie flat."

Bellamy lolled back, hands behind his head, legs outstretched, feet together and projecting over the edge of the table.

"Draw your feet up, heels resting on the table. Now, those feet back another twelve inches."

Bellamy bent his knees and drew in his feet.

"Now what?"

"Lie on your side."

Dutifully, Bellamy turned to his side but, within a minute, he was sitting up and dangling his legs over the side of the table.

"And now you've had your fun what's it all mean?"

"It means if you were living in the 'tween decks you'd be taking up nearly double the space allotted to each convict. Even for only a minute you were less than comfortable. Imagine, then, twenty-four hours a day, every day, in half that space. Take away fresh air, add filth and stench and chains - and you've some idea of conditions in the 'tween decks."

Walton shifted in his chair.

"The women aren't so badly off."

Arndell sneered.

"Not so badly off? Well, I suppose twelve square feet for the next twelve months may seem adequate to you - if not for you. Rather your conscience than mine. If ever a history of this voyage comes to be written then, by God, the name Francis Walton'll be made to stink worse than bloody-handed Attila the Hun."

The master of Friendship snatched up his chart.

"If you and Bellamy can produce a better plan for the convicts let me see it," he said and he stormed out of the cuddy.

Bellamy flung back his head and roared with laughter.

"Walton'll've gone to his convicts. One sniff as he opens the hatch'll be enough."

Suddenly the marines officer was serious.

"Never underrate Walton. There's a fair sprinkling of grey in that beard of his. He knows his arse from his elbow all right. He'll be putting up with the smell while telling the convicts their freedom's now in the hands of assistant surgeon Thomas Arndell."

Coming face to face with Walton at.the head of the companionway Arndell stepped aside and held out a hand. Walton ignored the gesture.

"Inspected the 'tween decks, Francis?"

Walton was gruff.

"Yes."

"And you agree?"

"Brought it on themselves. Convicted criminals."

"Convicted of what, mostly? A sixteen-year-old lad grabbed a chicken to impress some country wench then let it go free. But the magistrates didn't let the lad go free. Six months in a Thames hulk, working waist deep in water and mud for twelve hours a day. Then seven years' transportation.

"No hope, of course, of ever returning to his mother and father. But before those seven years begin you - we - chain and batten down the child in wetness and stinking darkness worse than a London cess-pit."

At the foot of the companionway Walton paused and turned.

"Their freedom's your responsibility from now on. All I stipulate is twelve men at a time, on a chain round and round the deck. Any attempted escape and it's a flogging for everybody."

"Women as well?"

"Why not?"

"I made to shake your hand a few moments ago, Francis Walton. The offer's withdrawn - indefinitely."

Chapter 25

As Henry Bellamy in scarlet tunic and tight buckskin breeches preened himself in front of the cuddy's mirror, the weary-eyed Walton glanced up from the array of charts.

"Even if the fleet sails within a day or two of assembling on the Motherbank, it'll be late December before we sight the coast of New South Wales."

Bellamy flicked insignificant specks from the scarlet.

"All the more reason for a few hours ashore this evening."

Walton stood up to stretch.

"If you're hell-bent on bedding some woman at the Cat and Fiddle again then remember....."

Bellamy's bushy eyebrows rose high.

"Didn't know you were an expert on Cat and Fiddle women, Francis."

Walton yawned.

"Nowt to do with women. Just get yourself aboard before high water in the morning. But in case you're still a-whoring at the Cat and Fiddle when we slip our moorings leave instructions for young Faddy. A warning, Henry. I never put back for anybody."

Bellamy, who had been drinking since late afternoon, rose to unsteady feet and saluted.

"Ay, ay, Cap'n Francis!"

Walton jerked his head in disgust.

"Damned if I see why you can't contain that woman-hunger till Teneriffe."

A clumsily-aimed hand landed on Walton's shoulder.

"If you can't see things like that, Francis, no bloody good me trying to explain. Leave the gangplank down till the last possible minute."

Amid a mounting clutter of water casks, ropes, cages of poultry and pig-pens, Thomas Arndell, deep in thought, was pacing the deck as Bellamy appeared from below.

"Restless, leech-man?"

"Not much taste for my books. And I can't sleep."

"Can't sleep? Half an hour with a Plymouth doxy'd make your eyelids heavy enough."

Arndell grimaced.

"Not much taste for whores."

"Only convicts?"

"My taste for convicts is no greater than yours. My pity is, though."

As Arndell watched the marines officer negotiate the narrow gangplank then stagger off into the night, a look of disgust mingled with contempt spread across the pale features.

In the cuddy the surgeon filled a goblet with brandy. He coughed and spluttered as he attempted, and succeeded in, swallowing the liquor at a single gulp. He replenished the goblet but this time he sipped very slowly.

He turned to inspect his pale, handsome features in the mirror. His hand smoothed the rich black hair and, as if he had been holding secret discussion with his half-smiling reflection, he nodded. He drained the goblet and taking the brandy bottle under his arm he climbed to the upper deck of the Friendship. At the head of the companionway he paused briefly, took a deep breath then with uncertain steps he made for the trapdoor leading to the women's prison in the 'tween decks.

A marine at once barred the way.

"Halt."

Arndell parried the musket barrel with the brandy bottle.

"Dr Arndell," he said softly.

"Sir?"

"I need the convict seamstress again."

The light from the moon was sufficient for Arndell to see at once the lewd expression on the face of the sentry.

"Risk it if you like, sir, but I wouldn't chance my oldest pair of breeches in the middle of that lot."

The marine kicked back the bolts and raised the trapdoor an inch. Immediately the peace of the night was rent by shrieks and screams and waves of bawdy laughter.

"I'll be ready with a cutlass, sir."

"Cutlass?"

"Them bickering whores. More respect for the flat of a cutlass than the muzzle of a musket. A couple of slaps across the arse and they won't be able to sit down for a fortnight. Besides, no ammunition aboard yet. And it's not much fun shoving a musket muzzle where you could be shoving something else. Best of luck, sir."

Stepping to the now wide-open trapdoor Arndell was promptly seized by the smell, warm and sour on the crisp night air. Handkerchief pressed to his nose, he knelt over the opening.

"The convict seamstress," he called.

Martha Kerwin appeared.

"Who wants her?"

"The surgeon."

Arndell thrust forward the bottle of brandy.

"A pleasure, sir," Martha said seizing the bottle then thrusting Margaret up the ladder supplied by the sentry. "Remember, Margaret," she hissed, "offer him a warm, soft seam for our benefit."

The guard hoisted Margaret to her feet on deck, dragged up the ladder, slammed and bolted the hatch.

"Good evening, seamstress."

Gulping deep draughts of fresh air Margaret did not immediately respond.

"We set sail in the morning," Arndell went on," and there's sewing to be done for the shipboard hospital before the fleet assembles off Portsmouth."

Margaret's voice bore overtones of deep suspicion.

"Isn't it rather late? And sewing by lantern light's not easy."

"The chief surgeon's boarding us at Portsmouth. He'll insist on seeing what provision we've made for the sick." For the benefit of the guard standing within earshot Arndell raised his voice. "Bandages urgently needed. I'll permit work in the cuddy with plenty of lanterns. Come."

Arndell led the way to the cuddy.

"Where's the muslin, the linen, the scissors?" Margaret glanced at the bare table then she pointed to the cuddy's solitary lantern. "And that light's no better than the prison deck."

Arndell's words were scarcely audible as he drew Margaret to him.

"More than enough."

She struggled to evade the searching lips but Arndell's all-consuming hunger gave him added strength. His hold on Margaret's protesting, quivering body was savage and, when his mouth failed to make contact with Margaret's mouth, he covered her face, her neck and her bared shoulders with an avalanche of frantic kisses.

Then, as suddenly as he had seized Margaret, Arndell freed her and stepped back. For a moment thrown off balance because of the fetters Margaret staggered and she would have collapsed on the cuddy floor but for the table.

"Oh, please, please forgive me. The chains, I'd forgotten."

Once more he attempted to take Margaret's unyielding, agitated body in his arms.

In wild fury Margaret thrust him aside.

"I fail to understand this - this hunger for a body fouled by your gaolhouse. And I've already told you - I am not for taking - ever."

Arndell dropped to his knees.

"Fail to understand, you say? Night and day my whole being craves for you. I can't sleep, my books no longer appeal, I cannot.... For God's sake, woman, show some pity...."

Margaret Dunne, ragged, unkempt convict-woman, looked down on the immaculately garbed young surgeon and her hand briefly touched the jet-black hair.

"Pity? I can't offer pity - or anything else."

"But I'd do anything...."

"You've been kind, you've been foolish. Foolish to yourself, deadly dangerous to me."

Arndell's tone was incredulous.

"Dangerous? How?"

"You're a fine-looking man, Thomas Arndell. There's muttering among the women. Jealousy. Hunger in those 'tween decks for a body like yours. Already I'm terrified......"

"They'll do you no harm, I swear. I'm getting more and more frantic."

"A waste of time."

Arndell scrambled to his feet.

"I'm going crazy for you, woman."

Margaret took Arndell's face between her hands.

"Listen, Thomas Arndell. I'm sorry, I could never, never love you."

"Why, why not?"

"For months and months of hell I've struggled for one man. I'd struggle through ten thousand more hellish months for him. And that man isn't you, Thomas Arndell."

Margaret drew her hands away.

"Who is it?" Arndell said.

"Jonathan Pettifer."

"Pettifer ? Scarface Pettifer? I - I don't believe....."

"You must."

"Since that chance encounter when he was carrying the corpse?"

"No, no, no. Months - it seems like a century of hell - ago. When we were both - both..... - Oh, what's it to you?"

"A great deal."

"I daren't think about the past....."

"Well, you'll have to think about the future."

"No worse than the here and now."

"Infinitely worse. D'you imagine there's going to be some sort of life here or Botany Bay or anywhere else with Pettifer? Convict with convict? Believe me, there's not the faintest hope. And the government's made no plans for getting you back to England. No thought whatsoever about your survival."

"Survivors of Newgate and the Thames prison hulks can survive whatever Botany Bay has in store."

Arndell gently drew Margaret's hands away from his face.

"Don't imagine you're bound for a land flowing with milk and honey. More likely slow starvation or swift death from the spear of some blackamoor. Very little fresh water, even less food. When stores run short it won't be the marines and the sailors who suffer......."

"If Jonathan and I can't live together we'll die together."

Arndell clasped Margaret's hands between his own.

"Certainly you'll die but almost certainly not together. Pettifer'll be as much a slave as one of those blackamoors captured in droves on the coast of Africa and shipped to the Americas. He'll be whipped to labour, brutalised and systematically starved. But your fate.....No, never."

"Never what?"

"Taken by some ruffian marine. To be used and used, sold again and again until you're gaunt and disease-ridden, until you're dead."

"You - you say you love me, Thomas Arndell?"

"Yes."

"You'd do anything for me?"

"Yes, yes."

"Anything?"

"Anything."

"And also for Jonathan?"

Arndell was silent.

"'Also for Jonathan?' I said."

Arndell shrugged.

"Well....."

Margaret pointed to the cuddy locker.

"Medicaments in there?"

"A very wide range."

"Then I ask for, beg you for, the simplest of things - a fatal potion for Jonathan and myself if ever......"

Chapter 26

On a calm morning in the month of March, 1787, the convict transport *Friendship* slipped her moorings at Plymouth's Deadman's Quay. In full sail the brig would have been capable of a substantial turn of speed but her progress up the English Channel towards Portsmouth was little more than leisurely. Francis Walton was a mariner for whom vast areas of canvas aloft held little appeal.

The vessel had been under way for half an hour when Thomas Arndell, a woollen muffler wound tight about his neck against a sudden brisk wind from the north east, joined Walton at the helm.

"Keeping your promise, Francis?"

"Promise?"

"Exercise on deck for the convicts."

"This sudden nor'easter'd kill 'em."

"Not so swiftly as the filth and the rats in your 'tween decks."

"All right, all right. Make arrangements with Bellamy," Walton muttered testily, eyes never for one moment losing sight of the grey waters of the Channel.

"Nowhere to be found."

"Hm, ignored my warning then. Hopped ashore last evening."

"Hopped? Staggered more like. I saw him."

"I warned him about sailing. Get Faddy."

Bellamy's second-in-command, sub-lieutenant William Faddy, was writing a letter in the cuddy.

"The ship's master requires eight armed guards. He's agreed the male convicts can be brought on deck for an hour," Arndell said.

Faddy, fair-haired and slight, little more than a boy, was hesitant.

"Captain Bellamy....."

"Isn't available, I know," Arndell said quickly. "Probably wandering around Plymouth seeking an express coach for Portsmouth. So you're in charge."

Faddy rose from the table, face twitching.

"T-too risky."

"But Captain Bellamy agreed. Not all the convicts at the same time, of course. In batches. Men this morning, women this afternoon. Linked by chains they'll give no trouble. By mid-day all the men'll have had sixty minutes of fresh air and I'll've had a chance to look at each one."

Faddy swallowed hard.

"I think we'll wait for Captain Bellamy."

Arndell's manner was airy.

"Very well, Mr Faddy. Wait if you consider waiting best. But Bellamy's unlikely to be aboard for several days. And if, as I suspect, there's typhus or cholera in the 'tween decks then at least I shan't feel responsible for..."

There was no mistaking Faddy's alarm.

"Typhus, Dr. Arndell?"

"Didn't I tell you?" Arndell said softly.

"No."

"Widespread sickness among the male convicts."

"Then shouldn't you be treating it in case it spreads right through Friendship?"

"It could well do that. Ever ventured into the 'tween decks, Mr Faddy?"

"No."

"Then you won't appreciate the difficulty of seeing, never mind treating, a sick man down there. On deck I could look all of them over in a couple of hours. - But, I appreciate, for a junior officer it's a very big decision to take. As you say, leave it to Captain Bellamy."

Faddy shifted uneasily on his chair.

"I - er - I need time," he said to Arndell now halfway up the steps of the companionway.

The surgeon paused and turned his head.

"Time, Mr Faddy, could be running out fast. I can only hope Captain-lieutenant Bellamy will be waiting for us in Portsmouth. I'll tell the ship's master. He'll have to think of other ways of protecting his crew."

"What sort of ways, Dr. Arndell?"

Lips pursed, Arndell slowly shook his head.

"Tell me the disease and I'll suggest the best protection."

Faddy's face resumed its twitch. He licked his lips.

"I'll - er - I'll instruct the marines," he said quickly. "But any escape attempt they'll use their muskets. Yes, muskets."

A smile spreading across his face, Arndell stepped on deck and bent low to pass through the opening in the barricade. As speedily as their irons permitted, the convicts clambered from the 'tween decks gaol and, marshalled into their messes of six men each, a long chain was threaded between their manacles. Pale and haggard, the men in each group huddled close to each other against the bite of icy March winds.

Arndell, his back to the barricade, nudged Faddy standing nearby.

"Not the faintest chance of escapes, unless six at a time hobble across the deck and plunge overside together. Look at 'em. Chained safe as the corpses swinging from Newgate's gibbets."

Faddy, features strained, stayed silent.

"If you don't issue the order soon they'll all freeze solid to the planking," Arndell went on.

Faddy's voice quavered.

"Guards!"

Muskets at the ready, marines took up stances along the barricade and down the centre of the deck.

"Convicts! In a clockwise circle - march."

Head down, hunched against the biting wind, Jonathan, leading with his mess, shuffled forwards.

Arndell joined him in the sluggish progress around the deck.

"They tell me there's sickness in the 'tween decks," Arndell said quietly.

"Well?"

"I'd like to know more."

"Maybe too late. Unless conditions in that hell-hole get better quickly there'll be little point in sailing to Botany Bay. The only creatures likely to land there alive are the rats and lice and cockroaches."

"Go on."

"What more is there to say? Even the Thames hulks let us free every morning so we rarely fouled ourselves and each other. But for weeks now hardly anybody's been away from that stinking dungeon. Look at the state of us, the state of me."

Arndell appraised Jonathan's feet, bound in rags, the torn breeches, the grimy remnants of a silken shirt, the haggard features, the matted hair.

The surgeon shook his head and displayed open palms.

"I've battled for days to get even this - this trivial freedom for you." He pointed to the trailing convicts. "You must all help yourselves. Use the easing chairs, keep clean."

Jonathan burst into a laugh so loud that a marine at once swung round with his musket. Irritably Arndell waved the man aside.

"You don't begin to understand, surgeon. We've become animals, packed so tight down there it's impossible for most of us to get anywhere near the easing chair. In days, Mr Surgeon, this ship'll be a floating cemetery."

As, for the tenth time, Arndell circled the deck with Jonathan, Faddy, face blue with cold, joined him.

"Long enough for this lot, Dr Arndell. My marines'll see 'em below."

Frowning, Arndell seized Faddy by the arm and dragged him to the barricade.

"They're entitled to a full hour and they've had barely ten minutes. And I haven't identified the sickness yet."

"Not surprised. You've questioned only one of them so far."

"A mess captain, a man with some medical knowledge. I've learned enough to realise the situation's desperately serious. Those men need all the fresh air and exercise you can allow. You've done a splendid job, Lieutenant Faddy, agreeing to their freedom, splendid. Feeling cold?"

Faddy shivered.

"Frozen."

"Leave the supervision to me and the marines. Go below, have some rum. Maybe we can do without

Captain Bellamy but we'd be utterly helpless without you."

Faddy stiffened.

"But my men take orders from me, not you."

"Instruct them, then."

Immediately Faddy had gone below Arndell rejoined Jonathan as the convicts continued their trail round the deck.

"Your co-operation would be useful, convict."

"At a price, surgeon."

"Convicts are in no position to strike bargains."

"I'm not without influence in the 'tween decks."

"That may well be but....."

Arndell stumbled over a coil of rope and would have pitched headlong but for Jonathan's manacled arm.

"See, even in chains, I can help."

The surgeon laughed.

"Very well. The bargain. Urge the men to keep clean. I'll see they have soap and plentiful water and extra easing chairs. And I'll keep pressing for more and more time on deck."

"Or the chief surgeon could take you to task?"

"Yes."

"My side of the bargain - seeing Margaret Dunne."

Arndell drew breath in sharply. The side of his neck was flushed.

"Impossible."

Jonathan quickened pace so that the rest of the convicts were compelled to follow suit. Every head was raised, every eye and ear directed towards Jonathan and Arndell.

"See how they follow the leader, Dr. Arndell?" Jonathan said in a harsh whisper. "Margaret, now. You can find some way - just as I can find some way of passing the gaol-house sickness to the whole of the ship's complement, including yourself."

"Convict, you must be mad."

"No, Mr Surgeon. Knowledgeable - and bloody, bloody desperate."

Chapter 27

Linked by a chain through their manacles, the convict women, heads down, had been circling the head of the aft companionway for almost an hour when rain and heavy squalls suddenly seized hold of the Friendship. Spurning the frantic efforts of the helmsman, the vessel yawed and bucked and rolled, pitching the women, helpless in their irons, this way and that before finally hurling them to the deck.

"Up, up, up!"

The marines sprang at the hapless women, repeatedly goading with their muskets.

Martha Kerwin, ankle irons entangled with the manacles of another convict woman and the linking chain, struggled frantically to regain her feet and at the same time dodge a vicious jab from a musket muzzle, but she stumbled. The other woman shrieked in agony as tangled manacles threatened to rip off her hands.

The marine was on the point of administering a further savage jab when Arndell, leaping from the lee of the mainmast, sent the man sprawling.

"Help them up and see them below. See them all below."

Martha Kerwin was the last of the shuffling, rain-soaked women to reach the gaol-deck trapdoor. Gingerly she urged her shackled legs over the edge and then appeared to lose her grip on the coaming.

"Help, help!"

The corporal of the guard dived forward to give Martha a final push. At once she grabbed his ankle. Arms high in the air, he teetered briefly on the brink then, with Martha, plunged into the gloom of the prison below.

Scores of long-nailed fingers seized the man and he was dragged, feet first, along the alleyway between the bunks to the bulkhead athwart the ship. There Martha sat firmly on his head, another convict sat on his chest while a third and fourth sat on his legs.

"Flogging, the lot of you," the corporal spluttered through blood gushing from his nose.

Martha playfully patted the man's cheek.

"No threats, soldier-boy. Just instructions. Instructions to your men. Tell them we want brandy and sugar and tea - at once," she said.

"Fat old sow."

Martha bounced up and down.

"Tell 'em."

"Go to hell."

"You'd have to come with me."

"My men'll fire."

"The first bullet for yourself."

"Branson, Cogan, Bell – fire!"

The muzzles of three muskets ranged the gaol-deck but there were no bullets.

"Into your bunks, everybody," Martha rasped then she flung herself behind the corporal and, looping her wrist manacles around his throat, she drove a knee into the man's back.

"You'll hang," he gasped as the irons bit deep into his windpipe.

"Too late for you to witness the ceremony, soldier."

The man battled to reply but no sound came.

"I couldn't hear," Martha whispered, for a moment relaxing the pressure.

The man's voice was hoarse.

"Fire!"

"They wouldn't be so foolish, corporal. You're in line for the first bullet."

In the gloom of the gaol it was impossible for the marines on the upper deck to identify any target yet they themselves stood out in stark relief against the light of the fading afternoon. One of the women, taller than the rest, wormed along the alleyway between the bunks towards the trapdoor. She leapt for the opening and seized the muzzle of a musket pointing into the prison.

There was an explosion and a bullet thudded harmlessly into the gaol planking. The marksman, forefinger trapped behind the trigger of his musket, plunged head first into the 'tween decks. Clawing hands seized and dragged him beyond the view of the remaining guards on the deck above.

Martha's grip on the first captive marine was now ferocious.

"Foolish, foolish, corporal. While you've still breath left, tell 'em. Brandy, sugar, tea."

Like a cat playing with a doomed mouse, Martha eased her grip only to restore it with even greater ferocity.

The man's struggles were wholly ineffective.

"You'll - you'll hang."

"Then you and your man are going first. Chains in position, ladies?"

A chorus of women's voices drowned the agonised gurgling of the second captive guard. The corporal, hands to his blood-spattered face, mumbled, "Water, water." And Margaret who so far had remained in her bunk, dropped into the alleyway.

"Back," Martha hissed. "They'll fire."

"He's begging for water," Margaret whispered.

"He gets water when we get brandy, tea and sugar."

"Let me give him water."

Martha laughed briefly.

"Well, if it'll help to keep him alive a bit longer..... "

The corporal gulped the water avidly. With a moistened rag Margaret wiped his blooded face.

"Now, soldier, while you've still got voice enough to tell 'em - or they'll be getting two dead marines," Martha said.

Francis Walton appeared at the trapdoor.

"Release them, convict, or I'll have you close-ironed to the deck - then slung overboard."

"First the brandy, tea and sugar," Martha called back.

Walton disappeared from view then within minutes he had returned.

"Tea for you," he bellowed.

Still grasping the throat of the corporal, Martha half rose to her feet and at once her head and shoulders were drenched with scalding water.

She screamed in agony.

"And - and now a dead corporal for you."

A faint gurgle escaped the man's lips.

"Make yours say something," Martha called, gasping, to the women holding the second marine.

Then a hand seized Martha's hair, dragging her head back.

In the confusion Thomas Arndell had dropped unnoticed into the 'tween decks.

He was terse.

"Scalded. Treatment or you'll never have a face again."

Shoulders hunched against the low ceiling Arndell dragged the shackled wrists away from the corporal's neck and hauled Martha Kerwin to her feet.

Then he glimpsed Margaret.

"Water for the corporal. Tell the rest to free the other man. And you," he said to Martha, tugging her hair, "on deck."

Walton was seated at the table when, Arndell, leading Martha Kerwin by her shackled wrists, entered the cuddy.

"That filthy blowse - out."

"One moment, Francis."

"'Out', I said. A hundred lashes from the bos'n and every one of your Newgate scum on deck to witness the treatment."

Grim-faced, Arndell motioned Martha to a chair.

"Scalding's punishment enough. Look." Arndell took Martha's chin and turned her face to the light. Her naked left shoulder, her cheek and her neck were harshly crimson against the remaining pallid skin. "Worse than a hundred lashes."

"Two hundred lashes then."

Arndell gave Walton an indulgent, paternal look.

"You'll calm down, Francis. You'll calm down."

Leaping to his feet Walton sent his chair careering across the cuddy floor to crash against the bulkhead.

"My ship, don't forget."

"Yes, Francis." From a locker Arndell took a bottle labelled 'Lime Water' and a jar marked 'Florentine Oil' and he started to anoint Martha's ravaged skin. "Yes, your ship but the surgeon's final decision on punishments." He pointed to Martha's shoulder where blisters had already begun to appear.

"This is when we need a hospital."

"No hospital nonsense aboard this ship."

Walton made to storm out of the cuddy but Arndell barred his path.

"You're ducking the problem, Francis."

"Out of my way."

Arndell stood his ground.

"Settle it before Surgeon White and Captain Phillip come aboard."

"Already settled."

Arndell slowly shook his head. Martha Kerwin, whimpering, teeth clenched, eyes tight closed, was swaying to and fro on her chair.

"How can this poor, misguided creature possibly survive without expert attention?"

"She was asking for it."

"In desperation."

"I've told you, Arndell. No hospital."

There was a half-smile on Arndell's face.

"No threat of lashes either?"

"We'll see," Walton snarled and rushed out, slamming the cuddy door behind him.

Arndell tapped Martha on the head.

"Away now. Take these." He handed her the lime water and oil then led her on deck.

As Martha turned to negotiate the ladder dropped into the prison deck by a guard, Arndell surreptitiously slid a bottle of brandy down the front of her bodice.

"Mr Walton's very best," he whispered, winking.

Chapter 28

By the time that Friendship dropped anchor off Portsmouth, the carpenter had partitioned the women's 'tween decks to provide space for a hospital. The partition was in the form of a grille so that occupants of the hospital would be visible to any guards inspecting the women's prison but the only access was by way of a newly-created trapdoor in the upper deck.

Scarcely had the carpenter driven home the final nail than Thomas Arndell was descending the ladder to inspect his new domain.

"No great privacy for the sick," he said, thrusting a hand through the dividing grille. "I expected a solid bulkhead."

"Mr Walton's orders. Make it too private, he said, and every one of the women'd find she'd got some ailment."

"And only six bunks."

"Mr Walton's orders."

Arndell climbed to the upper deck and made his way to the women's gaol. Martha Kerwin was there, hunched on the edge of a bunk, arms tight about her, rocking to and fro. Arndell placed a hand on her head.

"Let me see."

Eyes no more than slits above red and blistered cheeks glared at Arndell.

"Go to hell."

"Still applying the ointment?"

Martha nodded.

"Convict Dunne will nurse you."

He turned.

"Where are you, Margaret Dunne?"

"Here."

Margaret clambered from an upper bunk.

"Convict Kerwin's blisters. Regular treatment with ointment. You are to tend her. Follow me, both of you."

On deck a guard lifted the new trapdoor and Arndell motioned Martha to descend the ladder into the hospital.

"Take a bunk. Convict Dunne and I'll be with you in a few minutes," Arndell said, beckoning Margaret to follow him down the companionway.

In the otherwise empty cuddy Arndell's manner changed at once.

"I - I still can't sleep," he blurted out. "More and more desperate for you, Margaret. Please......"

He attempted to put his arm round her. She shrank away.

"No, no. Impossible."

"I arranged the sewing specially. I've now planned for you to tend the Kerwin woman. Not for the sake of her blisters - for you. There'll be special food and other comforts...."

"My only comfort would be Jonathan...."

"More and more freedom. The officers are looking for a laundress, a seamstress, a woman in the galley from time to time...."

"You don't begin to understand. Yes, you are kind, very. But I'm no laundress, no seamstress. At home my father and I had servants, several. I want nothing, I want nobody but Jonathan!"

"Please, please, I beg you. I could completely assure your future."

"Thomas - Thomas, you're a good man, you're a kind man but we have no future whatsoever together."

Arndell tightened his fists, combining supplication with determination.

"Without me you haven't any future. Not the faintest hope of getting back to England - except with me. And life in New Holland, if ever you reach there, and marry your apprentice tanner...."

Margaret eyed Arndell askance.

"Apprentice tanner?"

"Convict Pettifer."

"Jonathan, apprentice tanner?" Margaret smiled. "Who told....? Jonathan's an apothecary, a Ludgate apothecary. Nobody more able, according to his master, Matthew Gross, since Nicholas Culpeper!"

"I don't believe....."

"Don't believe what?" Francis Walton said, bursting into the cuddy.

Arndell swung round to face the master of Friendship who was closely followed by a stranger, a man of about thirty years, burly, bluff, unruly-haired.

"Dr. Arndell," Walton said to the stranger whose hand at once enveloped that of Arndell. "Thomas, this is Dr. White, chief surgeon."

John White's smile was broad and ready.

"We didn't meet in London but my friends at Surgeon's Hall were suitably impressed," White said. His eyes turned to Margaret. "Your wife?" He then glimpsed the manacles. "Hm, I see." White's manner was jocular. "I didn't really think men like you chained their women."

Arndell's neck and cheeks suddenly were pink.

"She tends the sick. She's a seamstress as well."

White gave Walton a knowing wink.

"Yes, I understand," he said.

The pair burst into laughter but the moment that a man, slightly built, in naval uniform, appeared at the cuddy entrance, both lapsed into silence. White at once stood to attention.

"You know Mr Walton, sir, master of the Friendship?"

The newcomer, balding, thin-faced, aquiline-nosed, acknowledged the ship's master with a faint bow.

"Yes, indeed," he said in a resonant voice wholly belying the slight frame.

"And Dr. Arndell, sir?"

"No."

"My assistant surgeon. Aboard Friendship. Arndell, this is Captain Arthur Phillip, Commander-in-Chief and Governor-Designate of New Holland!"

Arthur Phillip's smile revealed the absence of one front tooth. The delicately shaped hand seized the young surgeon's hand in a grip that made him wince.

"To be precise, Dr. Arndell, not New Holland but New South Wales."

Phillip eyed Margaret and her manacles.

"How many convicts?"

"Seventy-six men and twenty-one women, sir," Arndell said.

"Children?"

"None, sir."

"All well provisioned?"

"They've not eaten so well for years," Walton said quickly.

Phillip nodded approval.

"Clothing?"

Walton, pursed lips, was silent.

"The women are in rags." Arndell pointed to Margaret's tattered cloak. "Nothing came," he said.

"Pursue the contractors and Naval Ordnance."

"But if we sail Sunday......" Arndell said.

"Then pursue at once, Dr. Arndell. At once."

Arthur Phillip beckoned John White.

"'Tween decks now."

Margaret following with Arndell, Phillip, White and Walton left the cuddy.

Bent low because of the ceiling, in an alleyway between two rows of bunks in the gaol deck, Arthur Phillip put a handkerchief to his nostrils and grimaced. He glanced at the cluster of ragged, unsmiling women and promptly returned the handkerchief to a pocket.

"Little hope for them in these foul conditions," Phillip said in a low voice to John White. "Even less hope for the sick."

"If they could have clean clothes, if they were on deck more often...." Arndell said.

"Aren't they on deck most of the day?"

"No, sir."

"Why not?"

Arndell smiled wryly.

"Danger of escape."

"Escape?" Phillip frowned. "Escape, how? Fettered ankles, manacled wrists, six fathoms of water. Nonsense. They're to be allowed on deck all day. This stinking hole must be thoroughly cleansed."

Arndell went up the ladder ahead of Phillip. One foot on the bottom rung Phillip paused then turned.

"Ladies, we'll be sailing into the unknown together"

At the far end of the gaol deck a woman spat out, "Some in more comfort than others."

Phillip peered into the gloom but failed to identify the woman.

"Let me remind you - and the rest - I'm in no way responsible for your present situation."

Another convict woman elbowed forward so that she and Phillip faced each other, a foot apart.

"Pretty words."

The Governor-General Designate of New South Wales eyed the woman with faint amusement.

"Maybe. To tell you I'm not this or that is no comfort, I agree."

Phillip moved to sit on the edge of a bunk. He rubbed the back of his neck and thrust his head back. Emboldened by their spokeswoman the rest of the convict women gathered round.

"A four-foot ceiling day and night brings on worse ills than a crick in the neck," one said.

Arthur Phillip continued to rub the aching muscles.

"Four feet, six inches to be precise, madam. I'll do whatever's possible to help during the voyage, I promise," he said as he rose to his feet. "Take what comfort you can from the fact that you are all together. I am very much on my own."

Impatiently striking the back of his hand with the palm of the other, a man was standing alone on Friendship's upper deck. He wore a velvet tricorne hat, high-waisted coat of quilted blue silk and lavishly-embroidered waistcoat. The cream buckskin breeches were fastened below the knee with blue ribbon, the shoe buckles were clearly made of gold.

"Governor Phillip?"

Interrupted in his train of thought, Arthur Phillip acknowledged the raised tricorne and exaggerated bow with some irritation.

"Yes?"

"You have a berth for me."

"Indeed?"

"That was the information from Sirius, sir."

"See Mr Walton, the ship's master."

"Where.....?"

Phillip pointed to the companionway.

"The cuddy."

The stranger repeated his bow and went below where Walton and Arndell and also Bellamy, who had now rejoined Friendship, were drinking at the cuddy table.

"Mr Walton?"

"Yeh," Francis Walton said.

"You have a berth for me."

"Have I?"

"I hope so. I'm part owner of your ship. Turnbull McQuaid."

Chapter 29

The convict women, many of them in tears, huddled together in groups, anxious hands seeking other anxious hands, their ragged and filthy clothes contrasting sharply with the freshly-holystoned planking of Friendship's upper deck.

The morning sunshine which greeted them as they emerged from the gloom of the 'tween decks brought no pleasure. It was Sunday, the thirteenth day of May in the year 1787, and the convict fleet was now several leagues on its voyage to the penal settlement in what was to be the state of New South Wales.

The Isle of Wight safely astern, Francis Walton handed over the helm to a seaman then he joined Thomas Arndell standing by the companionway watching the women.

"Brutal," Arndell said, nodding towards the convicts. "Soon the Bay of Biscay and they're still in those flimsy rags. The end for some of them, probably."

Walton responded with an impatient shrug.

"I've told you. The Ordnance Office and the contractors. Clothing's their responsibility, not mine."

"I thought Captain Phillip's instructions were....."

"Ordnance doesn't take instructions from naval officers. Considers requests, that's all."

"But Phillip's a governor."

"If Phillip happened to be the Almighty Himself, Ordnance'd do no more than note his prayer."

"So no fresh clothing at all for the miserable wretches?"

"Only if Phillip buys some in Teneriffe."

"Teneriffe? Problems long before we reach the Canaries." Arndell paused briefly. "An idea. Plenty of spare sails?"

Walton eyed the surgeon cautiously.

"Enough."

"And, if necessary, more could be bought in Teneriffe and Rio?"

"Possibly. But what.....?"

"A moment, Francis. You've no great enthusiasm for excessive canvas aloft?"

"Not unless I know a ship's even keeled, well ballasted."

"And you don't know Friendship yet?"

"A few leagues are no great guide."

"Problem solved. The women aren't likely to compete with London's ladies of quality but at least they'll be warm. I need every inch of canvas you can spare, Francis."

* * * * *

"Faster, faster, faster!"

Using their musket muzzles with mounting savagery, two marines goaded the male convicts round and round the forward deck. The faster the men marched, the marines knew, the sooner they were likely to falter and stumble, then, panting, beg to go back below long before their permitted spell in the sunshine had expired.

As a musket jabbed at his fetters, the man in front of Jonathan, Timothy Jinks, stumbled and he would have been sent sprawling on the planking but for Jonathan's steadying hand.

"Thanks," Jinks whispered.

The thud of a musket butt across Jinks' shoulders produced a scream of agony.

"You talk too much, convict."

With even greater ferocity the guard struck Jinks a second time.

"God give me a knife," the convict muttered beneath his breath.

Jonathan, about to speak, glanced up and saw that Arndell, accompanied by Turnbull McQuaid, had joined the marines at the opening in the barricade. He lowered his head and hissed through clenched teeth, "A knife's too swift."

"The swifter the better," Jinks replied.

"Lingering effects give time for reflection."

Jinks turned briefly. The guard, now pre-occupied in goading another convict, had not heard the exchanges.

"Too subtle for me, Pettifer."

"A key to Arndell's medicine locker's worth a thousand knives."

"But how could a convict....?"

A blow from a musket butt caught Jinks off balance and Jonathan, with a dozen other convicts, collapsed, an agonised jumble of arms, legs and bodies on the planking.

Jonathan, dragging on the chains, struggled free of the sweating bodies and, an arm round Jinks, lurched to his feet.

Again the marine jabbed with his musket but this time Jonathan was able to thrust his companion clear.

"On your feet, the lot of you!"

Deep in conversation with McQuaid and, for a moment unsighted by the mainmast, Arndell had not seen the convicts fall but he paused in mid-sentence at the raised voice of the marine guard. He leapt forward and seized the man's shoulder.

"Discipline, yes. Brutality, no."

The rest of the convicts struggled to their feet. Arndell pointed to blood spattering the dry sand on the planking.

"Whose?" he said.

The guard spat.

"Don't ask me. The scum're always fighting."

"Yours, Pettifer?" Arndell said.

"Mine and others, sir," Jonathan said, lifting his manacles then indicating those on the wrists of Timothy Jinks.

There was blood on both sets of irons.

"Free them," Arndell said to the marine corporal.

"Captain-lieutenant Bellamy's orders.....!"

Arndell at once seized the padlock key hanging from the corporal's belt and removed the chain that linked the convicts.

"Who else is bleeding?"

Every convict lifted his manacles.

McQuaid, face blank of expression, looked on in silence.

"See the convicts below, corporal, except Pettifer. I want him in the cuddy," Arndell said, his voice tense.

Arndell was inspecting the contents of the medicine locker as Jonathan, pitched headlong into the cuddy by a marine, landed at his feet. The surgeon hauled him upright and helped him to a chair, then he turned his attention to the medicines once more.

"Now, what would the tanner's apprentice suggest for treating minor flesh wounds?" he said, half-smiling. "Herb robert, say?"

"Too astringent."

"Oh? Was that its effect on the cow hide? So astringent it made even the dead skin twitch!"

Jonathan smiled, "I've heard Persian balsam and hog's lard can be soothing."

"And I've heard something else. I've heard you're no apprentice tanner but an extremely accomplished apothecary."

"Apothecary?" Jonathan shook his head." You're mistaken. Maybe confusing me with Daniel Stocksbridge. Daniel was widely experienced in surgery."

"No mistake, Pettifer. You were apprenticed to Matthew Gross in Sea Coal Lane!"

"And - and Gross told you?"

"I could almost hear Gross himself speaking when you said herb robert was too astringent. And I couldn't, for one moment, believe Margaret Dunne's a liar."

"Margaret?"

"Extremely proud of your apprenticeship to Matthew Gross."

"Margaret told you?"

Arndell nodded.

"Why did you withhold the information?"

Jonathan's smile was wry, "Likely to do me more harm than good."

"How?"

"No stomach for cutting into maggot-ridden, rat-gnawed corpses while the surgeon, at a discreet distance, looks on."

"And you honestly believe I'd use your skills in that way?"

"Yes."

"We'd work together."

Jonathan rattled his manacles.

"In these?"

"Arthur Phillip intends freeing everybody very soon."

"I want rid now."

"Imagine your reception in the convict deck, the only one without shackles. They'd take you for a spy. Garrotte you while you slept."

"Maybe, maybe." Jonathan was thoughtful for a moment. "No post mortems?"

"We'd share the more gruesome tasks. And none undertaken out of morbid curiosity, I promise."

"One more thing."

"Well?"

"Arrange for me to see Margaret every day."

Arndell pursed his lips.

"Extremely difficult."

"Easy enough for the seamen to get to the women in their gaol deck."

"Without my knowledge."

"The marines know."

"I'll stop it at once."

"Am I to see Margaret?"

Arndell turned to the medicine locker and, with exaggerated precision, began to line up bottles and jars.

"Grave problems, I'm afraid."

"No graver than battling entirely on your own for the health of one hundred and fifty souls aboard Friendship, month after month after month, Thomas Arndell."

Chapter 30

There were high seas running when, two hundred miles south-west of the Scilly Isles, the convict fleet hove to. Arndell and Walton stood together on deck, clinging to the rail as Friendship bucked and rolled and yawed, seemingly impatient to be under way once more.

"You get your wish, Mr Leech-man. A signal from Arthur Phillip," Walton said.

"Signal?"

"Convict irons to be struck off."

Arndell's face lit up.

"Splendid. When?"

"The smith's at work already. First whisper of trouble though and the irons go back. Tell your friends in the 'tween decks I've ordered the bo's'n to re-wire his cat-o'-nine-tails."

All of a sudden the Friendship's poop was awash and in spite of the canvas awning stretched from stern to companionway both men were at once drenched from head to foot.

Wiping water from his eyes, Walton laughed.

"With Mother Atlantic on our side, they could be far too busy dodging salt water to give us any trouble. Those 'tween decks'll be wet as the bottom of the ocean."

Arndell, breathless from the Atlantic's onslaught, gasped, "We've - we've got to do something!"

Walton, shaking water from his sodden hat sneered.

"Such as?"

"Give 'em buckets and brooms."

The ship's master raised an imperious finger,

"We'll inspect," he said.

Gingerly, hand over hand along the ship's rail then from iron ring to iron ring in the barricade the pair reached the opening. Two marines on guard were struggling to dry their muskets.

Walton pointed to the hatch cover where, to admit more light and air to the gaol deck, a stout grille had replaced the solid wooden trapdoor.

"Tell 'em the chains'll come off if they're good. And let 'em know about the bo's'n and his pussy-cat claws."

Arndell waited for a momentary even keel then lurched to the gaol-deck grille.

"Open," he said to the marine sitting, hunched and soaked, on the coaming.

The man kicked the bolts and lifted the grille. At once he and Arndell were bundled aside by a surge of bodies frantic to escape from water swirling, knee-deep and rising, in the gaol deck. Arndell flung a lightning glance over his shoulder. The guard had already scuttled through the barricade on the heels of Walton and the other marines. By the time Arndell reached it the door had been slammed and bolted on the far side. He turned to face the drenched convicts. The hands of one of them were already at his throat when Jonathan battered his way through the angry mob.

"Fools, fools. It was the surgeon who got rid of the irons. Next man who so much as touches him goes overboard with a broken neck."

The crowd surged away and then at the cry, "Man overboard!", the convicts stumbled across the heaving deck to the ship's rail. In spite of a battle against the heavy northerly swell, the escaper was already twenty yards away from Friendship's larboard side and swimming strongly.

The barricade door was flung open and six marines, Francis Walton close behind, charged through.

"Back, back, scum!"

The marines opened fire.

Clawing, punching and kicking each other in a frantic effort to avoid the bullets the convicts scrambled back to the hatch opening and within a minute not one of them remained on deck.

Walton bounded to the ship's rail. The strokes of the fugitive were still strong but, against the powerful Atlantic swell, they were now almost as nothing. Slowly, relentlessly the swell sucked him back to the ship's side.

"Ropes," Walton shouted.

Turnbull McQuaid had now joined Walton.

"Let him drown."

"Don't be a fool, Mr McQuaid."

"What's the point of rescue?"

A pair of ropes snaked over the deck and, seizing both, a seaman clambered overside.

"Ever seen a man drown?" Walton said.

"Never," McQuaid replied.

"A swift, quiet business. Too swift, too quiet. Arms high above the head for an instant - then nothing. I didn't want him rescued. An example, though, for the others."

The escaped prisoner, hauled out of the water, lay and gasped, face down on the planking.

"I don't understand. First the marines open fire on the mob and not a single casualty. Then drag a man out of the ocean," McQuaid said.

"Bellamy ordered volleys over their heads. Madness killing off cargoes just yet." Walton took a step forward. "See that man-o'-war?"

McQuaid nodded.

"Waiting to take Arthur Phillip's despatches about convict numbers to the Admiralty. The minute this swell subsides there'll be a boarding party from Sirius to check our friends in the 'tween decks. And corpses don't count, Mr McQuaid."

"Killing was justified," McQuaid said. "We were faced with a murderous riot."

Walton strolled to the rescued convict, still prostrate on the deck. McQuaid followed.

"Of course killing was justified," Walton said as if addressing a child. "Of course it was. But your profits slump while I work my way out of a job."

"What d'you mean?"

"Shoot most of Friendship's convicts and the rest'd be crammed aboard the other transports, Charlotte and Scarborough and Lady Penrhyn. And then Friendship's back to the Thames, Admiralty charter torn up. Kindly allow me to run Friendship in my own way, Mr McQuaid."

McQuaid's expression was thunderous. With the toe of his gold-buckled shoe he jabbed the side of the still-gasping convict.

"No doubt you'll be administering our best brandy."

"My bo's'n does the administering and it won't be brandy."

The boatswain and his mate were standing nearby coiling the ropes used to haul the convict out of the water.

"Take him, strip him and fasten his wrists there," Walton said, pointing to a pair of iron rings set high in the timbers of the deck barricade.

"Ay, ay, sir."

The two seamen dragged the now-naked convict to the barricade where, feebly protesting, hands above his head, he was roped to the rings. A small cask was thrust between his feet and the base of the barricade so that his quivering body was stretched taut at an angle to the deck.

Arndell leapt through the barricade opening and seized the boatswain's shoulder.

"Stop, stop!"

"Mr Walton's orders."

"Set him free!"

Walton, McQuaid at his heels, stepped from the ship's rail.

"Mind your own business, Arndell," Walton snapped.

"Barbarism, Francis."

The convict began to moan.

"Water, water."

The boatswain looked to Walton who shook his head.

"For God's sake at least quench the poor wretch's thirst before you begin your Roman holiday, Francis," Arndell said, voice quivering with rage. "And, better than water, enough rum to knock him senseless."

Walton sneered.

"Bad heads and sore backs go ill together. You should know that, Mr Blood-letter." He turned to the boatswain. "Give the scum some water." He signalled the marines at the hatch opening. "Bring 'em all on deck."

The first lash from the cat-o'-nine-tails dragged a scream from the hapless prisoner and a concerted groan from the assembled convicts. By the twentieth lash the convict audience was still groaning but the victim, body no longer taut, was silent.

Walton raised a hand.

"Enough," he said, and pointing to the hatch grille. "Get 'em below."

The flogged man, cut down by the boatswain's mate, lay bleeding and inert on the deck.

"Very competently handled," McQuaid said, patting Walton's shoulder.

"Bloody savagery," Arndell said through clenched teeth. "What now?"

Face devoid of expression, Francis Walton glanced at the convict lying now in a pool of blood that slowly crept across the planking. He pointed to flesh ravaged as if some giant fork had been repeatedly dragged across it.

"Now, show us the sort of surgeon you are, Thomas Arndell. Smooth out the creases from that."

"Your tongue digs a well of hatred for yourself, Francis," Arndell replied as he knelt to the brutalised, motionless creature on the planking.

By this time, McQuaid had gone below. Walton, grim-faced, about to follow him, paused. Arndell was struggling desperately to stem the flow of blood. Slowly Walton shook his head.

"No easy decision, Thomas. It could well save you from another attack," he said, voice remote, and then was gone.

Arndell got to his feet.

"The convict Pettifer," he called to the marines guarding the hatch coaming. "Send him. Quickly."

Arndell dragged off his tunic and shirt and tore the latter into strips.

"Bind him," he said to Jonathan who had now joined him, handing over the strips of cotton shirt. "Those two broken spars and my tunic will make a stretcher."

Chapter 31

There was a burst of cheering from the women as Jonathan and a marine guard struggled down the hospital ladder carrying the flogged convict. They crowded the grille-bulkhead, fighting for a glimpse of the man whom Jonathan and the marine were now laying, face down, in an upper bunk.

"He needs mattress and coverings, bandages to staunch the bleeding and ointment," Jonathan said to the guard.

The man stepped back to the ladder.

"My orders were 'take him to the hospital', that's all."

"Look at him."

The guard flung a disinterested glance in the direction of the convict, moaning and writhing on the bunk's rough-sawn timbers, already drenched with blood.

"He'll soon be gone and corpses don't bleed, convict."

"This is a hospital, as much for you as for him." Jonathan pointed to blood now dripping on the lower bunk. "In half an hour it'll look like a slaughter-house."

Still crowding the grille, the women began to chant, "Slaughter-house, slaughter-house."

The marine swung round and rammed a vicious musket muzzle at them.

"Shut up, filthy whores," he rasped and was on the point of driving Jonathan up the ladder when Arndell clambered down, laden with bedding and a roll of muslin.

The surgeon dismissed the marine and, with Jonathan's help, slid a muslin-covered palliasse under the convict's body then applied an ointment to the savage lacerations.

"What is it?" Jonathan said.

"Navelwort."

"For deep wounds I prefer loosestrife."

Arndell's tone was was brusque, dismissive.

"We all have preferences. Lift him," he said and he began to swathe the tortured body in muslin from armpits to waist. He drew a bottle from the pocket of his tunic.

"Anodyne."

"Which?"

"Laudanum."

"No."

"Oh, yes."

"Torture."

"What d'you mean?"

"Laudanum induces sweating," Jonathan said. "Body swathed in muslin and what happens? Salty sweat seeping into raw flesh. Poor devil'll go crazy. I suggest diacodium."

"We'll agree to differ then," Arndell said, pressing the bottle of laudanum to the convict's lips. "Not enough privacy here." He nodded in the direction of the women, faces glued to the bulkhead grille. "We'll have a floor to ceiling canvas curtain." He gave Jonathan a covert wink. "Ladies should never be exposed to sights of savage wounds and strange sicknesses. And the place must be kept clean. I'll find some female convict to...."

The rest of Arndell's words were drowned by a piercing shriek from the sick convict who suddenly jerked to a sitting position, frantically struggling to tear away the muslin that encased his body.

"I warned you, surgeon," Jonathan whispered.

Arndell leapt for the trapdoor.

"Remove the muslin. I'll be back."

Jonathan had barely taken away the swathes of blood-and-sweat-soaked muslin before Arndell re-joined him, grasping another jar of ointment, a small phial and more bandage. In silence the surgeon swabbed the man's lacerations and applied fresh ointment.

"Loosestrife?" Jonathan said.

"Yes."

"And diacodium?"

Arndell handed Jonathan the phial.

"Give it as soon as the effects of the laudanum subside."

Jonathan glanced at the man in the bunk. His eyes were closed. He looked towards the dividing bulkhead. On the far side the women, their interest waning, had moved away.

"Dare a convict congratulate a surgeon?"

"A competent apothecary might," Arndell said, grasping Jonathan's hand.

Shortly after Arndell left the hospital a marine raised the trapdoor and bawled, "Convict."

A slight, cloaked figure was thrust through the opening. Jonathan got to his feet and the trapdoor slammed into place.

The figure threw back the hood.

"Margaret!"

Hunched beneath the low ceiling they locked in a passionate embrace until, at length, Margaret, gasping, begged to be free.

"A miracle, dearest, together like this," she whispered, first her fingers then her lips lightly caressing the scar on Jonathan's cheek. "A miracle!"

He took her fingers to his own lips.

"No miracle, my love."

"I've prayed and prayed..."

"And I've been bargaining."

"Bargaining?"

"With Thomas Arndell. Adept, he may be, at sawing limbs but he knows as much about medicaments as the leeches he keeps in his glass jars."

Jonathan flung a swift glance at the brutalised convict who, at that moment, began to stir then groan. He raised the man to a sitting position and mopped the sweating brow.

"Just one example of Arndell's skill. Murderous wounds from the bo's'n's lash, then Arndell drives the poor wretch crazy with the wrong ointment, the wrong sleeping potion."

"But Thomas Arndell's a very kind man..."

"And pathetically ignorant."

Jonathan gently eased the convict into a lying position, face down. The man stirred momentarily then drifted into a drugged stupor.

"Without a single musket, without a single cutlass I could soon be ruling this ship," Jonathan said softly, drawing Margaret to him once more.

"How, my love?"

"A hundred and fifty people aboard, most of them crammed like rats in a cess-pit. One, just one, suffering from gaol fever and in days, without proper medicine, Friendship's a floating coffin."

"But surely Thomas Arndell could....."

"On his own he'd be scarce able, or knowledgeable enough, to do a thing."

"There'd be help from the other ships, surely."

Jonathan shook his head.

"Nobody struggles for contact with gaol fever."

"Then you must help Thomas Arndell, my darling."

"So far as it fits my aim, yes. And my aim, for you and for me, is revenge."

Margaret's ragged bodice only fragmentarily concealed her shapely breasts. She took Jonathan's head between her hands and pressed his face deep into warm and yielding flesh.

With all the anguish and despair and longing inexorably mounting since one sunny morning in September on Tower Hill they took each other, frantically, savagely, tenderly again and again. And yet again.

It was late evening so that scarce a vestige of light crept through the trapdoor opening when a marine kicked back the bolts.

"Convict whore, out."

Margaret gave Jonathan a farewell kiss and scaled the ladder. As she scrambled to her feet, Jonathan heard her scream in protest then a man's coarse laughter. He leapt for the trapdoor but the grille slammed ruthlessly over his head. He thrust both hands through the grille and the marine's heavy shoe stamped on them. Again he heard Margaret's scream.

He stumbled blindly to the edge of a bunk, crushed and bleeding fingers pressed hard to his mouth.

"Sweet Christ, give me, give me my revenge," he muttered, spitting blood.

Chapter 32

Although the convicts' shackles had been struck off by the time Friendship and the rest of the convict fleet were approaching calmer waters north of the Canaries, the captives created few problems for the marines and the ship's company. Even the most spirited, after weeks of seasickness, were left quiet and listless. Arndell, himself a victim of Friendship's helpless plunging and rolling across the Bay of Biscay, struggled daily with mounting numbers of ailing convicts.

"Too soft-hearted, leech-man," Bellamy mumbled over his goblet of brandy. "The more they suffer the less trouble. Who cares whether they sink or swim?"

Arndell regarded the marines officer with ill-disguised distaste.

"I do."

"You do what, Arndell?" Francis Walton said, as he came into the cuddy.

Bellamy guffawed and, one eye screwed up, pointed to Thomas Arndell.

"He's got hold of the idea our mission's to land live convicts in Botany Bay."

Throwing up both arms, Arndell made to leave the cuddy.

Walton pointed to Arndell's vacated chair.

"Sit down again, Thomas. If getting convicts all alive-o to Botany Bay's the same as getting me and my ship there in one piece, I agree. I'm not so sure about Shortland's ideas, though."

"Shortland?" Arndell said.

"Naval agent. With Phillips aboard Sirius. Insisting on forty leagues a day - forty bloody leagues every day."

"Beyond Friendship's capacity?"

"No, no. But I'm not risking wet feet and soaked blankets for any naval officer's promotion prospects. Shortland'll have to be content with thirty leagues."

"And if it's better for the convicts to sail slowly then we must sail slowly," Arndell said.

In mock despair Walton put the heel of his hand to his forehead.

"My God, how many more times? Official interest in the convicts' welfare ceased the minute we weighed anchor on the Motherbank. D'you imagine Pitt and Sydney and the rest lie awake wondering if the scum of Newgate and the Thames hulks are getting warm blankets and fair shares of brandy? D'you think Arthur Phillip even, stuffing his guts with roast duckling aboard Sirius, stops for one second to send up a prayer for your stinking friends in the 'tween decks?"

"Well, Phillip must have some concern if only because my stinking friends, as you term them, are the settlers for his new colony," Arndell said.

Bellamy refilled his goblet.

"The fewer convicts crawling ashore in Botany Bay, the fewer Phillip's problems."

"And more provisions for those of us left," Walton added.

In silence, Arndell made to leave a second time and once more Walton urged him back to his chair.

"Something more, Thomas. Friendship's not very big and most of the time we're living up each other's backsides...."

"Well?"

"Nothing much happens aboard that doesn't escape notice."

Eyes narrowing, Arndell glanced briefly at Bellamy, whose smug expression made it clear that he was privy to what Walton was about to say.

"Go on," Arndell said to the ship's master.

"It's obvious you're favouring two particular convicts....."

"The wench with auburn hair, "Bellamy said.

"And a tall dark youth with a scar-face," Walton said.

"You're making fools of us - and yourself - Mr Surgeon."

"Fools? In what way, Francis? The sick are well tended by the girl and she's a very useful seamstress. The man's got an outstanding knowledge of medicaments."

"And knowledge of a lot more besides." Bellamy's grin was obscene. "Spending half his time with the convict women. They're not all fat old harlots."

Studiously ignoring Bellamy, Arndell said, "Risks far outweighed by the benefits."

"Benefits to the convicts are no concern of mine," Walton said.

Arndell nodded.

"Friendship's only a small vessel, yes, Francis?"

"Too bloody small."

"Yet you keep on telling me about no official interest in the welfare of the convicts."

"Go on, go on," Walton said testily.

"In tiny ships like this, the interests of the convicts are the interests of everybody aboard. Any malady rife in the 'tween decks can't be kept in check by hatch covers, no matter how savagely battened down."

Face fiery red, Bellamy lurched unsteadily to his feet.

"Walton has twenty five seamen, I've got twenty-five marines. Fifty men, yes, fifty, all of 'em hungry for a woman..."

"With the promise of the bo's'n's cat if I catch any of 'em with the convict whores," Walton said. "And don't forget seventy-six male convicts. If Henry and I can't maintain discipline over our own men, what hope of controlling the savages from the Thames hulks? If they ever got to the women..."

"What has all this got to do with me?" Arndell said, puzzled.

"Pointing the way. Too much freedom for your pair of favourite convicts. You mixing too freely with the 'tween deck whores."

"But, Francis, I must tend the sick, convict and free alike. That's why I'm here. And it's common sense, surely, using the skills of the convicts Dunne and Pettifer."

Walton gave an impatient wave of his hand.

"In future, a seaman or a marine'll accompany you and your tame convict whenever you enter the women's gaol deck or hospital."

Arndell gave a hopeless shrug.

"All I can say is, make sure he's not over-squeamish about bloody fluxes, suppurating sores and scurvy scabs," he said and he stormed out of the cuddy.

On his way to the women's gaol later that afternoon Thomas Arndell was intercepted by a seaman, fresh faced, fair and of build slighter than normal for a youth of seventeen.

"I'm to accompany you to the women," the youth said in confident tone.

Arndell's smile was indulgent.

"Special knowledge of medical matters?"

The youth seemingly puzzled, shook his head.

"And strong stomach?" Arndell went on.

"I've been at sea a full twelve months and never once been sea-sick," was the reply.

"Then you'll not be disturbed by a jaundice and you'll stay with it until the ipecacuanha has induced the necessary vomiting. Or maybe you advocate tartar for an emetic." Arndell paused to knock back the bolts of the grille then clambered down. The young seaman ignored the proffered hand and leapt lightly into the gaol deck.

"Not so eager," Arndell said. "Now, when you examine the woman with the boils, hold muslin over your nostrils. I've yet to come across a fouler stench. Then there's the woman so bloated she can't manage to struggle out of her upper bunk."

As the atmosphere, heavy with the stench of stale vomit, assailed his nostrils, the young man pressed a hand firmly over his nose and mouth. At the sight of a woman lying in a ground-level bunk, half-naked wasted body covered in sores, he started back and his head thudded against the low ceiling.

"Oh, hell."

Arndell's laughter was not wholly unkind.

"Even I forget sometimes the ceiling's only four and a half feet." The surgeon's voice dropped to a whisper, "See how the women manage, crouching and shuffling, day after day."

"Horrible."

"If -er - if you wish I'll suggest to Mr Walton you're unsuited to the job of - er - supervising me"

"Certainly not."

"Well, then, I do it this way. I crouch and worm along each of these." Arndell pointed to a series of narrow alleyways separating the tiers of bunks. "I look into every bunk. If there's a sick convict I examine as best I can and arrange for medicines. Serious cases I move to the hospital. Come."

The young seaman folded his arms.

"Better if you came with me, Mr Surgeon. I'll lead the way."

"As you wish."

Arndell pursed his lips and followed.

Elbowing the women aside, the youth hurried along an alleyway. At the sound of a scream then a thud Arndell plunged forward. He was met by a solid phalanx of bodies.

"Go back, Mr Surgeon!" Martha Kerwin hissed.

"Set him free. He's only a boy," Arndell roared.

"Mr Surgeon, I beg you, go back."

A second scream, higher pitched than the first, followed.

"Let him go!"

Battling against the human barricade Arndell was steadily forced back to the open space beneath the hatch.

"I insist."

Martha Kerwin was stronger than most women. She seized Arndell from behind, dragged him to the floor and pinioned his arms while another convict, heavy with dropsy, sat firmly on his legs.

"I - I'm sorry to do this, Mr Surgeon," Martha said.

Arndell's struggles were ineffectual.

"Let him go. I insist."

A third scream filled the gaol deck.

"Too late now, sir," Martha whispered to the back of Arndell's head.

"What - what d'you mean?"

"Please go back on deck, sir."

"Not until the boy's free."

Again Martha whispered.

"They won't let him go now till the ceremony's over."

"What ceremony?"

"Old Nick's wedding."

"They'll mutilate him?"

"No, no. But one bridegroom, twenty brides. All of 'em putting wedding rings on him."

"On - on him?"

"And the fit gets tighter and tighter as they practise their favours - till he's ready to burst."

"My God, they wouldn't......"

A series of screams, mounting in intensity, rent the foetid atmosphere of the gaol then a babble of excited female voices.

"It's over now," Martha said.

"Over?"

"The first one. Only the first. Twenty brides couldn't all be satisfied at once, could they, Mr Surgeon?"

Chapter 33

Followed by the surgeon, two marines carried the young seaman to the hospital, already so over-crowded that there was barely space for Margaret to move from one patient to another. Those for whom there was no bunk, men and women alike, were huddled on palliasses in the alleyways.

The marines laid the seaman, naked except for a sheet of blood-stained sail canvas, at the foot of the ladder.

"A bunk, absolutely essential," Arndell said to Margaret.

"There isn't one. Scarcely even floor space."

Arndell took a lantern and, picking his way between the recumbent bodies, he inspected every bunk. He paused at one to touch a forehead and to raise the lid of an eye, then he went back to Margaret now tending the seaman.

"One spare bunk. The convict who had convulsions," he said, shrugging.

When seamen had removed the corpse to the upper deck Arndell and Margaret carried the apprentice seaman to the empty bunk.

"Attend to the others. This is no work for a woman," Arndell said.

Alone now, Arndell drew aside the canvas. From waist to knee the youth was deep-scored and bleeding as if the talons of a score of eagles had taken their toll. His genitals were no more than a clutch of raw, blood-soaked flesh.

"Arndell."

The surgeon glanced up to see Henry Bellamy at the hatch opening.

"Yes?"

"Come here."

Arndell covered the boy and made his way towards the trapdoor.

"I'll send Jonathan," he whispered to Margaret, bending over a sick man, then he clambered to the upper deck.

"Keen on discipline, Henry?" he said quietly to the marines officer.

"You know damn well...."

"Then show it by addressing me as 'Surgeon' or 'Dr Arndell' when marines and seamen and convicts are within earshot."

"Words, words. Which of your poxy women raped the seaman? We'll hang and draw and quarter the lot. Get 'em on deck, strip 'em naked and make 'em parade till the guilty ones own up. I'll show you discipline, Arndell."

Swaying, Bellamy would have toppled but for the surgeon's restraining hand.

"Go get a bucket of cold water for that head of yours, Bellamy. Sober up then we talk. In the cuddy and with Francis present."

Francis Walton, lips pursed, shook his head.

"Naked? No, no!"

Bellamy thumped the cuddy table.

"Naked, naked."

"What a fool the man is," Arndell said as, at that moment, he strode through the doorway of the cuddy. "Can you imagine a score of naked women in full view of sailors and marines? What kind of discipline could you impose after that?"

Walton laughed.

"Oh, in another hour or two he'll come to his senses. Won't you, Henry?"

Once more Bellamy thumped the table.

"Punishment now, now. Threaten keel-hauling, walking the plank and swinging from the yardarm - just for a start."

"But no stripping, Henry," Walton said.

The marines officer lurched to his feet and blundered towards the doorway.

"I'll drag 'em out and strip 'em myself."

Arndell solemnly shook his head.

"Impossible." He dangled a key. "The women's gaol's padlocked."

"Locks can be smashed."

"No, no, Henry," Walton said. "Cool off for a couple of hours then - and only then - we'll get the women on deck."

Muttering, cursing, Bellamy stumbled out of the cuddy and struggled up the companionway to Friendship's upper deck.

Arndell rose to follow but Walton barred his way.

"He'll not interfere with the padlock. Tipsy, yes, but even paralytic, Henry would never go so far when any of his marines are in sight."

Walton steered Arndell back to his chair.

"I'll deal with the convict vixen - after we've dropped anchor."

"Dropped anchor?"

"By tomorrow mid-day we'll've made Santa Cruz and Henry should be easier to handle then. When he's been up-ending more bottles than usual his mind always goes crazy about naked women."

* * * * *

There was scarcely a ripple in the water, the sky azure, cloudless, and the sun extravagantly warm that June morning in the year 1787 when the brig Friendship and the rest of the convict fleet dropped anchor in the roads of Santa Cruz.

In anticipation of bountiful supplies of fresh water, Francis Walton had ordered that the normal ration for the convicts be trebled that day.

There was no mistaking the extreme sarcasm in Arndell's tone.

"How generous, Francis. How incredibly generous."

"Common sense," Walton said. "Use up all the casks aboard and fill up on fresh. Last chance, maybe, before Rio. And something else - twenty grimy women lined up on deck in the hot sun until we find the ringleader. Imagine the stench. Tell'em to wash, Thomas. Let 'em have soap for a change."

When Thomas Arndell arrived to unlock the trapdoor of the women's gaol, he found Henry Bellamy feverishly pacing up and down the deck, freshly uniformed and revealing nothing of the previous night's drunkenness.

"I've been waiting a full ten minutes, leech-man," Bellamy snarled and to emphasise his annoyance he slapped his tightly-breeched thigh.

"Waiting for what?" Arndell said lightly.

"You - and the key to the whore-house."

Bellamy stabbed hard with a forefinger at Arndell's chest.

"Contain yourself, Henry."

"The key."

Arndell's smile was benevolent.

"Francis insists on the women washing before questioning," he said, as if talking to a petulant child.

Bellamy opened wide his hand.

"The key."

"Very well, Henry. Into the gaol deck with you. Only one problem." Arndell pointed to Bellamy's cutlass. "Not well enough armed."

"Against twenty miserable, feeble women?"

"Twenty miserable, feeble, stinking women. They haven't had a wash for a month. In addition to the cutlass, I suggest a supply of linen to protect your elegant nose".

Bellamy glanced at his resplendent uniform and snorted.

"See they're all on deck in an hour," he rasped then hurried down the companionway.

Even more sullen than usual, the women crowded the foot of the ladder as Arndell attempted to join them in the 'tween decks.

"What's afoot?" Martha Kerwin asked.

"You're all to have a wash, ladies."

Martha turned to her fellow prisoners.

"Pretty news, ladies. Don't drink your precious quart of water today - wash in it and go thirsty."

She held wide her open palms to Arndell and, even in the gloom of the prison deck, he could not fail to see the ingrained filth.

"For weeks on end they treat us like cattle and then, suddenly, we are 'ladies'. And all ladies wash themselves - even if dying of thirst."

"Listen, listen," Arndell said. "As much water as you wish for both washing and drinking. And as much soap."

His eyes roamed the women, "Margaret Dunne."

Margaret wormed her way through the throng.

"Yes?"

Arndell motioned her to climb the ladder.

"Urgent work in the hospital, Dunne."

At that moment, alone together on deck, Arndell whispered to Margaret, "You'll stay there till evening. Take back almonds and sweetmeats for the others. Plenty in the hospital."

He stepped back to the hatch grille and called to the women below, "Water a-plenty on deck. Come up two at a time, wash, then line up along the ship's side."

"Line up, why?" Martha Kerwin said.

"When you've washed, Mr Walton'll explain."

Elizabeth Ware and Charlotte Dudgeon were the first to clamber on deck and make for the water butts. Charlotte flung aside her cloak and bared herself to the waist. She had scarcely turned her back and plunged her face into a bucket of water when a sentry from the barricade swung her round, hungrily appraising the firm and ample breasts.

"I - I could help," he said thickly.

"Maybe," Arndell said, suddenly appearing from the opening in the barricade. "But not the sort of help you have in mind. Back to your post."

At length all the women had washed and now they idled in the warmth of the June sun. Although many were hollow-eyed and listless from bouts of seasickness, none looked skeletal any more. To those who had relentlessly struggled for survival in the foetid dungeons of Newgate, where even a crust of stale bread was a much-prized rarity, their daily ration of salt beef, pork, butter and flour represented a banquet.

Although Francis Walton cared little for the future of his convict passengers, he was careful to comply with Admiralty requirements and the prescribed scale of foodstuffs was relatively generous.

The corporal of the guard, Henry Bellamy close on his heels, appeared from the companionway and marched down the deck.

"Stand up straight and in line."

The women, muttering resentment, shuffled into line, their backs to the ship's rail.

"Straight, straight."

Bellamy swaggered past, pausing here and there to lift a chin with the blade of his cutlass.

"You, was it you?" he said glaring at a woman, square-faced and pale, quivering in fear. "Did you foul that boy?"

The woman cowered.

"N-no, sir."

The cutlass blade lifted the chin higher forcing the wretched woman to splutter,"No, no, no."

Bellamy sniggered, stepping back to eye the woman from head to toe.

"Hm, maybe not."

It wasn't the cutlass blade but Bellamy's hand which lifted and held the chin of the next woman.

"There's a certain look about you, convict."

"I - don't know what......."

The grasp on the woman's chin was now so savage that the rest of her words disappeared in a choking gasp.

"What a fool you are."

Bellamy released the hold and swung round.

"Who said that?"

The women shifted uneasily. None spoke.

"Who - said - that?"

Bellamy thudded the ship's rail with the flat of his cutlass.

"You stay here, the lot of you, all night if needs be, until I know who called me a fool."

Head held high, Charlotte Dudgeon stepped out of the line of convict women and confronted Bellamy. The cord which criss-crossed the front of her bodice lay loose.

"Yes, I called you a fool. Couldn't you see?"

"See what, convict?"

Charlotte burst into laughter.

"Men make that woman vomit. She loves little girls. In fact she'd rather take a sow than one of your marines or a sailor boy."

With a pronounced and provocative sway of her hips, Charlotte stepped back in line. She was a tall, shapely woman of about thirty, straw-coloured hair that contrasted sharply with dark brown eyes and a complexion of a freshness that wholly belied many months in gaol. She winked at Bellamy.

"You, was it?"

Charlotte studied the silver-buckled shoes, the white stockings concealing substantial calves, tight buckskin breeches and a crimson tunic that few men of her acquaintance would have filled so impressively.

"Send a man next time, Captain Bellamy, not just a boy. And if you can't find a volunteer then come yourself."

The lustrous eyes, provocative lips, and, as Charlotte changed her stance, the now half-naked breasts brazenly taunted the marines officer. Walton, Arndell, marines and convict women looked on and waited. Bellamy took a deep breath. His voice was unnaturally high.

"Maybe you weren't alone but you can bear the punishment for the rest of the convict scum," he said and raising his cutlass he sliced Charlotte's skirt from waist to hem, then swung round on the corporal.

"Strip her naked, dress her up in a barrel, then a scold's bridle to curb that saucy tongue."

The corporal made no move.

"Go to it, go to it."

Bellamy swung on his heel and almost ran to the opening in the barricade.

Chapter 34

Arndell clambered from the men's gaol deck. Pale and sweating, he stumbled to the ship's side where he leaned to snatch repeated gulps of fresh air.

"Ill?" Walton said, eyes roving over the multitude of vessels riding at anchor in Santa Cruz roads.

Arndell went on gulping the air.

"Nauseated."

"By Atlantic airs?"

"Lack of 'em. Both 'tween decks are screaming out for thorough cleansing."

Walton's tone was caustic.

"Plenty of idle hands there."

"The stench of stale vomit, urine....."

"Whose fault's that?"

"Mine and yours, Francis."

"And what d'you expect me to do?"

"Empty both gaol decks for twenty-four hours."

"Impossible."

"It's warm and dry on deck. The convicts could spend a night in the open air while the gaols are lime-washed and treated with burning brimstone."

"Men and women together, Arndell? You must be mad."

"They wouldn't be together. The deck barricade, remember."

"And d'you imagine six feet of timber with a few iron spikes on top are likely to keep 'em apart?"

Still leaning on the rail Arndell buried his head in his hands.

"The situation's desperate, Francis, desperate. What an opportunity. Months, maybe, before another one turns up again. Anchored in calm waters, good weather."

"All right. The men on deck all morning, the women all afternoon. Arrange for the cleansing that way."

Arndell raised a weary head.

"You don't even begin to understand. Cleansing every square inch of timber means hours and hours of work. Then hours and hours again for the brimstone fumes to subside. The fumes as lethal to humans as to the rats and the cockroaches. Damned if I can stand idly by as you sign the death warrant of all those miserable creatures in the gaol decks."

Francis Walton thumped the ship's rail.

"I am not allowing the men and the women on deck at one and the same time."

"But you'd agree to a full twenty four hours each, longer if necessary?"

"Er - yes."

Arndell smiled.

"Then the women can have a day and a night on deck while their gaol is cleansed and the men can follow with the same."

"Only if Bellamy agrees. He'll have to mount additional guards," Walton said.

"Then have words with him, Francis. Incidentally, where is our gallant captain of marines at the moment?"

Walton grimaced.

"Well, he's unlikely to have jumped overboard but I'll wager he's drowning just the same."

"Drowning?!"

"A couple of jeroboams of wine disappeared overnight and I tripped over an empty one outside his cabin this morning. Keeping himself to himself, I'd say. Far from proud over yesterday's performance with the cutlass. A disaster for discipline. Or he could be pondering over other matters."

"Such as?"

"The naked bosom of that convict whore," Walton said.

"Which, I can now assure you, is adequately covered," Arndell said with a smile. "I took it upon myself to remove the water butt and bridle and give the woman some more discreet garb. Now that you seem to be in expansive mood, Francis ....."

"Am I?"

"I need the jolly boat."

"Why?"

"Ashore for fresh medicines."

"I can't spare a seaman."

"One of the convicts....."

"Your medicaments friend?"

Arndell nodded.

"And if he attempts escape?" Walton went on.

"He won't."

Walton was persistent.

"But if he does?"

"I'll shoot him."

Walton's head nodded in approval.

"Sense at last. All right. I only hope the islanders are more generous with medicines than their water. We could be a very parched ship by the time we put into Rio."

Walton was standing with Arndell at the ship's rail as seamen lowered Friendship's jolly boat and Jonathan swung overside to take a pair of oars.

"Pistol?" Walton rasped

Arndell tapped the lower pocket of his tunic.

"He should be fettered," Walton continued, jerking his head in the direction of Jonathan now aboard the boat.

"Imagine the interest," Arndell said," when we step ashore and walk through the streets. No, Francis, I'm a surgeon, not a turnkey. In any case, the convict'd refuse to go in irons."

Arndell clambered overside, swung into the jolly boat and took the second pair of oars.

When they were beyond earshot of Friendship, Arndell called to Jonathan, "If you attempt escape I'm ordered to shoot."

Jonathan, shipping his oars, turned, "And would you?"

There was an off-shore swell so that, with only one pair of oars in the water, the boat began to nose southwards and away from land. Jonathan folded his arms, sat back and smiled.

"At this moment you seem to need me as much as I need you, Mr Surgeon. But maybe my escape would be some benefit to you. In due course."

Arndell feathering one oar, pulled determinedly on the other, yet the jolly boat continued to nose away from land. He was panting from the exertion.

"What d'you mean?"

"Margaret. In love with her, aren't you?"

Arndell's complexion, pink from the exertion of rowing alone, turned a fiery red.

"You over-estimate your situation, convict," he snapped.

"And you, surgeon," Jonathan said slyly, as he laid hands to his oars and the jolly boat was once more heading for shore, "underestimate my intelligence."

In silence the pair continued rowing until they came to a stone jetty. Jonathan, mooring rope in hand, leapt ashore and secured the jolly boat to a bollard.

"For the composing pills. Catch," Arndell called, flinging a haversack to Jonathan.

"Opium? Tck, tck, tck," Jonathan said with mock seriousness, thrusting out a hand to help Arndell on to the jetty.

"Nothing better. Seasickness is going to be with us all the way to Botany Bay."

"Opium. Vicious stuff. More addictive than tobacco. Why not columba root?"

"I -er I don't know it."

"Like so much else in your world, your limited world, of medicaments, Mr Surgeon."

The glowering Arndell, jaw set tight, quickened pace.

The ill-assorted pair, a slight and meticulously garbed surgeon and a tall, ragged convict, had reached the outskirts of Santa Cruz when the latter broke the silence.

"You go in front?" he said lightly. "Easier for a bullet in my back if I decide to bolt."

Arndell stopped and turned.

"You'd be a fool, we'd both be fools. I - er - I think I'll have need of you, Pettifer." Arndell's face relaxed into a smile and he thrust out a hand, "and you could have need of me."

The women were lounging on deck in the afternoon sun when Jonathan, grasping a bulging haversack, and

Arndell came aboard. Arndell perused the women then, turning to Jonathan, he gave a covert wink and said in a voice loud enough for all to hear, "The hospital, convict. Cleansing, brimstone and liming."

Jonathan promptly swung his legs over the open hatch and dropped into the hospital. Every bunk was empty. Margaret was there alone. She rushed to him.

"I can't - I can't go on!"

Jonathan's arms encircled her and he held her close.

"You must, you must. You know precisely how to handle Thomas Arndell now."

"It's - it's not Thomas Arndell. It's Turnbull McQuaid."

Jonathan held Margaret at arm's length.

"McQuaid? McQuaid's a thousand miles away."

"He's on board this ship."

Still holding Margaret away from him Jonathan, slowly shaking his head, eyed her with incredulity.

"Never."

"When I was brought here this morning, I saw Turnbull McQuaid on deck with Francis Walton."

Jonathan laughed.

"You must be - must be mistaken, love."

"Nobody dresses like Turnbull McQuaid. And I'd recognise that high-pitched voice anywhere."

"He spoke?"

"To Walton."

"Did he notice you?"

Margaret shrugged her shoulders.

"He gave no sign."

"But if it really is...."

"He is aboard, dearest. It was McQuaid, I know."

"Then why ever is he bound for Botany Bay?"

"I'm - I'm terrified."

Suddenly Arndell appeared at the hatch opening.

"Terrified? Of what?" Arndell said, joining Margaret and Jonathan.

"One of the marines," Jonathan said quickly.

"Which? Bellamy'll deal with him. Now, an emergency, Pettifer. Midwifery?"

"No, no."

Arndell pointed to the hatch opening.

"A chance to learn. Quick!"

One moment it was daylight and the next, or so it seemed, the whole expanse of Santa Cruz roads was plunged into darkness. Surrounded by her fellow convicts, head cradled in the lap of Charlotte Dudgeon, a woman lay moaning and alternately gasping on the planking.

Jonathan at his heels, Thomas Arndell rushed forward.

"Give the woman air, give her air. Guards, the women below, at once."

Arndell motioned a marine to bring a lantern closer then, snatching a sheet of canvas covering from a water cask, he dropped to his knees and gently swathing the stillborn child, he handed the tiny bundle to Jonathan.

"The hospital," he said briskly to Charlotte Dudgeon still cradling the woman's head. "And you," he said over his shoulder to a figure looking idly on, "give a hand to get her through the hospital hatch."

When they had gone, Jonathan, still holding the dead child, said,"Burial service?"

Arndell's face was devoid of expression.

"Just overside," he said.

He picked up a length of chain from the deck, bound the canvas-wrapped body, then quickly stepped to the ship's rail.

In the rhythmic slap of a heavy swell against Friendship's timbers, the single splash was scarcely audible. As Jonathan joined Arndell at the ship's rail, the surgeon retched.

"Neither of us greatly skilled in midwifery," Jonathan said.

Arndell's voice was faint.

"Or burials," he said.

"I hate to admit it, but I'm delighted we bought your composing pills as well as columba root in Santa Cruz, Dr. Arndell."

Chapter 35

It was not until the light from a lantern swinging from the aft mast revealed briefly the man's features, that Charlotte Dudgeon recognised the marine helping to carry the sick woman as Captain-Lieutenant Henry Bellamy. The convict woman gasped and was on the point of dropping her burden, when Bellamy pressed an urgent finger to his lips.

"Shh."

Lifting the sick woman himself, Bellamy clambered down the ladder into the hospital.

"She's had a child," he said gruffly to Margaret.

The woman was whimpering. Margaret covered her gently with a blanket.

"Where - where's the child?"

Bellamy jerked a thumb in the direction of the upper deck.

"Ask the surgeon," he said, then leapt for the ladder and Charlotte Dudgeon waiting nervously for him in the shadow of the mast.

"No need to be scared," he said, his rough hands seeking a way through the coarse bodice to her breasts. His voice was strained, "I - I want you, woman!"

"Then take me - if you can."

Charlotte was by no means a small woman nor was she a weak one. The slap on Bellamy's cheek was loud and savage enough to be heard from Friendship's larboard to starboard.

"You - you bitch."

His mouth, wide open, clamped hard over the convict woman's mouth, his knee thrust deep between her ample thighs and, trapped in a brutal embrace, the struggling Charlotte began to gasp and choke.

At the sound of footsteps from the companionway, Bellamy quickly freed his captive and, hand clamped firmly over her mouth, he dragged her to the starboard rail. Concealed by upturned water casks, he held her firmly and he watched as Thomas Arndell made for the hatch-grille of the hospital.

When the surgeon dropped out of sight, Bellamy swiftly led the convict woman down the companionway. The door of the cuddy was ajar and, at the table, Turnbull McQuaid and Francis Walton were deep in argument. Bellamy paused for a moment, smiled, then, propelling Charlotte ahead, he steered her to his cabin.

Bellamy immediately dived for the bunk which took up most of the floor space of his quarters and drawing Charlotte on top of him he began to drag off her clothing. She wriggled free and clamped her teeth over his anxious, probing fingers.

"Owch."

"You - you want me to stay?"

Bellamy's reply was gruff, urgent.

"By God I do."

"A long time?"

Bellamy arms encircled her thighs.

"Yes, yes."

With an extraordinary display of strength, Charlotte once more struggled free of the marine officer's clutches and, rolling off the bunk she got to her feet and stood upright, her back pressed to the door.

"No need for such frantic haste, Captain," she said, then pointed meaningfully at an array of bottles and goblets on a shelf above the head of the bunk, "Many a long day since I tasted brandy."

Bellamy jerked to his feet and cursed as his head struck the low ceiling.

"Poor, poor boy." Standing over him, Charlotte drew the head of wiry hair to her lips. "That'll make it better. And brandy could make more things even better."

With shaking hand Bellamy filled two brandy goblets and, when he raised his head, he was faced by Charlotte's full and naked breasts, nipples pert and crimson. He tossed back his brandy and, before the convict woman had chance to take even the first sip, he dashed the goblet from her grasp and dragged her back to the bunk. He threw himself on top of her and this time there was not the faintest hope of escape.

The intensity of his lovemaking drew a series of wild and frantic gasps from her, "Please, please. Not - not so...... Oh, oh....."

An urgent thudding on the cabin door roused Charlotte, but it was only after repeated jabs with her elbow that Bellamy finally stirred.

"They're calling you," she whispered hoarsely.

The thuds resumed with greater urgency. Bellamy yawned and stretched his arms.

"Bloody wonderful. You were bloody wonderful, woman."

"Somebody hammering on the door," Charlotte said.

Bellamy sat up.

"What is it?"

"The master wants you, Captain Bellamy."

Charlotte wormed free of Bellamy's arms and, naked, rolled off the bunk to seek her clothes.

"Tell him I'm coming."

Bellamy slid an arm around Charlotte's buttocks as she bent to retrieve her skirt.

"Back to the bunk, woman."

He dragged her into the bedclothes and once more thrust deep between her thighs.

"Never satisfied?" Charlotte murmured as, at length, she eased herself away.

Bellamy's only reply was to embrace her yet again, then bury his face between her breasts.

The thudding on the door resumed.

"What is it?"

"Urgent, captain. And there's breakfast in the cuddy."

With reluctance Bellamy drew away from the convict woman and, struggling to his feet, he began to dress.

"Stay where you are. I'll bring food."

Charlotte glanced around the tiny cabin.

"Stay?"

"Anxious to be back in the prison deck?"

"No, no, but I'll want to....."

"Empty cask over there," Bellamy said with a coarse laugh. "Use it while I'm getting the food for you."

* * * * *

At first light, a marine summoned Margaret to the hatch opening of the 'tween deck.

"Surgeon - hospital," he barked.

Tending the woman who had given birth, Arndell glanced up as Margaret joined him. The woman, in high fever, persisted in kicking aside the blood-stained blankets while Arndell, with equal persistence, covered the emaciated, sweating body again and again.

"I'll hold her. You pour this down,"he whispered urgently to Margaret.

Margaret regarded the bottle askance.

"How much?"

"All of it."

"She'll choke."

"No, no."

Arndell moved the woman to a sitting position and, as she opened her mouth in protest, he rammed a piece of wood between her teeth.

"Pour now."

The sick woman gulped and spluttered. Most of the medicine, however, found its way down her throat.

Arndell withdrew the piece of wood, lowered the woman to the straw palliasse and covered her with a clean blanket. He gasped with relief. Taking the bottle from Margaret, he held it up to the light and nodded.

"Enough to fell a couple of oxen," he said, a note of satisfaction in his voice.

With a moistened rag, Margaret mopped sweat from the ivory-like face now in deep repose.

"Save your effort," Arndell said.

Wet cloth in hand, Margaret paused.

"Curious man, Thomas Arndell."

"A sensible one."

"Too much medicine, too little comfort."

"Comfort's wasted on her now. Enough laudanum to put twenty women to sleep."

Margaret's eyes narrowed.

"You've made me poison her?"

"No, no. With the laudanum she may survive painlessly till nightfall. Without it, screaming agony for days on end. Then death."

The Friendship shuddered and lurched to larboard and Margaret suddenly found herself in Arndell's arms. He planted a hungry kiss fully on her lips.

"No, Thomas, no."

Arndell, lips quivering, held Margaret at arm's length and anxiously scanned her face.,

"I'm - I'm still frantic for you."

Again the convict ship lurched, more savagely this time, and the pair were pitched to the decking.

"No, no, no, Thomas."

Anchor at last freed from the seabed in Santa Cruz roads and now riding on an even keel, Friendship had begun to nose southwards with the rest of the convict fleet.

Margaret, weeping, dragged herself free of Arndell's embrace and stumbled to the edge of a bunk.

* * * * *

The spruce Walton had already eaten breakfast when Bellamy, unshaven, tousled hair, shirt unbuttoned, joined the ship's master in the cuddy.

"Where in hell've you been? Twice I sent an apprentice looking for you. Wasn't a roll-call of marines necessary?"

Bellamy seized a jug of porter and drank deeply.

"Whaffor?"

"Before sailing!"

"When?"

"Well, we weighed anchor half an hour ago. If any of your men are still ashore, they'll have to stay. But I daresay we'll manage with fewer marines."

Bellamy's teeth buried deep into a hunk of cheese and he took another draught of porter.

"What d'you mean?"

Walton regarded the marines officer with ill-concealed scorn.

"Good discipline can be imposed without an armoury of muskets and cutlasses. By, say, setting a good example," he said.

Bellamy ceased chewing.

"What're you getting at?"

"The convict Charlotte Dudgeon, Henry."

Bellamy guffawed, spluttering fragments of cheese across the cuddy table.

"The very best discipline. I taught that bitch a lesson she's never likely to forget. The rest of 'em saw it all."

Walton slowly shook his head.

"Not all, exactly. But I saw it all. On the other side of that door last night. And in the alleyway I heard more from your cabin. I suggest you get rid after nightfall. And quickly!"

Bellamy drained the porter jug, then wiped his mouth with the back of his hand.

"Go to hell."

"Nightfall, Henry. Unless you're bent on making my job impossible."

"Nonsense."

"If the captain of marines can take a convict woman, why can't the rest of the marines? Why not every crew member? Then the male convicts. You're on the way to making my ship a floating whore-house, Henry Bellamy. I've no fancy for embarrassing you. Nor any fancy for mutiny. So nightfall, Henry, not a minute later."

"A pox on you."

"Imagine, me having to ask the captain of marines to arrange a stem-to-stern search of Friendship for a missing convict woman, and then she's found in....."

"All right, all right."

* * * * *

It was a pitch black Atlantic night when Bellamy emerged from the companionway, Charlotte Dudgeon following. He came to a sudden halt, his hand in warning behind him.

"Wait."

Bellamy strode purposefully across the deck to the barricade where a sentry leaned over the butt of his musket, dozing. He kicked the musket's barrel and the man lurched forward.

"Wake up, wake up."

"Sir?"

"There's a convict woman skulking at the head of the companionway. See her to the prison deck. If you're not back at your post in two minutes, I'll have you court martialled for falling asleep on duty."

Chapter 36

Despite his own intense passion for Margaret Dunne, Thomas Arndell constantly struggled to arrange meetings for her with Jonathan Pettifer in the only possible place aboard the convict transport, its tiny, makeshift hospital.

Occasions of privacy for the pair, however, were pitifully rare. Each bunk held its sick occupant and those for whom no bunk was available lay on palliasses in the narrow alleyway.

As Friendship sailed south towards the tropics the benefit of the earlier cleansing and disinfecting of her 'tween decks was rapidly lost. The conditions in which the convicts, men and women alike, were existing grew fouler by the hour.

Daily the sun's heat became more savage and the stench in the gaol decks increasingly vile as the sweating, unwashed prisoners lay night after night on sodden palliasses repeatedly soaked whenever the squat-sailing transport Friendship struck heavy Atlantic swells and the seas sluiced over her hatches.

Hitherto, Arndell had prepared and stored his medicines in the ship's cuddy but as sickness aboard Friendship continued to mount he persuaded Francis Walton to allot him space and a bench in the armoury, a tiny room immediately below the cuddy and adjacent to a cabin shared by the marine guards.

It was here that Jonathan was now afforded the daily opportunity to practise and demonstrate the skills in medicaments that he had learned from Matthew Gross in Sea Coal Lane.

At first there was growling resentment among the male convicts over Jonathan's increased freedom but this was promptly silenced by the astute Thomas Arndell. With Thomas's secret connivance, Jonathan was able to smuggle extra tobacco, sugar and the occasional bottle of rum or wine into the men's prison deck.

The filthy and cramped conditions of the convicts were not, however, the sole causes of their sickness. The ration of drinking water, green and brackish, was barely sufficient to assuage thirsts fuelled by tropical temperatures while the food, although by no means ungenerous in quantity, was either stale or so uninviting as to be almost inedible.

Biscuits were infested by black-headed maggots and the cheese was either seething with red worms or, to rotting teeth and tender gums, it seemed as hard as seasoned oak.

Similarly, the food for the ship's company and marines grew increasingly unpalatable. In the cuddy, Turnbull McQuaid's delicate features contorted in exaggerated revulsion at the flavour of the salted pork. He sluiced it generously with red wine then lowered his head to take a tentative sniff.

"Filth, Walton, filth," he growled, thrusting his plate to the other side of the table. "I couldn't possibly stomach muck like that."

Francis Walton regarded the shipowner blandly.

"It's as well you're getting a taste of your own medicine, Turnbull."

McQuaid snorted.

"My own medicine? Nothing wrong with the victualling, nothing at all. You haven't the vaguest idea how to keep food in good condition."

Walton's smile was patronising.

"Your ship, remember."

"Partly mine."

"Enough to be aware of its limitations."

"What d'you mean? Friendship's well found, she sails safe and squat."

"Too squat. I detest a vessel that ships half the ocean even in a moderate swell. I've never seen decks so often awash. That's why the victuals don't suit your gullet. Impossible to keep 'em dry."

"How many years at sea, Walton?"

"A quarter of a century."

McQuaid's tone was snide and, at the same time, malevolent,

"And you still forget to batten down the hatches."

"And you forget, McQuaid, our cargo's human beings not bolts of cotton or woollens. Like it or not - and I don't much like it - the convicts need daylight access to the upper deck. You'd have my crew for ever battening down and opening up."

"Why not batten down permanently?" McQuaid said.

"And risk wholesale deaths?"

"Well, you'd get your money and I'd get mine. I gave no undertaking to land one hundred live convicts in Botany Bay. Did you?"

"No, but I'm fairly keen to stay alive. And the surgeon's convinced if we don't look after the convicts not one of us aboard, convict, marine and crew alike, will ever make Botany Bay."

"The fool."

"An old woman, Arndell maybe, but no fool. King's evil, convulsions, consumption, all there in the 'tween decks. Feed the prisoners, give 'em air as much as possible and we keep the sickness within bounds. Batten down, as you suggest, and, within a week, a cargo of putrefying corpses."

McQuaid left the table, filled a wine glass and drank deeply.

"What's our next port of call?" he said.

"Port Praya, God willing."

"God willing?"

"We need good weather. Catspaw winds more often than not and a nasty hungry reef to the east of the bay. A heavy swell and you've got the perfect mix for losing a ship... I'll tell you more when I've had a word with the look-out. Now, can I ask you something, Turnbull?"

"Why not?"

"Ever since you came aboard I've been wondering why you were going to Botany Bay. It's going to be a hell of a lot different from the luxuries of Wheel House Square."

McQuaid smiled and said in bantering tone, "I came to keep an eye on my ship."

"Is that all?"

"Can you imagine any other reason?" McQuaid said.

Walton was hesitant.

"Come on, Francis," McQuaid continued," speak your mind."

"I - er - I think you've been heavily involved in running contraband...."

"Tell me more."

"So your friends at court have suggested voluntary exile until....."

McQuaid burst into laughter.

"Extremely perceptive, Francis," he said, slapping the ship's master across the shoulders, "I'll finish the sentence for you - 'voluntary exile until the dust settles'."

Walton nodded, "Useful having friends in high places."

"Yes, indeed. And if ever....."

"Thanks." Walton sipped his wine sparingly. "Now, I'd better take over the helm."

Alone now in the cuddy, McQuaid rose from the table for a sight of himself in the mirror. He raised a goblet to the reflection.

"Well done, Turnbull, damn well done, sir," he said in a loud voice to the smiling image. "If the astute Francis Walton hasn't noticed - and he clearly hasn't - you can feel proud, extremely proud......"

McQuaid's reverie was interrupted by a confusion of sounds overhead, running feet, shouts, wildly flapping sails. He swiftly drained the goblet and bounded for the companionway.

"What's happened?"

Walton's knuckles were ivory white as he savagely clenched the wheel.

"Not going to make it."

"What d'you mean?"

"Use your eyes, man."

An offshore breeze from the Cape Verde Islands had dropped to little more than an occasional puff. Already HMS Sirius lay becalmed while the rest of the fleet, Friendship on its eastern perimeter, was starting to drift in helpless cluster around the warship. At the same time, an onshore swell gently but inexorably nudged every vessel closer and closer to a spit of broken water, at once recognisable as the outline of a submerged reef.

"Signal from Sirius, sir. 'Get an offing'!" the lookout yelled.

Walton, cursing, spun the wheel savagely to larboard but Friendship, squatting low in the water, was even more sluggish than usual in response.

"Idle, bloody bitch," he roared, hurling his full weight against the wheel.

Slowly, almost imperceptibly, Friendship's bows bobbed away from the rest of the clustered fleet and, in spite of wind flurries now from every point of the compass, Francis Walton was once more in control.

McQuaid loosened his anxious grip of the starboard rail.

"Brilliant seamanship, Francis."

Walton spat.

"Seamanship? You'd've seen a lot better but for that nanny-goat Arthur Phillip."

"But the danger of going aground, Francis."

Again Walton spat.

"Pah! Backing and filling for an hour, I'd've made Port Praya all right even in this tub of yours. We need fresh water. Desperately." Walton's index finger ranged over a row of butts. "Every one of 'em empty. And what's left's all stinking green. In twenty four hours I could've shipped enough to see us to Rio and the Cape."

Friendship, now on a steady south-easterly course, had left the rest of the convict fleet comfortably astern when Walton handed over the helm to a seaman. Arndell and Bellamy, who had been standing in the bows, came through the doorway of the deck barricade.

"Not putting into port?" Bellamy said.

"What does it look like?"

"Why not?"

"Ask bloody Phillip."

"So when do we ship more rum, more brandy?"

"We're frantically short of fresh water and medicines," Arndell said.

Walton threw up his hands.

"Bloody, bloody Phillip's nanny-goat orders. Henry, you drink too much and you, Thomas, shipped, I'd've thought, enough medicines in the Canaries."

"But the sickness, absolutely raging in the gaol decks. They're screaming for water. They get it. It's foul and they vomit."

Walton threw up his arms.

"Wine, below." he said.

* * * * *

It was the first time that the four, Walton, Bellamy, Arndell and McQuaid, had sat in the cuddy together. For much of the voyage McQuaid, suffering like the convicts from recurrent bouts of seasickness, had remained in his cabin.

Walton filled a goblet and passed it to Arndell. The latter, who normally drank sparingly, now sipping with obvious relish, drained the goblet.

"Good stocks of wine?" he said to Walton, filling a range of goblets.

Walton smiled.

"Enough to see us to the Cape - if Henry here topples overboard in the near future."

"We could ship more before the Cape if necessary?"

"In Rio, yes."

McQuaid toyed with the stem of his glass.

"Not bad condition. You keep your wine better than your water, Francis." He turned to Thomas Arndell, "Why this sudden interest in wine, Mr Surgeon?"

Arndell winked and nodded his head.

"A little each day for the convicts would be highly beneficial. Give the miserable wretches something to look forward to."

"Wine for convicts?" McQuaid said. "They've got water."

"Not fit for herring," Arndell said.

"They brought it all on themselves."

"And we want to add to their misery?"

Bellamy, so far silent, emptying goblet after goblet, placed a hand on Arndell's shoulder.

"Have another drink, Mr Leech-man."

Ignoring Bellamy, Arndell turned to Walton, "How many goblets of wine a day is my ration?"

Walton gave an amiable shrug, "Three or four. A whole bottle if you like."

"Then will you arrange for the daily ration to be left in my locker?"

"Why?"

"I can then pass it on to your miserable captives of the 'tween decks, Francis."

Chapter 37

When the Friendship was struck by a freak equatorial rainstorm, the convicts had already been battened down for the night, frantic with thirst. For days on end most of them, too feeble to clamber on deck, had not stirred from their bunks where, unable to eat the dry food, they lay panting, licking the sweat from their naked bodies in desperate attempt to slake their thirst.

In the summer sunshine the planking of the upper deck, inadequately caulked, had become snuff-dry and shrunken. Rainwater now seeping between the cracks ceaselessly dripped on the prisoners who were quick to spread out scraps of canvas and every available container to funnel and collect the fluid.

Cloudy with the powder from the holystone blocks used for scrubbing the deck, tainted by tar-caulking and salt, fouled by filthy canvas it was still the very liquid of life to the desperate convicts. As every prisoner held canvas or vessel to one dripping crack, he pressed a mouth to another crack.

On deck Francis Walton ordered the erection of awnings to catch the rainwater and by early morning, when the storm had abated, every butt on Friendship's deck was overflowing.

Arndell, followed by Bellamy, emerged from the companionway into brilliant sunshine and glancing along the rows of water casks he smiled.

"No more frantic convicts, thank God," he said.

"And plenty of clean shirts," Bellamy said as, brushing past Arndell, he strode to the hatch of the women's prison deck and summoned one of the guards from the barricade.

"Is there a woman who can wash shirts and stockings?"

"I don't know, sir."

"Find a volunteer. Say it's for Captain Bellamy's shirts. There's a convict woman, Dudgeon, I think..."

"Yes, sir."

"Well, don't just stand there."

* * * * *

For an hour Henry Bellamy paced up and down the after-deck, pausing time after time by the women's gaol hatch.

"The laundress," he said to the guard whenever he paused but the reply was always, "She's coming, sir."

Finally Bellamy rasped, "Go fetch her."

The man gave a wry smile.

"I beg your pardon, sir, but...."

"But what?"

"Daren't risk myself down there, sir. Nobody dare. I passed on the message, sir. All the women'll be on deck for daily exercise in a few minutes."

Bellamy snorted.

"Escort her to my cabin the minute she appears," he said and, turning on his heel, he went below.

At mid-day there was a gentle tap on the door of Bellamy's cabin. He hurled himself from the bunk and flung wide the door.

Bonneted, radiant, Charlotte Dudgeon stood silent in the narrow alleyway. Bellamy quickly drew her into the cabin and, closing the door, studied her at arm's length. His eyes ranged hungrily over her face, the full and shapely bosom and the broad hips.

"It's you, really you."

"Of course."

"But you're so....."

"Different? Only because I've been able to wash, use soap."

Bellamy drew her to him and buried his nose deep into the rich golden hair.

"Sweet as a spring meadow," he said, his lips seeking hers.

Charlotte allowed the lips to linger no more than briefly before drawing away from him.

Her tone was impish.

"I thought you wanted a laundress," she said.

With a mounting nervous urgency, Bellamy began to unfasten the lacing of her bodice.

"That's what I thought, too," he murmured, his hands gently cupping her naked breasts.

It was early evening when Bellamy tumbled from his bunk and began a search for his clothes in the dimly-lit cabin.

"I'll get food and drink from the cuddy," he said.

Charlotte urged herself to a sitting position and, legs over the side of the bunk, arms encircling Bellamy's hips, she buried her face in the hairs of his chest.

"I'd rather have you than food. Come back to the bunk."

Bellamy took her head in his hands and turned her face upwards.

"I - I couldn't....." he said gently.

Charlotte's hand sought and caressed his groin.

"Shh. Quiet."

"I mean it. I just couldn't...."

Her finger nails bit deep into his flesh, then she pushed him aside.

Her tone was bitter, scornful.

"Couldn't? Only twice all afternoon and you say you couldn't?"

Bellamy had now collected his clothes scattered across the floor and he began to dress.

"When we've eaten....."

"Eaten? Call yourself a man? No real man should need chicken and brandy before proving himself."

"Please, please, Charlotte. I'll give you everything..."

The convict woman, eyes blazing, shot naked from the bunk and dragged a dress quickly over her head.

"If twice is your everything, soldier-boy, then you're certainly not the man for me," she said, lacing up her bodice.

"Don't - don't taunt," Bellamy said. "I'd been frantic for you for so long. That second time. Like a torrent. It - it drained me. Please, please stay."

Charlotte thrust him roughly aside and finished putting on her clothes.

"Maybe one of your marines would...."

"No, no."

"Why,'No, no'? If you've got no desire for me, why stand in the way of somebody who might? Why, Henry Bellamy?"

Bellamy stood limp, gazing at the convict woman.

"It's more than your body I want, Charlotte."

"More than my body?"

"Damn you, woman, damn you," Bellamy said and, turning his back on her, he dragged on his breeches.

Charlotte tapped him on the shoulder.

"What are trying to tell me?" she said softly.

"That I'm in love with you, damn your hide."

Both her hands now on his shoulders, she struggled to turn him but he was unyielding.

"Say that to my face, Henry."

Bellamy's voice quavered, "I - er - I've never said things like that before."

"Say it again and say it to my face."

Struggling into his shirt, Bellamy turned and for a moment, his head was hidden.

"I love you," he said.

Charlotte dragged down the shirt to reveal flushed features and quivering lips.

"Think what you're saying. Do you know me, really know me?"

Bellamy's nod was emphatic.

"Yes."

"Certain?"

"Yes, yes"

Charlotte's smile was warm, gentle.

"There's scarcely an earl in London who hasn't at one time or another bedded me, Henry. Twice I've had a prince, once a prime minister....."

"I - I don't care, woman."

"But you've got to."

Firmly Charlotte drew Bellamy to the edge of the bunk where they sat and held hands.

"You can never, never talk me out of it... Listen, Henry Bellamy. I was fifteen when the lord of the manor took me the first time. Soon, it became more often than his wife."

"Makes no difference whatsover."

"It must."

Bellamy put a finger to Charlotte's lips.

"The past doesn't matter."

"But it's got to, it's got to. The past decides the future. I've had three children. Two of such important blood they were handed to wet nurses straightway - and I never saw either of them again. Then....."

Again Bellamy's finger went to Charlotte's lips.

"I don't want another word."

She pushed aside the finger.

"I insist, Henry, I insist. I'm the sort of woman no one man could ever satisfy."

"I could."

Charlotte shook her head so that the long golden hair tumbled free about her shoulders.

"Five minutes ago, you were attempting an escape to bolster yourself with cold chicken. I tell you here and now, I'd never, never remain faithful. Never. Take me, make love to me here as much as you wish but, if and when we reach Botany Bay, I'll not stay with you."

Bellamy's grasp on Charlotte's hand tightened.

"Rio. We'll skip ashore in Rio and never come back."

Charlotte, laughing, returned the pressure on her hand, "Just the same, Henry, I'd never stay. And how could you make a living in South America, you a soldier all your life? I'd have to earn enough money, in the only way I know, for both of us."

"Never that."

"What other way? Nothing offers so much profit - and pleasure."

Bellamy slid from the edge of the bunk and, still holding Charlotte's hand, he dropped to his knees.

"Until this minute I'd never begged for anything in my whole life....."

"Oh, get up Henry, get up."

Bellamy scrambled to his feet. Charlotte's kiss was lingering and tender.

"Did you ever wonder why I was aboard a convict ship?" she said.

"Not really."

"It'll explain why I'd never make you a wife. I'm already married. to a Bow Street magistrate. Night after night he used to lash me to the bedpost and thrash me with a riding crop."

"No!"

Charlotte lifted her dress to reveal her naked stomach.

"Scars. Scars don't come from love tumbles in the hay, Henry Bellamy. After the thrashing…" Charlotte was silent for a moment, "after the thrashing he'd rape me, still lashed to the bedpost."

"And you stayed?"

"Sometimes it could be pleasurable, mostly it was hell. But there was never any escape. While he dispensed justice at Bow Street, I was kept behind barred windows and locked doors. I smothered his child."

"His - but yours."

"It looked exactly like him. It had his fingers, his ears. I couldn't ever….. My husband's fellow magistrates were being lenient, they said. For one fleeting moment I'd been crazed, they said. Fourteen years in the colonies'd teach me life was sacred.

"It's true I'm crazed. I'm crazed all the time, but not the way the magistrates said. I'm crazed for men.

"Tell me again you love me... Then love me, Henry - please."

Charlotte ripped apart Bellamy's shirt as he battled to extricate himself from his buckskin breeches.

"I - don't - care," he murmured into Charlotte's wide open mouth as he thrust deep between the welcoming thighs.

* * * * *

The waters of the Atlantic, silver and black and grey, fretted against the bulwarks of the convict transport Friendship, snugged down for the night by that wariest of mariners, Francis Walton, so that progress on the vessel's southerly course was barely a cable's length in an hour.

Deep within the shadow of the companionway top, Bellamy embraced Charlotte, then turned her in the direction of the marine who guarded the hatch cover to the women's prison deck.

"Laundress, remember," he whispered with urgency. "No further explanations."

Momentarily unsighted by the aft mast, he did not see Charlotte as she reached the hatchway, but he heard a grunt as the convict woman roused the dozing sentry. Then there were ribald words in a male voice followed by the sound of a slap.

Bellamy's anxious features broke into a smile. Charlotte was demonstrating that she was a woman of spirit and, no matter how frustrated she may have felt over Bellamy's inadequacy earlier in the evening, she had no taste now for a common, though lusty, marine.

Chapter 38

"The last of the columba," Jonathan said to Thomas Arndell, as he pressed dry brown roots into a mortar for pounding into fine powder.

"Then back to composing pills," Arndell replied jocularly.

"What we need are decoctions of oak bark, of penny-royal..... oh and a dozen other things," Jonathan said.

"Nothing like that aboard."

"Amazing. Didn't you inspect stores before we sailed?"

"Walton assured me they were satisfactory."

"Walton?" Jonathan laughed. "What could an ex-deck swabber know about medicines?"

"The contractors....."

"Leaving such vital things as medicine to chandlers and quayside labourers? Amazed you didn't check Walton's statement. I'd've thought your first job boarding Friendship was detailed attention to health, convicts' and crew's alike."

"It was - and it is."

"You allowed the women aboard still in their stinking gaol rags."

"I did everything I could for them."

"That, on the face of it, seems virtually nothing."

Arndell, even paler than usual, put a hand to his forehead and drew it back to stare at the sweat on his palm.

"I'm only one man, remember, Pettifer," he said.

Having finished pounding the columba root, Jonathan thoughtfully trickled the fine powder between his fingers.

"Barely enough to allay half a score of nauseas," he said.

Arndell's mouth opened to reply but he coughed, vomited and then collapsed over the armoury bench. Jonathan lifted the surgeon bodily to an upturned cask. With a rag soaked in water, he sponged away the vomit from Arndell's face and wiped as best he could the front of the leather jerkin.

"Take this," he said, raising Arndell's head and putting a horn beaker to his lips.

"Hm? What is.....?"

"Lime water and columba root."

Arndell sipped the water but his lips closed tightly against the columba root powder.

"Composing pills," he murmured.

Jonathan smiled to himself and cast an eye along the rows of jars at the back of the bench.

"Where?" he said.

"The cuddy."

"Can you go for them?" Jonathan said.

Arndell shook his head.

"Well ,if I so much as set a foot beyond that door, I'd be clubbed senseless."

"Hell." Arndell lurched to his feet, swayed for a moment then collapsed. "Guard, guard," he called in a choked voice.

"Guard!" Jonathan bellowed, kicking open the armoury door.

A marine stood on duty in the alleyway.

"What, convict?"

Jonathan pointed to Arndell, slumped over the upturned cask.

"The surgeon needs medicine from the cuddy."

"Let him get it."

"Dr. Arndell's ill, very ill. Tell the master."

The guard spat.

"I take no orders from convicts."

"Well, at least use your head, man. Even you can see he isn't exactly brimming with good health. And if it happens to be the plague...." Jonathan paused and waited for the re-action.

"Plague? God help us."

"He will if you help yourself. First step, call Mr Walton."

Jonathan was urging more lime water between Arndell's pale lips when Walton appeared in the doorway of the armoury.

"Plague?"

Jonathan glanced meaningfully over Walton's shoulder at the marine in the alleyway.

"Medical matters are best discussed in private, sir," he said." Come inside and close the door."

"If it's plague, I'm not getting any closer," Walton said.

"Then dispense with the musket protection, sir."

With a wave of the hand Walton dismissed the sentry.

"Well, convict?"

"I don't think so."

"You don't think so? Why drag me down here then?"

"Dr. Arndell's in dire need of medicines from the cuddy. I'm not allowed to go out and he can't...."

"Why not?" Walton rasped.

"Set him on his feet and try, sir."

The ship's master hauled the surgeon upright, but at once Arndell slumped forward and would have collapsed but for Jonathan's timely arm.

"See what I mean, Mr Walton? If Mahomet can't go to the mountain, the mountain must go to Mahomet."

Walton looked puzzled.

"What?"

"A saying. As Dr. Arndell can't get to the medicine locker, the locker will have to come to Dr. Arndell."

"Aboard my ship I take no orders from anybody, convict."

Jonathan jerked his head in the direction of Arndell, slumped over the upturned cask.

"Then we leave the surgeon.....?"

"He'll be well enough in an hour or so to run his own errands."

"In that hour or so, if there's any repetition..." Jonathan pointed to the remnants of vomit spattered over the armoury bench and his voice dropped to a harsh whisper "...Friendship could well be without its surgeon."

"Damn you," Walton snarled. "What - what is this medicine?"

"Pills, sir."

"What pills?"

"Catapotium tranquillum opii, sir. The bottle could be labelled 'cat. tranq. op.' or 'opii. cat. tranq.'. A matter of usage."

"If I thought you were trying to make me look an idiot, convict....."

"I'm trying to save the life of the surgeon, Mr Walton. Every single moment could be vitally important."

Walton tapped Arndell on the shoulder.

"Well, Thomas?"

Forearms pressed to his stomach, Arndell muttered almost inaudibly, "For God's sake, Francis."

Walton nodded to Jonathan.

"Go ahead convict," he said and, as he followed him to the deck above, he called to the guard-room, "Take the surgeon to his bunk. It's not the plague, I've decided."

In his cabin, Arndell lay sweating and pale.

"Dr Arndell," Jonathan whispered.

The surgeon stirred.

"Composing pills," he mouthed.

Arndell's lips parted sufficiently for Jonathan to administer the pills then a sip of lime-water.

"How long, convict?" Walton said, looking on, as Arndell's head settled back on the pillow.

Jonathan palmed the distended stomach, felt Arndell's pulse, then listened for seconds to the stertorous breathing.

He shrugged.

"Several days at the very least," he said.

"Pettifer!"

A marine kicked back the bolts of the gaol hatch and Jonathan clambered on to the deck where he flung himself prostrate to gulp the sweet dry air of dawn.

"Up."

The butt of the marine's musket jabbed Jonathan's shoulder blades and he reluctantly stumbled to his feet.

"Mr Walton will see you."

Jonathan peered intently into the man's yellowed eyes.

"Not feeling very well, guard?" he said blandly.

"What's that to you?"

"Sickness is part of my trade."

"Well?"

The man's breath was like vapour from a cesspit. Jonathan edged away.

"Acquainted with the plague?" he said.

Suspicion mingled with fear on the man's sallow face.

"You? The plague?"

Jonathan shook his head.

"No, not me. Don't know about you, though. Fires in your head, belly rumbling? One moment furnace hot, the next chilled to the marrow? A thirst not even a whole cask of water would satisfy?"

The marine surveyed Jonathan with mounting terror.

He stiffened.

"You're - you're trying to frighten me, convict," he said, thudding the planking with his musket butt.

"Frighten you, guard? With symptoms like that you've got every reason for feeling fright."

"Symptoms? What symptoms?" Francis Walton said, appearing at that moment in the barricade opening.

Jonathan pointed at the sentry.

"He may be suffering from the plague, sir."

"Sure, convict?"

"A possibility. The surgeon ought to decide."

"If I thought you were taking advantage because the surgeon's sick I'd....."

"Is he no better this morning, sir?" Jonathan said.

"Spewed twice all over his cabin." Walton indicated the barricade opening. "Better take a look at him."

"First, please allow the men on deck and give them breakfast there."

The flat of Walton's hand landed on Jonathan's face.

"Instructions come from me, convict."

Jonathan's scarred cheek was now deep crimson.

"I'm - er - I'm sorry you had to strike me, Mr Walton," he said in slow,level tones. "Seemingly, forbearance is something to be learned in your ship's gaol decks rather than in its cuddy."

Tight-lipped, nostrils flaring, Walton turned to summon a marine.

"Let 'em on deck - and feed 'em," he snarled then jerking a thumb to indicate that Jonathan was to follow, he strode away.

There was scarcely room for both Jonathan and Walton to stand alongside the bunk in Arndell's tiny cabin. The surgeon lay pale and, apart from bouts of stertorous breathing, quiet. The bedding was damp from the sweat of the night.

Jonathan lightly felt the sick man's stomach and checked his pulse rate. His touch raised a faint glimmer of recognition on Arndell's face and one eye opened for a moment.

"Composing pills," Arndell said in a voice that was little more than a whisper.

"Of course."

Walton, who had stepped back into the alleyway, looked on in silence.

"Well, convict," he said after Jonathan had pressed the pills between Arndell's lips,"is he any better?"

"A little."

"On his feet in an hour or so?"

"More like a week or so."

"Impossible."

Jonathan shrugged and turned to give Arndell a sip of lime water.

"A change of bedding could hasten recovery - if you're in a mood to accept orders. Now I'd like to join my fellow prisoners for breakfast."

Outside the cuddy Walton paused.

"Follow, convict," he said and he closed the door behind them. "Breakfast in here. Tell me, plague aboard?"

Jonathan eyed the ship's master thoughtfully.

"A variety of sicknesses but the plague, I think not. Something from the hulks, something else from Newgate, something from too much salt pork, too much foul water, too many rats, too many cockroaches."

"But the guard with the plague?" Walton said.

"I don't think so. Are others in the guardroom the same?"

"Not to my knowledge."

"Then nothing more, maybe, than a belly's revolt against too much porter or lees of wine gone sour. But I'm not the ship's surgeon, remember, Mr Walton."

"Until Thomas Arndell's on his feet again, you could be. I'm sending a signal to Sirius. If Chief Surgeon White agrees...."

"Access to medicines?" Jonathan said.

"Under my instructions, yes."

"And control of the hospital?"

"Inspection twice every twenty four hours. There's a bunk in the fo'c's'le for you until the surgeon's fit again."

Jonathan had breakfasted alone in the cuddy, washed and changed into a clean shirt, tunic and breeches supplied by Walton, when he was rejoined by the ship's master.

"A warning, convict. Take more upon yourself than I order and it's back to the 'tween decks - in irons. And if a single marine or seaman dies - a flogging."

"But I can't help....."

"Be very careful, convict. Do as I order and, who knows, you might find yourself the first ticket-of-leave man in Botany Bay."

Chapter 39

Margaret was changing the dressings of a wounded seaman when Jonathan joined her in the hospital.

"A miracle," she said softly as her fingers lightly traced the lines of crimson scars on the seaman's back. Ten days earlier, as demonstration of the brutal skills of the boatswain's mate with his cat-o'-nine-tails, the scars had been wounds that bared the bones of the man's lower rib cage and twelve inches of backbone.

Jonathan inspected the scars.

"Barbarism. Walton's determined his men do no more than cast a hungry eye over the ladies in the 'tween decks," he whispered to Margaret. "This man should survive but I don't hold out much hope for the bos'n's mate. There'll be a swift garrotting in the fo'c'sle the day this man leaves hospital."

Jonathan tapped the seaman's shoulder.

"Still painful?"

The seaman smirked.

"It's been worse."

With a groan, the man raised himself on his elbows, arching his back.

Jonathan looked on approvingly.

"See, the skin stretching without any sign of rupture."

Margaret smiled, "Miracle man."

"Thomas Culpeper, not me. Enchusa ointment. The man could be up and about in a week."

Margaret drew Jonathan out of the seaman's earshot.

"Isn't he well enough already?"

"The longer he stays, the better the healing. Proving beyond doubt I'm a miracle man… And the more we see of each other."

"He says we'll reach Rio in a few days. Our chance to escape?"

Jonathan gently clasped Margaret's hands and shook his head.

"I could never condemn you to that, love. Strange people, strange language, no money…"

"You're an apothecary. You could earn money, a lot of money."

Jonathan bit his lip.

"An apothecary but no medicines, nowhere to live. The herbs I know best are mostly from the southern parts of England. We'd starve, my darling."

Margaret's grasp on Jonathan's hands tightened.

"I - I can't go on much longer like this. Treating wounds and sores in here or spending night after night in that stinking prison deck. Please, we must do something…"

"The moment Arndell's better I'll get him to help, I promise."

"What can Thomas Arndell do? He couldn't arrange for me, like you, to sleep in the fo'c'sle. The other women envy me, hate me. I take them sugar and other comforts but their whingeing and grumbling go on and on. Why can't others tend in the hospital, they want to know. And they point to Charlotte Dudgeon - 'Why can't others launder the officers' linen?'"

Jonathan kissed her.

"I know, I know. I do all I can. But I'm still only a convict and have to tread very, very warily. Walton gives me a free hand and at the same time threatens flogging and fetters. Thomas Arndell, I'm certain, will find some way when he's well enough. But remember, the longer he's kept in his bunk the more powerful I become - for both of us."

Margaret drew herself away.

"No, no use," she said, beginning to weep. "I'll go alone."

Jonathan pressed fingers gently to her lips and embraced her.

"Nonsense."

"Maybe an apothecary couldn't make a living in Rio but a woman could."

"Margaret, please."

She forced herself out of his arms and he would have embraced her again but a marine, at that moment, slammed back the hatch grating.

"Convict. The cuddy."

* * * * *

"Bloody fool, Francis," Bellamy muttered as he continued to pour wine.

The goblet overflowed and the liquid spilled over the cuddy floor. Walton waved aside the proffered drink, "You're blind drunk."

Sprawling back in his chair, Bellamy belched.

"But I still see you're a fool. Playing into the hands of a convicted footpad."

"Footpad?"

"The one who puts on all the airs about pills and potions."

"Footpad, was he?"

"What's it matter? He's a convict with the run of the ship. First I see him with Arndell, then disappearing into the hospital, then making the most of the galley."

Walton shrugged.

"He knows how far he can go. One step out of line and it's flogging then chains. Arndell sick, what else d'you suggest? The man works hard enough. The hospital goes well… A clever fellow, cleverer than Arndell, maybe."

"Playing right into the hands of a convict." Bellamy said with scorn.

"Not as bad as playing into the hands of that 'tween decks washerwoman, Henry. Washing your shirts. How many shirts d'you wear in a day? Every one of your marines is laughing at you. 'Off to be laundered again' they say as the Dudgeon woman's hauled from the 'tween decks. One of my men was flogged for breaking into the women. Know what he said?"

"What?"

"'Will you be flogging Cap'n Bellamy as well?'."

Bellamy lurched to his feet and, grasping the table edge succeeded in remaining upright. He drew in his chin.

"I'll have you know, Francis Walton, I intend to marry."

The ship's master, who had carried on much of the conversation while poring over navigation charts spread across the cuddy table, glanced up.

"Marry?" he said." Marry?"

Bellamy shifted a trifle uneasily, "What's wrong with that?"

Walton threw back his head and guffawed, "You, getting married? By Saturday morning we'll be lying off

Rio de Janeiro. Sunday, if I know you Henry, you'll be bedding some black-haired Rio society beauty, the Dudgeon woman completely forgotten."

Bellamy's grasp on the table edge was even more savage.

"I intend to marry Charlotte Dudgeon."

"Oh, sit down, Henry. Fill up your goblet. We'll talk later - when you're sober."

"Talking'll make no difference."

"There'll have to be talk, serious talk. I don't imagine Arthur Phillip'll approve."

Bellamy sneered.

"Phillip? What about his Brooks woman?"

"Who?" Walton, said, puzzled.

"Calls herself Elizabeth Brooks. Wife, she says, of Thomas Brooks, bo's'n aboard Phillip's ship."

Walton eyed Bellamy with suspicion.

"I know nothing about that."

"The more you know about a man's private life the more - or the less – you trust him, Walton."

"I'd trust Phillip to the ends of the earth."

"With your wife? Not if she's a charmer. Phillip took Brooks aboard Sirius not because he's any good as a bos'n, but because Elizabeth's rare bliss in bed."

"How did Phillip come across her?"

"She and Brooks were aboard the 'Europe' with him."

Walton threw up a dismissive hand.

"Pah, a drunken man's fantasies. I don't believe...."

"There's more. The woman's name isn't Brooks. She was never wed to Thomas Brooks. Her husband's a carpenter in Plymouth Dockyard."

Walton shook his head in mounting disbelief.

"How d'you come to know all this?" he said suspiciously.

Bellamy gave a broad wink.

"Weeks kicking my heels at Plymouth waiting for a ship's careening and re-arming. A man of some taste, Phillip. I told you Elizabeth was bliss in bed...."

"You mean you....?"

"Yes. But when I met her again in London, she wanted no more of a mere lieutenant in the marines when she'd found favour with a naval captain by the name of Arthur Phillip."

"All right, Henry, I'll accept your story. But Phillip's in command and I can't see him countenancing a marriage between a marines officer and a convicted whore."

"Whore? Convicted whore?"

Bellamy was a powerful man but, in his drunken state, his aim was wild. His fist, a yard wide of its target, Walton's jaw, encountered nothing more than thin air and he toppled, striking his head on the edge of the cuddy table.

For a moment Walton surveyed impassively the silent crumpled figure. Blood oozing from a wound in Bellamy's temple began to spread across the bare oak floor. The ship's master went to the door of the cuddy and called to the guard,

"The convict Pettifer. At once."

Bundled down the companionway, a musket butt at his back, Jonathan paused at the cuddy door and knocked.

"In."

Walton was still panting after dragging the unconscious Bellamy and propping him up in a corner.

"A fall," he said, pointing to the marines officer. "Patch him up."

Jonathan knelt beside the inert figure. The trickle of blood from the head wound was becoming a flood.

"Linen, quick."

Walton, looking on, did not respond.

"Mr Walton, linen if you please."

"A blood-letting can be highly beneficial, convict."

Jonathan shot to his feet, thrust Walton to one side and seized a bundle of linen from the cuddy locker.

Chapter 40

Immediately aft of the deck barricade, the ship's carpenter had built a wooden caboose, no bigger than a sentry box, where a woman convict would be allowed to prepare food.

This did not mean that Walton was becoming more indulgent towards his prisoners, but it was an indication of a mounting disenchantment with the quality of food aboard Friendship.

A substantial part of the stores already was stale and almost inedible when shipped in Plymouth, three months earlier. Most had been bought at a cut price from local chandlers by contractors such as Turnbull McQuaid, whose prime concern was not for the welfare of seamen, marines or convicts but for swift and handsome profits.

In spite of its quality, however, one of the women, Maria Cogan, an accomplished cook convicted of attempting to poison her drunkard husband, proved well able to transform worm-ridden flour and rice into moderately palatable dishes. The rock-hard beef and pork, by soaking in sea water then boiling with herbs, she skilfully converted to a substance moderately acceptable to the palate and no longer disastrous to teeth and stomach.

Alive to the possibility of being poisoned by Maria, Walton was careful to insist upon the exclusive direction of her skills over the stove in the caboose. She was allowed to prepare food for the rest of the women convicts then, at some moment of distribution, carefully varied from mealtime to mealtime, the ship's master diverted some of the best to the table in the cuddy.

As a further precaution, Walton warned Maria, in front of the rest of the women, that if any stomach ailment seized any officer or official she would have her head shaved, she would be flogged daily for a week and then, chained inside the caboose, pitched into the Atlantic ocean.

* * * * *

Henry Bellamy lay quiet in his bunk, but the moment that Jonathan removed the blood-sodden bandage from the marine captain's head, he jerked up on an elbow.

"Out, get out," he barked and the sudden exertion made the blood spurt afresh.

"A further dressing's needed," Jonathan said.

"Out, out. I never take treatment from Arndell. I'll certainly take none from a stinking convict"

The wild fist aimed at Jonathan caught Walton a glancing blow on the chin as he peered over the former's shoulder. Already blood was soaking pillow and blankets.

Walton ruefully rubbed his jawbone.

"Idiot. You're bleeding to death."

Bellamy, gasping, dropped back.

"Fetch Arndell, then."

Walton and Jonathan exchanged swift glances. The latter shook his head. Arndell's recovery was sluggish. As yet he was wholly incapable of stirring unaided from his bunk.

"Arndell's not well enough."

"Get Faddy."

"Faddy's no surgeon."

"Faddy. Get him."

"Carry on staunching the blood," Walton whispered to Jonathan and he left the cabin to return at once with Lieutenant William Faddy, Bellamy's second-in-command.

"Faddy's here," the ship's master said.

"Leave us. You and the convict - go," Bellamy muttered thickly.

Walton motioned to Faddy to take the linen from Jonathan and continue the pressure on Bellamy's gaping wound. Then, with Jonathan, he slipped into the alleyway.

"I'll consult Arndell," Walton said.

"No need. In any case Arndell's better left undisturbed. Given a few minutes I can find a specific for the haemorrhage."

Walton sneered.

"Bellamy'll never let you treat him."

"No problem. I prepare it, you or Faddy do the rest."

The sleeves of Faddy's tunic were blood-stained to the elbows when Jonathan and Walton returned to Bellamy's cabin.

"Henry," Walton whispered tentatively.

Bellamy reluctantly opened one eye and his lips formed "What?"

"I've seen Arndell. Too feeble to crawl from his bunk. He prescribes this." Walton held up a broad strip of linen, liberally coated with green ointment. "Guaranteed to stem bleeding..." here Walton paused, "if, he says, you can stand up to the initial pain."

Bellamy's voice was faint and hoarse.

"Stand up to anything."

"Then turn your face to the bulwark, Henry."

Jonathan stepped swiftly between Walton and Faddy then, motioning them to grasp Bellamy's arms and legs, he swiftly stitched up the gaping wound then, after pressing the ointment-laden linen over the flesh, he swathed the marines captain's head with muslin.

"Three days undisturbed," he whispered to Faddy and, handing him a half-filled goblet, "he'll sleep after this."

As Jonathan and the ship's master stepped into the alleyway Friendship lurched violently and both were flung to the floor.

"The helm," Walton bellowed, stumbling to his feet and as he staggered to the companionway the rest of his words were engulfed in an ear-shattering thunderclap.

For one fleeting moment it seemed that the convict ship was about to turn turtle. Almost on her beam ends she paused, timbers shuddering from stem to stern. Then as if giant hands had laid hold of her topmasts, she was urged back to an even keel.

On deck lay a bewildering mass of wrecked water casks, scattered crates and tangles of rope. Scores of hens, escaped from their damaged pens, ran clucking excitedly in and out of the debris.

At the helm, Walton shouted, "So much for supper, convict," and he pointed to the barricade. The caboose where Maria Cogan had been cooking the meal was now nothing more than splinters of timber scattered over the Friendship's deck.

"What happened?"

"A water cask. Hurtled across the deck. Smashed the caboose like an egg-shell," Walton said.

"And the woman?"

"Start looking for another cook."

"Overboard?"

Walton nodded.

"Turning about for her?"

"For one woman convict?"

"A human being," Jonathan said.

"She was. Five minutes ago. Squashed flat by a water cask. I saw it all."

The storm now abated, Walton handed over the helm to join Jonathan at the ship's rail. William Faddy, a hand covering one eye, appeared on deck.

"A tumble when the storm hit us?" Walton said.

Faddy removed his hand to reveal a closed eye, the surrounding flesh red and swollen.

"Bellamy. Demanding a woman."

"Even after the sleeping potion?" Jonathan said.

"Sent it flying and demanded a woman."

"So?" Walton said.

"So I told him my first concern was his wound and – well…" Faddy pointed to his eye, "…his answer."

"Was the woman called Dudgeon?" Walton said.

"Yes."

Walton was thoughtful for a moment.

"I wonder if she can cook as well?"

Chapter 41

Rife among the women convicts was a rumour that the Friendship would not sail into Botany Bay until after Christmas, yet although it was only early in the month of August, land lay less than half a mile to larboard and the convict fleet, strung out in a wide arc, lay at anchor in placid, sunlit waters.

With a flurry of excitement not seen since their irons were struck off in late May, the women, as best they might in the cramped, low-ceilinged 'tween decks, began to wash with their meagre ration of drinking water not only their sweating, grime-caked bodies but also such of their garments as had survived the long voyage in their floating gaol-house.

The bolts of the hatch trapdoors were kicked back and a short ladder thrust into the prison deck.

"Out, out!"

Battened down since early the previous evening in the foetid atmosphere of their gaol, the women clawed and fought like tigresses to reach the ladder first.

"One at a time, you filthy sows," a marine bellowed, jabbing indiscriminately with his musket.

Marshalled on deck the women were directed to the ship's side where the smith fettered their ankles, then chained them in groups.

Face pale and strained, Arndell struggled from the companionway and, leaning heavily on Jonathan'a arm, he stepped between the women and the guards.

"Why're they being ironed?"

"Orders."

"Whose?"

"Mr Walton."

Arndell turned to Jonathan, "Men as well?"

"I don't know. They're still below."

Arndell, frowning, limped towards the companionway and Jonathan followed.

"Wait here," Arndell said outside the door of the cuddy.

Walton, in impeccable uniform, was at breakfast.

"Back at last, hm? Something to eat?" Walton said in lively tone.

Arndell grimaced.

"Thank you, no."

"It's good, very good." Walton leaned confidentially across the table. "That Charlotte Dudgeon's a splendid cook. Never eaten such chicken. Something on your mind?"

Arndell took a chair.

"The women. In irons again."

Walton's fingers raked over the chicken on his plate and selected a piece which he ate and swallowed before replying.

"Yes," he said casually.

"Why?"

"Precautions. Decided, remember, to cleanse the 'tween decks when we reached Rio. The women'll have to stay on deck 'til dusk. Men the same. Fetters off when we sail."

"In God's name, why?"

"Only a short swim ashore. Rio wouldn't welcome our stinking convicts roaming its streets. Arthur Phillip has some kind of local reputation, remember. An officer in the Portuguese navy here years ago and thought highly of. The less we upset Rio and Phillip the better for us - fresh water, food, wine, spirits and livestock."

Arndell reached for the jug of porter.

"Madness, drinking on an empty stomach," Walton said with a wry smile.

Arndell, shrugging, gulped the porter. Suddenly swaying, he grasped the edge of the table.

"Ph- Phillip's orders, the irons?"

"No, mine."

"Then off with them. Off," Arndell roared and at once collapsed.

Walton rose from the table and lifting the surgeon bodily he carried him into the alleyway where Jonathan was waiting.

"Ah, you. Take him to his bunk, at once," Walton said sliding the inert Arndell over Jonathan's shoulder.

The mate was waiting for Walton in the cuddy.

"Captain Phillip's signal. Coming aboard."

Walton bounded up the companionway and without so much as a glance at the fettered women, catcalling and hissing as he crossed the deck, he passed through the barricade opening. Two marines were about to unbolt the trapdoors of the men's prison deck.

"Wait. Upper deck's to be kept clear."

"The convicts'll go crazy."

"Let 'em. No, no, promise something. Rum tomorrow if they're quiet today." The marines stood their ground.

"Go on, tell 'em, tell 'em."

The mate tapped Walton on the shoulder.

"Captain Phillip waiting to come aboard."

Spurning assistance from a seaman, Arthur Phillip vaulted over the ship's rail to the deck. He saluted Walton then held out a hand.

"A tight-looking ship, Mr Walton," he said, in a voice surprisingly loud and deep for such a slight individual. Walton indicated the barrier opening and as Phillip emerged on the after deck, the women's catcalls and hisses became even more vehement.

"One moment," Arthur Phillip said as Walton urged him towards the companionway. "The women's irons. Whose orders?"

"Mine, sir."

"Why?"

Walton pointed to the buildings of Rio, white and gleaming in the brilliant morning sun.

"Rio wouldn't welcome escaped convicts, sir."

Phillip's dark eyes narrowed. He strode over to the fettered women, sullen and, for the moment, silent. One, bolder than the rest, lunged forward to seize a button of Phillip's naval uniform. At once Phillip drew a knife and the woman shrank back in terror.

"You were wanting a keepsake, madam. I'm flattered, "Phillip said lightly and, cutting off the button, he gave it to her.

Firmly grasping the gift, the convict woman crept forward to kiss Arthur Phillip's hand.

"I - I'll treasure....."

"Make sure you do. If ever I find it's been used to make spurious dollars, you'll travel the rest of the voyage to Botany Bay in the coal-hole."

A second convict struggled to touch Phillip.

"You - you said, sir, 'the voyage to Botany Bay' but we're there already."

Phillip smiled ruefully.

"'Fraid not."

The woman pointed shorewards.

"But....."

"That, woman, is Rio de Janeiro, capital of Brazil. Six more months, ten thousand further miles of salt water then - and only then - Botany Bay."

The woman rattled her fetters.

"Six - six more months in these, sir?"

Phillip jerked his head in the direction of Rio.

"Planning to swim ashore?"

"Swim, sir?" The woman cackled. "I could easy drown in my own sweat."

Phillip gave a half-smile.

"Which of you ladies are planning to swim ashore?"

The women remained silent. He repeated the question.

"Too scared," the woman with the button then said.

"What, scared of a few man-eating sharks?" Phillip said.

"Your irons'll all be struck off by mid-day."

The cheering of the women convicts could still be heard when Phillip sat down at the cuddy table to inspect the Friendship's log book.

"How frequent are the floggings, Mr Walton?" Phillip said as he scrutinised the first few pages of the log.

Walton's tone was off-hand.

"Two, maybe three a week."

"The log suggests much less frequent. Some entries overlooked, perhaps?"

"Well, sir, floggings are sometimes decided in a hurry and....."

"I scarcely need remind you, Mr Walton, floggings imposed only after due deliberation and a log book entry every time, every time. I'd expect to see certificates from the surgeon....."

Walton shifted uneasily.

"The surgeon's been ill, sir."

"The fleet surgeon aware of it?"

"N-no, sir. But I've found a competent substitute."

Phillip's fingertip slid rapidly down the crew list.

"No mention here of another surgeon."

"An apothecary convict."

"Convict? A convict you say? Sufficient faith in a Newgate felon to tend the sick, officers, marines, crew and convicts alike?"

"Thomas Arndell is well satisfied."

"Indeed. And why was this - this apothecary convicted?"

"No idea."

"No idea, Mr Walton? You surprise me."

"No gaol records arrived with the prisoners."

"So you don't know whether this man snatched a chicken or defrauded some ailing, elderly widow-woman?"

"Yes - er - no, Captain Phillip," Walton stammered.

"Did it ever occur to you this convict might mix a dangerous potion and poison somebody?"

"The man's conduct's been good. Even Dr Arndell takes his concoctions."

Arthur Phillip resumed his inspection of the log book and after a while he said without looking up, "A strange confusion of standards, Mr Walton."

"How, sir?"

"You fear the convicts, shabby, penniless and unable to speak the language, will swim ashore through shark-infested waters......"

"Shark-infested?"

"That's what I told them. You fear escape yet no fears about the ministrations of a convicted scoundrel. I'll see Dr Arndell."

"He's a very sick man, Captain Phillip."

Arthur Phillip rose from the cuddy table, lips set and straight, dark brown eyes firmly fixed on Francis Walton.

"Ready?"

No natural light relieved the gloom of Arndell's tiny cabin where the surgeon, seated on the edge of his bunk, head close to a lantern, was struggling to read a book.

"Captain Phillip," Walton announced.

There was barely space for two to stand so Walton stepped back into the alleyway. Arndell rose uncertainly to his feet and shook Phillip's proffered hand.

"You've been ill, Dr. Arndell. I'm sorry. Please don't stand for me."

With a sigh of relief Arndell resumed his seat on the bunk.

"Thank you, sir. Yes, very ill."

Although Arthur Phillip was a man well below average height, even he was compelled to stoop because of the low ceiling. In the soft light of the lantern his pronounced aquiline nose suggested a hawk.

"But improving?"

"Yes, sir."

"Enough to discuss medical matters?"

"Of course."

"During your illness you recommended the services of a convict...."

"Er - yes, sir."

"A man claiming to be an apothecary?"

"Yes."

"You had independent details?"

"No."

"Then how were you aware the man was an experienced apothecary?"

"By lengthy conversations. His knowledge of disease and medicines as substantial as any I've ever encountered. But, of course, his mentor was Matthew Gross."

"Matthew Gross?"

"The Sea Coal Lane apothecary, London's foremost."

"Mm… Why's your man a convict?"

"One of the quirks of Bow Street justice. On his way from Rochester - where he'd been prescribing medicines - to London, he was set upon by two footpads, robbed, beaten, his horse stolen. He stopped a coach on the Dover road seeking help - and finished up aboard a Thames prison hulk, a convicted footpad."

Phillip gave a non-committal nod.

"And you have confidence?"

"More than in myself, sir."

Phillip put out a hand, "Good day, Dr Arndell. I hope you'll soon be well."

In the cuddy, Francis Walton was pouring wine.

"Did Arndell satisfy you?"

Phillip eyed Walton blandly.

"Substantially, yes."

"So we continue using the convict Pettifer?"

"Not without the fleet surgeon's authority."

"But we have two marines, three seamen and several convicts all sick, some needing medicines hourly and Arndell's in no fit state to dispense or administer them."

Phillip's expression remained bland.

"Signal Dr White to join me here at once. He's aboard the Scarborough, lying aft," he said, then resumed his inspection of Friendship's log book.

Chapter 42

The night foulness of the convict deck still heavy upon him Jonathan, though desperate to take Margaret in his arms, held her firmly but at a distance.

"Close, closer, love," she said.

Jonathan shook his head.

"First let me wash. I sicken even myself," he said.

In a corner of the hospital stood a water keg. Jonathan filled a bucket then, stripping to the waist, he soaped and repeatedly sluiced himself, a luxury denied his fellow prisoners in the 'tween decks but, at the insistence of Arndell, always available in the hospital. Margaret handed a towel to him, coarse to the flesh yet clean and sweet- smelling.

She rested her open palms on his bare chest.

"In Rio, they say, soap and water are commonplace," she said, a roguish twinkle in her eyes. "We could easily make the break."

Jonathan drew her to him and kissed her.

"To be penniless, starving beggars. I'd never condemn you to that."

Margaret ceased to fondle the bare flesh.

"You'd condemn me to this, though," she said, pointing to a range of bunks narrow as, but shorter than, coffins. "My option's either the stinking 'tween decks or battling here, mostly on my own. Remember, sickness isn't always a broken bone or flesh slashed by the cat-o'-nine-tails. No soap gets rid of the stench from burst abscesses or suppurating sores."

Jonathan pressed two fingers to her lips.

"I know, I know, dearest, but think, think........"

Margaret brushed aside his hand.

"I'd get a supply of food, there's a jolly boat moored to the stern. After dark we could....."

"No."

"Please."

"I can't let you take the risk. Arndell's cooped up in his cabin so my position grows stronger every day. But even when he's fully recovered he'll still be dependent on me."

Margaret thumped Jonathan's chest.

"You're still giving not a thought to the future for me."

"It's because I'm giving your future so much thought that...."

"Besotted with dreams of power. Escape to Rio or not? I want an answer now."

"No, my love!"

"Your final word?."

"Listen, listen. By the time we reach Botany Bay, I could have a standing equal to the chief surgeon, never mind an assistant like Arndell. If Arthur Phillip really plans a colony and not just a hangman's paradise, I could be - I could be principal apothecary of New South Wales."

"Besotted with thoughts of power."

"No, no, no. It's our future. You with a reputation for tending the sick, me with medical knowledge to make Arndell seem no more than a peddler in tansy for toothache.

"If we'd married and I'd taken over from Matthew Gross in Sea Coal Lane, our prospects wouldn't have been any better, maybe far worse."

Margaret sank down on the edge of a vacant bunk.

"I - I couldn't, of course, go alone. There is an alternative - marriage."

"Marriage, darling?"

"Not to you."

"Not....?"

"The man I refused months ago. He's on board."

"On board Friendship? Surely...."

"Turnbull McQuaid."

Jonathan, in spite of his astonishment, laughed.

"McQuaid's fifteen thousand miles away in Wapping!"

"Turnbull McQuaid is here aboard this ship. He's still desperate for - for respectability. That's why he came aboard. To start a new life, he says."

"You've seen him?"

"Here last evening for a few minutes after dark."

Jonathan eyed Margaret with deep suspicion.

"Strange. I've not set eyes on him..."

"Francis Walton found him naked in bed with a young midshipman soon after we left Portsmouth. The youth was given a flogging."

"And McQuaid goes scot free?"

"Not altogether. Walton ordered him to stay in his cabin or Arthur Phillip would be told...."

"I'll never, never let you marry that sickening beast. Never."

Margaret leapt from the edge of the bunk and flung herself into Jonathan's arms. She was sobbing.

"I - I loathe and detest and..... But I can't stand another day of this - foul breaths, sweat and damp and filthy sores. Just think. A chance to wear proper clothes, sleep between clean linen sheets ......"

"But your body next to McQuaid."

"No, no, never. There's space in his cabin for a separate bunk."

"But you'll be together."

"Meaning nothing. My love, will you not understand? I can't, I can't go on like this."

Margaret stepped back and pointed to her skirt, crudely fashioned from sail canvas, to the coarse osnaburg blouse and a clumsy shawl, also of canvas.

Jonathan bit his lip.

"I beg you, my love. Please. I promise I'll become so powerful aboard this ship that......."

"No, dearest. Be sensible. Francis Walton'd never let you get that far."

"He's gone a long way already."

"Too far, he fears. I've heard the whispers. The moment Thomas Arndell's on his feet, Walton'd do everything possible to pitch you back into the 'tween decks."

"Margaret, please,...."

A marine leaned over the hatch opening.

"On deck, convict."

"I'll be back, my darling," Jonathan whispered. "For God's sake, don't......"

The upper deck was bathed in sunshine, the air full of chatter from the convict women. Jonathan, emerging from the hospital was at once confronted by Francis Walton, Arthur Phillip and John White, the fleet's chief surgeon.

"The convict apothecary, sir," Walton said to Phillip.

"Your name?" Phillip said, not unkindly.

"Pettifer, sir."

John White nudged Walton.

"I'll test his knowledge of medicines. Where d'you suggest?"

The ship's master pointed to the companionway.

"The armoury. The surgeon's workbench there and stocks of potions and powders."

White beckoned Jonathan and when Walton was about to follow the pair down the companionway, the chief surgeon said dismissively, "Enquiries like this I conduct on my own."

Phillip and Walton had been pacing the deck for an hour when Jonathan and White re-appeared.

"The hospital, convict," Walton said.

"No, Mr Walton, the apothecary comes with me," White said exchanging covert glances with Arthur Phillip.

"Where, Dr White?" Walton said.

"Ashore. I need fresh supplies of medicines."

Walton made scant effort to conceal his annoyance.

"It was decided 'no convict on shore', sir," he said. "If this one goes there could be trouble with the rest."

White's tone was caustic, patronising.

"If you fear loss of control over your – er - passengers, Mr Walton," White lowered his voice, "then we'll not go ashore until they're battened down for the night."

"The convict'll have to tend the sick first, including Thomas Arndell. Arndell won't be very pleased with your plan."

"If you or Dr Arndell can suggest ways of taking the apothecary's knowledge with us instead of the man himself, I'd be grateful. Otherwise, Pettifer goes ashore in Rio with me."

Walton's expression was thunderous.

"As ship's master I require life and death control over the convicts......"

"Death, mainly, if you stick to your stiff-necked attitude. Is the jolly boat seaworthy?" White said.

Walton was sullen, silent.

"Is it?!"

"Of course."

"Then kindly see it's victualled for two days and nights."

Walton at once swung round on Phillip who had stood impassively looking on.

"Am I - am I to take orders like that, Captain Phillip?"

"Send the convict apothecary to tend whatever sick people there are. We'll continue in the cuddy," Phillip said.

With a flick of the wrist Walton dismissed Jonathan and led Arthur Phillip and John White below.

Phillip took a chair at the cuddy table.

"Keen disciplinarian, Mr Walton?"

"Impossible to run a ship otherwise."

"Then why the unseemly outburst on deck?"

Walton's face was crimson.

"I - I was....."

"Incensed, yes. A reaction by no means conducive to discipline. The convict women were watching and listening. No doubt they heard every word."

Walton began to bluster.

"I can handle....."

"With greater difficulty in future, I'd say. What's your knowledge of medical matters?"

"Practically nothing," Walton said grudgingly.

"And you solidly oppose the convict Pettifer going ashore to help Dr White with supplies of medicine?"

"Absolute madness."

"But you admit the convict's skill in such things?"

"I suppose so."

"Then a radical change in attitude wouldn't go amiss, Mr Walton. It'd be stupid not to use Pettifer's knowledge. Indeed, any knowledge or skills rotting away in those 'tween decks. God knows we'll need them if and when we reach Botany Bay.... And talking of Botany Bay, my responsibility's to land human beings there, not corpses. Now, shall we take a little wine?"

Chapter 43

Conversation between Arthur Phillip, John White and Francis Walton had been no more than desultory. Apart from brief reference to his service with the Portuguese navy some years earlier, Phillip, drinking sparingly, had remained silent but, when White reminded him that the town of Rio had been built largely by convict labour, his pale features lit up at once.

"But, of course," he said. "Unrivalled opportunity for guidance, training our own convicts to create a city at Botany Bay."

Walton refilled his goblet and sneered, "If you're thinking of the pimps, pickpockets and whores of the 'tween decks as craftsmen, you're going to be disappointed, Captain Phillip."

"Are they all pimps and forgers and so on?" Phillip said.

"Yes."

"And the apothecary?"

"An exception."

"Any other exceptions?"

"No."

"But, if there's no information from Newgate and the prison hulks, how can you be sure?"

"Experience of life."

White drained his goblet and got up.

"High time we went ashore," he said to Phillip.

"A moment, John. Mr Walton, I want you to record in the ship's log details of every convict."

"Such as?"

"Age, occupation, sentence."

White, glancing from the bland-faced Phillip to the angry Walton, said, smiling, "In your 'tween decks you could be entertaining unawares a host of bright angels."

"Every one with a cut-throat's knife," Walton snorted.

Phillip's features were again animated.

"I'd prefer carpenters and brickmakers. More immediate, though, I must see the captain of the marines."

Walton, without a word, went to the cuddy door.

"Captain-lieutenant Bellamy," he said to the marine on duty in the alleyway.

The marine, glancing over Walton's shoulder in the direction of Phillip and White now in earnest conversation, winked at Walton and said in a low voice, "Not to be disturbed."

Walton raised an eyebrow.

"Lieutenant Faddy, then," he said.

The guard nodded and, before Walton had settled down in his chair again, William Faddy joined them. He saluted briskly, and Walton made brief introductions.

"I asked for Captain Bellamy," Phillip said with some irritation. "Tell him he's to join my shore party in an hour's time."

Faddy looked to Walton who gave an almost imperceptible shrug.

"Yes, sir," Faddy said.

* * * * *

Charlotte Dudgeon, lightly kissing the forehead of the sleeping Henry Bellamy, began to dress but, before she had time to drag a shift over her head, Bellamy opened his eyes.

"Don't go," he murmured, his hand seeking to fondle her naked buttocks.

Gently she pushed him away.

"There's food to be cooked for the cuddy," she said as she went on dressing.

"Oh, let 'em starve."

"Then they'll go looking for another cook and laundress. But I'll stay if you'll stay."

"I couldn't possibly drag myself away," Bellamy said, his hand once more fondling the convict woman.

"I meant - don't go ashore," Charlotte said.

"Phillip's orders. You heard young Faddy."

"You'll not stay ashore, though?"

"Knowing you could be bedding with any one of a dozen men aboard? Not likely."

Charlotte smiled secretly. She drew on her skirt and laced up her bodice, then bent to peer into a mirror fastened to the bulkhead.

"D'you realise I've spent three whole weeks with you in this cabin?" she said, eyes glinting mischievously.

"Well?"

"Except when that husband of mine locked me up, I'd never spent more than a few days - and nights - with any one man."

"Twenty one days and nights of me too much?"

Charlotte turned from the mirror to appraise the naked barrel-like chest and the firm muscular arms. She bent over him and, kissing the firm handsome mouth, she gave an involuntary shudder as her face came into contact with unshaven skin.

"Not enough, Henry, not enough," she murmured.

"And not enough for me either, woman," Bellamy said, as Charlotte dragged the hem of her skirt up to her waist.

There was no mistaking the urgency of the hammering on the door.

"Captain Bellamy. The jolly-boat leaves in twenty minutes," William Faddy called. "What shall I tell Captain Phillip, sir?"

Charlotte tumbled from the bunk but Bellamy dragged her back.

"I'll be there, tell him," Bellamy bellowed and then, in a quieter tone, "If they're so anxious for me, they'll wait."

"But it's now too late for their meal," Charlotte whispered.

"I've already told you – let 'em starve."

"And be sent back to the prison deck? The less trouble I make the better, Henry."

"Five more minutes."

"No."

Bellamy, naked, rolled out of the bunk.

"Never ever refuse me, woman."

Once more they coupled, swiftly and with total abandon.

* * * * *

Arthur Phillip and John White sat together in the stern of the jolly-boat, in front of them Bellamy and second lieutenant William Dawes, the fleet's astronomer and navigating officer from HMS Sirius. In the bows Jonathan, wearing a cream shirt, leather jerkin and breeches, white stockings and silver-buckled shoes, sat on his own.

"What takes you to Rio, Dawes?" Bellamy said to the astronomer.

"Checking my navigation instruments. Make sure we finish up in Botany Bay, not the South Pole."

"No time for Portuguese beauties?"

Dawes laughed.

"I'm not saying my eyes'll be glued to telescopes every minute I'm ashore. If you chance on some spare, wealthy, lovely lady don't forget those who battle with sextants and errant timepieces."

"I'll choose wisely and well. For you. For myself, not interested."

William Dawes guffawed.

"Not interested? You? I'd've thought your mind was on nothing else since we sailed from the Motherbank. Reformed character?"

"You could say so."

"What else brings you ashore?"

"Search for small arms and musket balls. We're short."

Dawes leaned forward to whisper, "Arthur Phillip'll want to cut a dash, a smart uniformed captain of marines dancing attendance."

"But he'll need help with other things."

"Well, there's John White and there's the convict," Bellamy said, jerking his head in the direction of the bows. "He'll manage."

Dawes eyed Jonathan with sudden curiosity.

"Convict? Dressed like that I imagined he was the shipowner at least."

Bellamy snorted.

"If Walton and Arndell - and Phillip, ay, Phillip - aren't more careful he could well end up being just that."

"What d'you mean?" Dawes said, viewing Jonathan with mounting interest.

"He's a leeches, pills and potions man, an apothecary."

"Or so he says."

"Arndell and Walton seem to think so."

Dawes frowned.

"Dangerous, isn't it, a convict free like that?"

"Arndell's sick so the convict takes over. It doesn't worry Walton. Both Phillip and White," Bellamy jerked his head back towards the pair in the stern," seem quite happy. They must be, bringing him ashore. Helping White choose medicines. Bloody idiots. He could easily poison....."

Bellamy ceased abruptly as the bows of the jolly-boat nudged a stone jetty. Jonathan leapt ashore with a mooring rope and secured the vessel to a bollard. Phillip made to follow and, stumbling, would have landed sprawling on the jetty but for Jonathan's prompt arm.

Bellamy nudged Dawes as they both scrambled ashore.

"See that? The whore-spawn could be treating even Phillip himself before we make Botany Bay."

Chapter 44

Only the gentlest of breezes teased the Friendship's rigging during those warm days of August and September, 1787, and on orders from Arthur Phillip the convicts spent all daylight hours lazing on deck. There was fresh water in abundance, the allowances of bread and fresh meat and fruit were generous and Phillip had insisted that a pint of wine be provided daily for each prisoner.

Thomas Arndell, after his prolonged illness paler and more gaunt than ever, sat tight-lipped in the cuddy.

"You'll have to decide, Arndell," John White, the fleet's chief surgeon, said. "The Glatton sails for the Indies in a few days. I can arrange a berth. Then you take a chance on a passage to England from Trinidad early October. Craigie's itching to take over from you."

Arndell shook his head with some irritation.

"I don't want to leave," he said.

"But you're sick."

"I was. I'm now on the mend."

"Oh, be practical, Arndell. We're losing precious time. Nothing tackled since we dropped anchor a week ago."

Arndell massaged a creased forehead.

"But nothing could be done 'til the 'tween decks're dried out."

"Well, they're bone dry now. So when precisely can I expect a start?"

"Very soon."

"Fine. But, if I see no progress by Saturday, I'll feel bound to urge Phillip to relieve you. You're a good man, Arndell. Surgeons' Hall was well satisfied. But there's far too much at stake to...."

Arndell threw his arms wide in despair.

"But my plans are well laid. I've already told you it's pointless attempting anything until the timbers are thoroughly dry. While the convicts are on deck during the day I'm already having rat traps set. Then the sulphur, the gunpowder and the liming....."

"And the convicts vomiting all night because of the stench?"

"Infusion of columba root takes care of that."

John White pursed his lips.

"Hardly a treatment I'd recommend. And too costly for lavishing on whores and pickpockets."

"I do my best for them," Arndell said. "I must."

White gave his assistant a quizzical look.

"Could it be you're unduly influenced?"

"No. How?"

"I took the convict Pettifer with our shore party. Enthusiastic as you for columba root."

"My instructions," Arndell said.

"Hm. In terms of powder, what would be the size and frequency of the dose?"

Arndell was hesitant.

"Er....."

"The response from your convict was much swifter," John White said, rising from his seat. At the door of the cuddy he paused, "Over the next three days, Arndell, give consideration to your ability as ship's surgeon and also your status aboard the Friendship. I too will give the matters some thought."

Arndell wormed his way through the melee of convicts jostling for space on a deck already crammed with water casks, poultry cages, pig pens and other stores. He clambered on to the coaming of a hatch.

"Convict Pettifer," he called, glancing over the convicts.

Jonathan, disengaging himself from a cluster of men standing around the forward mast, pushed his way through the crowd.

"Yes, Dr Arndell?"

"You and the other mess captains, assemble in the 'tween decks."

Gone was the easy familiarity in Arndell's tone to which Jonathan had of late become accustomed.

"Why, Dr Arndell?"

"Orders."

With ten other convicts Jonathan brushed past the surgeon and dropped into the gaol deck. Arndell, recoiling momentarily as the stench of damp timbers and stale sweat attacked his nostrils, followed. The men, hunched together in an alleyway between the bunks were waiting, scowling, silent.

"This stinking hole must be thoroughly cleansed," Arndell said. "Get rid of the rats and the cockroaches, explode gunpowder, burn sulphur, wash and lime every inch of the timbers, every crevice....."

"While the rest loll in the sun on deck?" a convict at the back shouted.

"A foul, unpleasant job, I admit. But it has to be done while we're at anchor. Extra comforts, I promise. Rum and twice the ration of wine. And a special prize for the man who produces the most rat tails each day. So stake out your hunting patches."

The outburst of cheering was loud and spontaneous. The tension on Arndell's face slowly disappeared.

"Finish by Saturday and you'll have two more weeks of Rio sunshine. We won't be sailing until early September."

Patently anxious over White's threat to discharge him and send him back to England, Arndell devoted his every waking moment to the task of cleansing the 'tween decks, so that Margaret, free to come and go as she pleased, was left to her own devices in a hospital where all the bunks now lay empty.

From time to time, Jonathan managed to join Margaret. Bottles of rum, smuggled out of the armoury, effectively silenced any rumblings of discontent among his fellow convicts, left to their foul labours in the gaol deck.

"You've told McQuaid?" he said, one day.

Margaret shook her head.

"He came last night. No, my love, not what you are thinking. There was no mention of marriage." Margaret's eyes had a roguish glint. "It was about a fever."

Jonathan clasped her close.

"Don't - don't trifle, darling. And don't waste precious time."

Margaret eased herself gently from the embrace.

"Don't you want to hear about the fever - the lust?"

"McQuaid didn't.....?"

"No, no. His lust's like yours."

"Come here." Jonathan again enfolded her in his arms. "You're telling me he didn't attempt to take you?"

Margaret burst into peals of laughter.

"I'm talking about lust for power. Turnbull's jubilant. You know the fleet's taking aboard huge stocks of wines, spirits, cocoa, coffee, medicines, clothes?"

"Yes, yes," Jonathan said with mounting impatience. "But who pays?"

"The British government, the navy, I imagine."

"Who were never over-generous. And though Phillip's personal standing's high in Brazil, his credit's little more than modest."

"So?"

"So, Phillip, Walton, and the rest have to turn to wealthy shipowner and ship's chandler, Turnbull McQuaid. They need McQuaid badly. The incident with the young seaman and other incidents like it are conveniently forgotten."

Jonathan regarded Margaret with disbelief.

"Walton might be swayed - the Friendship belongs to McQuaid - but I couldn't for one moment imagine Phillip relenting."

"Phillip almost certainly doesn't know a thing about McQuaid and the seaman, dearest. Walton accepts no interference from anybody aboard any ship under his command. And he keeps most matters to himself."

"So either McQuaid's credit in Brazil's high enough or he has sufficient dollars and golden guineas....."

"Sufficient? The gold buttons on his tunic, the gold buckles on his shoes and the diamond rings on his fingers last night are enough to victual the whole fleet for half a year."

Margaret's laughter soared to hysteria and then she collapsed in tears.

Jonathan led her to the edge of a bunk.

Head in hands she sobbed.

"No nightmare was ever like this."

Jonathan gently stroked her hair.

"Sacrifice a little longer, just a little longer, my love."

Margaret brushed aside his comforting hands.

"Sacrifice? It's been sacrifice, sacrifice, sacrifice ever since that night of hell with the filthy press gang officer. I went through it for you, for us. And don't imagine marrying Turnbull McQuaid is any less of a sacrifice. The very thought of it sickens me as much - and more than - it sickens you!"

Jonathan drew Margaret to her feet and hunched beneath the low ceiling they faced each other at arms' length.

"McQuaid and his sort - abominations," he said through clenched teeth.

Margaret freed herself.

"But that's precisely why I can go through with this - this marriage."

"I'll not have you parading naked......"

Margaret's laugh was brief and mirthless.

"If there's one thing with no appeal for McQuaid, it's the sight of a naked woman, a thousand naked women. Now, if, for some trumped-up reason, Thomas Arndell insisted on examining me from head to foot, what would you say to that?"

"That's different."

"All that different? If I read the signs aright, any minute your surgeon friend could forget he was simply a surgeon."

"I don't think...."

"Maybe not. I'll tell you what I think, though. Our faithfulness'll be better preserved if I'm married to

Turnbull McQuaid than if I stay in the hospital or be sent back to the gaol deck."

In spite of her frantic struggle to escape, Jonathan picked up Margaret without apparent effort and carried her kicking and protesting to a bunk.

"We've waited too long," he said in a hoarse whisper." Far too long."

"You're- you're hurting……"

"What - what d'you imagine I'm suffering?"

"A - a lovely hurt though… Lovely… Please, please, darling, don't - don't stop…"

* * * * *

The convicts' memories of day-long sunshine on deck while the fleet lay at anchor off Rio de Janeiro in Guanabara Bay were soon to fade. Powerful westerly gales, thrusting the convict fleet across the Atlantic towards the Cape of Good Hope, hurled seas at it that constantly deluged the tiny ships, seeping through the hatch covers no matter how solidly battened down.

"Something's got to be done for my men," Bellamy said. "They're drenched and they're mutinous."

"The minute I'm given control of the weather, I'll do something, "Walton replied. "Your men, you, all of us, are lucky to be alive, seas like that coming at us full astern. I've known a poop-sea take many a vessel within minutes - and not a single spar, not a square inch of ragged canvas left floating."

"Alter course, then," Bellamy rasped

"And put her on her beam ends?! Stick to your soldiering and whoring, Henry. Leave ship-handling to me."

"Bloody incompetence," Bellamy barked and, hurling himself out of the cuddy, narrowly missed bowling Arndell over as the surgeon appeared in the entrance.

"Incompetence?" Arndell said mildly.

"You as well," Bellamy flung over his shoulder as he battled along the short alleyway to his cabin against the bucking and rolling of Friendship.

Arndell flopped in a chair.

"Seen the women, Francis?" he said.

"Oh, my God, what now? No, I haven't seen the women. I don't want to see the women. I've already seen enough of women. What the hell's the matter?".

"Washed out of their bunks. Ankle-deep in water."

"Then they'll have to bale out and swab. You're as bad as Bellamy and his marines and their damp toes I've got no control over the weather."

"Something'll have to be done, Francis."

With a resigned sweep of both arms, Walton rose from his chair and, as he got to his feet, the aft end of the cuddy tilted, forcing him to make a frantic grab at the table edge. A wine bottle careered across the table top, splashing its contents over Arndell's tunic and breeches before thudding, half-empty, on the floor.

"They'll have to bale out and carry on baling."

"But they're cold and wet."

"For God's sake, man. take some initiative yourself. You've leaned on me and that convict apothecary far too long. Time you solved your own problems."

"I will - given the chance. You say 'bale and swab' in the women's deck. With what? I ask a seaman for buckets and brooms. See the mate, he tells me. I see the mate. He says see the captain. Is it any wonder I seem utterly useless?"

A further onslaught of sea engulfed the poop of the Friendship. Her stem rose, her stern plunged and, like a shuttlecock, Arndell was hurled across the cuddy. Walton, smiling wryly, helped the surgeon to his feet and thrust him in the direction of a chair.

"See what I mean?" the ship's master said, edging back towards his own chair. "If you can't control your own body, how d'you expect me to control Friendship? You'll get your buckets and brooms, Thomas, my lad, when this lot subsides."

"When this lot subsides?"

"My crew aren't convicts, Thomas. I can't risk losing a single one of them. Crossing the upper deck, mainmast to hatch, is, at the moment, the quickest way to suicide I can imagine."

Chapter 45

Anxious lest she disturb the snoring Bellamy, Charlotte Dudgeon eased herself from an embrace slackened in sleep and, smiling, she quickly drew the black dress over her naked body. There was barely room for the restrained pirouette between the bulkhead and the edge of the bunk.

Bellamy grunted and stirred then rose to one elbow.

"Beautiful," he mumbled. "Wish the men of Rio could see what you can do with one of their dresses - nay, dammit, that's the last thing I'd want."

He struggled to make contact with the sensuously covered flesh and, but for Charlotte's timely arm, he would have overbalanced and landed on the planking at her feet.

"Have a care, Henry."

"Hell, what a woman."

Charlotte thrust aside his questing hands.

"I must go," she said, wriggling out of the new dress and swiftly donning coarse blouse, voluminous canvas skirt and clumsy shawl.

"Don't you like your dress? The best, most expensive I could find in Rio de Janeiro."

"I adore it," she kissed him lightly on the forehead, "but it's not for the prison deck. They'd tear it to shreds. Jealousy. Like a disease down there. All manner of delicacies I smuggle in, but still they resent my freedom."

Bellamy tumbled from the bunk, thrust his legs into breeches and dragged on shirt and tunic.

There was no guard in the alleyway nor at the head of the companionway so Bellamy summoned a seaman.

"Escort the convict cook to the 'tween deck hatch," he said, then went below.

The seaman glanced about him. The ill-lit deck was deserted. He dragged Charlotte to him.

"Hm, perfume. You smell a lot better than the others. Walk you round the stern?" he said, already steering her away from the prison hatch.

Charlotte's reply was an elbow into the seaman's midriff which drew an agonised gasp.

"Bloody whore." Rage and frustration storming across the blotchy face slowly gave way to a leer. "But, by God, you've got spirit - and a lot more besides." A rough hand momentarily squeezed a breast. "I can wait, I can wait."

He paused to eye Charlotte hungrily then, "Hell, no, I can't wait."

Savagely he pinioned Charlotte's arms behind her and again and again his wide-open mouth assaulted her neck and her face.

She screamed and, with all the strength she could muster, she plunged a knee deep into her attacker's groin. Then she leapt towards the hatch grating and frantically shook the shoulder of the dozing sentry.

"Let me down, let me down."

As Charlotte stumbled to her bunk she was assailed by a welter of clawing hands.

"Tea?"

"Honey?"

"Chicken?"

"Sorry. Only this tonight," she said, dragging a small bottle from the folds of her skirt. "More tomorrow, I promise."

One of the women at once seized the bottle and drained it at a gulp.

"Half empty," she snarled. "Too much time in the marine's bunk, not enough in the caboose."

Charlotte was roused by a broad hand clamping hard over her mouth.

"That perfume," a harsh voice whispered. "I knew I'd find you."

His hand remaining over her mouth, an arm roughly imprisoning her at the waist, Charlotte's attacker impelled her, furiously kicking and struggling, along the alleyway between the bunks. Then he thrust her forward and she stumbled through an opening in the floor to land on bolts of canvas stowed in the hold below.

At once, the seaman was on top of her, ripping her clothes, thrusting his tongue so deep into her mouth that she was scarce able to utter a sound.

She drove a clenched fist between the man's body and her own then, with every ounce of strength she could muster, she lunged at his lower jaw, at the same time sinking her teeth into the writhing tongue.

Gasping, the sailor rolled away and she struggled to her knees. Over her head there was an opening, dimly discernible as square from the light of a solitary lantern in the gaol deck above. Blood from her attacker's tongue seeped from the corner of her mouth. She retched and vomited.

"We've been waiting half an hour, convict," Walton growled, as Charlotte laid breakfast dishes on the cuddy table.

"But well worth the wait," Arndell said, eyes and nose savouring a plate laden with roast chicken drenched in wine and fennel sauce.

Bellamy and Charlotte exchanged covert glances. He nodded and began to eat. As soon as Charlotte had left the cuddy, he said, "Fortunate to get any breakfast today."

Walton snarled.

"Too long in your bunk, was she?"

"Too long under one of your seamen. The one who broke into the 'tween deck."

"What?"

"During the night."

"One of your marines, you mean."

Bellamy's smile was confident.

"No marine dare. A seaman, I said."

"The convict's word?"

"Parade your crew on deck and I'll show you."

Arndell shook his head.

"No, no. Identity parades settle nothing but old scores."

Bellamy, mouth crammed, guffawed, splattering the table with fragments of chicken.

"How many men aboard Friendship with only half a tongue?"

"None, so far as I know," Walton said, frowning.

"Then I'll let you into a secret. One."

Walton's eyes narrowed.

"You trying to tell me.....?"

"Charlotte Dudgeon's not only a splendid cook but a woman of spirit as well. The sooner you get the hole in the planking of the 'tween decks fastened up, the safer the rest of your seamen's tongues."

The hold beneath the prison deck of the women was crammed with tent canvas, spades, felling axes and other materials for establishing the settlement at Botany Bay. Through these stores lay an alleyway, two feet wide, two feet in height, revealing at the far end a square of timber in the low ceiling. Walton, Arndell and Bellamy wormed their way to the opening. Walton tugged and dislodged the square.

"The women," Bellamy whispered.

Walton laughed.

"Don't be scared. They won't attack. They can't. They're all on deck," Walton said as he examined the timber in the light of a lantern.

"By no means freshly cut," Arndell said.

"A well-worn path from the foc's'le to the women, Francis," Bellamy said, laughing uproariously.

Followed by Arndell and Bellamy, Walton returned in silence to the cuddy and took a chair at the end of the table.

"We'll see your man with the half-tongue," he said to Bellamy.

"Your man, Francis, not mine. But I'll get him."

Faced by Arndell, Bellamy and Walton, the seaman sat on the edge of a cuddy chair, a blood-stained rag pressed to his mouth. Walton's clenched fist thumped the table.

"Did you break into the women convicts during the night?"

The man removed the rag. Blood started to trickle from his mouth. He fought to speak but little more than a gurgling sound escaped from his lips.

"Is that 'yes' or 'no'?"

The man, frowning, shook his head.

Walton sprang to his feet and seized the seaman by the hair.

"Did you creep through a hole in the 'tween deck planking and take a woman?" Savagely, Walton shook the captive head. "Answer me. Did you?"

"Y-yes. L-like all the others."

Walton flung the seaman aside.

"Then save the rest of your blood for the bo's'n's cat. Get out."

Arndell followed the man in his headlong departure for the door, then carefully closed it.

"You can't have him flogged, Francis. He's not the only one using that way to the women. Besides, he's lost enough blood already."

"Put him in irons then 'til he's fit for the cat," Bellamy said.

"Barbaric as usual," Arndell said, eyeing Bellamy with distaste. "Wise to keep your mouth shut, Henry. If it hadn't been your bedding partner, would you have troubled to mention the incident? You can satisfy your hungers in the comfort of your cabin, but seamen have to hunt for some dark and stinking corner."

Meantime, Walton had been laboriously making an entry in the ship's log. 'Isaac Deadleaf. Damage to ship's timbers: raped convict woman. Fifty lashes. Sentence to be carried out this day.' He sanded the ink liberally, puffed the surplus sand from the page, then read the entry aloud.

Arndell's tone was incredulous.

"Damage to ship's timbers?."

Walton gave him a knowing wink.

"To Arthur Phillip, fifty lashes for raping a woman'd be far too much. For wanton damage to a ship maybe not enough."

A marine roped the seaman's wrists and ankles to iron rings in the deck barricade, then he stuffed a rag into the man's mouth and gagged him. Grasping the cat-o'-nine-tails, the bo's'n's mate began, to the roll of a marine's drum, scourging the hapless captive.

By the twentieth drum-roll, the victim of Walton's savage sentence, face now deep purple, no longer tautened against the hissing lashes.

Arndell, teeth clenched, leapt forward and seized the cat-o'-nine tails.

"Enough, enough."

The bo's'n's mate, the tails of his cat limp and dripping blood, poised high ready for the next lashing, looked to Walton who stood, arms folded, impassive.

"Carry on."

Still grasping the cat, Arndell wrenched it from the hand of the bo's'n's mate and stood resolutely between the man and his victim.

"I said 'Enough'."

Walton remained impassive.

"The sentence was fifty lashes."

"But not a death sentence," Arndell roared. "I told you. The man isn't fit enough for punishment like that. Five more strokes and he could be a corpse."

Bellamy grabbed Walton's arm.

"Bloody leech-man," he said. "Let's see who's the master, Walton."

Shaking free of Bellamy's hold, Walton turned to the bo's'n's mate, hesitated for a moment and said, "A bucket of salt water - then cut him free."

As Walton strode swiftly away Bellamy hastened to catch up with him.

"Why, Walton, why? Scared of your pills-and-potions man?"

Grim-faced and silent, Walton hurried down the steps of the companionway. In the cuddy, he closed and bolted the door.

"Arndell could have been right. Not a convict, a seaman, remember. Flog a seaman to death and it could be mutiny. Or wholesale desertion the minute we reach the Cape. You're not much help, Henry."

Bellamy looked puzzled.

"Me?"

"Everybody aboard knows your taste for the convict Dudgeon. Arndell'd not hesitate to tell John White, White would tell Arthur Phillip, then all hell'd be let loose. Bloody women. I wish we were rid of 'em... One solution, I suppose."

"What?"

"Leave the opening in the floor of the 'tween decks but bolt it on top. It'll be up to the women then!"

"Lunacy, Walton, bloody lunacy."

"Maybe, Henry, maybe, But it was you who started it all."

Chapter 46

Jonathan and Arndell looked on in silence as Margaret bathed the seaman's ravaged, twitching flesh.

"Yarrow ointment," Arndell said," when she's cleaned the wounds."

Jonathan's smile was patronising.

"Cleansing encourages bleeding. I suggest herb robert."

"Will we ever agree?" Arndell said whimsically.

"Not until you realise there've been enormous strides in specifics since the days of Nicholas Culpeper."

Arndell's shrug of the shoulders seemed to be an admission of defeat as he moved closer to inspect the seaman's lacerations, so savage that here and there ribs and back bone lay stripped of flesh.

"I'd say the thongs of the cat were laced with strips of metal. Bloody savages," Arndell, shuddering, said in a soft voice. He put his mouth to the ear of the motionless seaman. "Show me your tongue."

With a groan the man rolled to one side and opened his mouth to reveal a tongue that was little more than a stump of raw flesh.

"Well?" Arndell said to Jonathan, who was leaning over the surgeon's shoulder. "And what does the successor to Nicholas Culpeper have to say?"

"The man's own spittle's his best medicine. Honey with gold of pleasure could be a comfort. And a generous ration of rum certainly wouldn't go amiss."

So far as the low ceiling permitted, Arndell straightened up and said to Margaret, "Did you hear the apothecary's opinion?"

Glancing proudly in Jonathan's direction, Margaret smiled and nodded.

"Give his ideas a trial," Arndell went on and, about to clamber on deck, he turned a smiling face to add loudly, "The seaman will need attention day and night. Until we reach the Cape at least."

* * * * *

In the late afternoon of 13th October 1787, the convict fleet dropped anchor in Table Bay. Aboard Sirius, Arthur Phillip sent a signal to all vessels that crewmen, marines and convicts alike were to toast King George now that half the voyage to New South Wales was behind them.

But Phillip took care not to reveal that the ships would not be in sight of dry land again until they sailed into Botany Bay, almost eight thousand miles distant. Nor did he warn those prisoners, clad in nothing more substantial than their gaol-house rags, of the bone-splintering cold to be encountered crossing the southern oceans.

"What problems since Rio?" Arthur Phillip said, as he and Francis Walton paced the deck of Friendship early the following morning.

"A very wet ship."

"But sails well?"

"Well enough, I suppose. Too much ballast so she sails squat."

"Jettison some."

"And risk capsizing? No breeze to steady her and she rolls like a floating bottle."

At the head of the companionway, Phillip paused.

"I'll inspect the log," he said brusquely.

Walton followed him down the steps to the cuddy where Turnbull McQuaid sat alone, drinking wine. McQuaid bounced to his feet and bowed to Arthur Phillip whose only response was a peremptory nod.

The ship's log lay open on the table.

"Not exactly an idle ship," Phillip said, scanning the pages and giving a smile of approval to Walton. "One hundred and forty miles in twenty-four hours. Sirius'd be hard put to achieve that."

"Friendship was built for speed, sir," McQuaid said.

"If not for comfort," Walton said quickly. "And I suspect the builders had in mind an escape from proper harbour dues."

Phillip laughed.

"As we're not likely to be paying harbour dues in Botany Bay, the point's no more than academic, Mr Walton. But I'd welcome an explanation."

"Harbour dues're based partly on the depth of a ship. It's assumed worldwide a vessel's depth is half her beam."

Phillip nodded.

"So a narrow ship never pays its fair share of dues, I see. And she's speedy," he said and, turning to McQuaid, he went on, "Is that how you built the Friendship?"

"Yes - er - yes. In our cut-throat business that's the way it has to be, Captain Phillip."

"And as long as there's cut-throat business, ships'll go on rolling, their holds take a soaking and the crews put up with a life of pitching and misery," Walton snorted as he filled three goblets.

McQuaid looked to Arthur Phillip.

"May I now ask something?"

"Of course."

"Why d'you ask these questions?"

Phillip contemplated his goblet of wine.

"Fifteen hundred pairs of feet all stepping together on to the shores of Botany Bay could create problems. I've a plan for the swifter part of the fleet to go ahead, survey the Bay with its hinterland and find supplies of fresh water. The Friendship's to be in my flying squadron."

A look of cunning spread across the face of Francis Walton.

"What a damn nuisance our women convicts're going to be," he said.

"And a hindrance, Mr Walton. All female convicts'll be transferred to the Charlotte, Lady Penrhyn and the Prince of Wales."

Walton's smile was broad.

"Damn glad to get rid of the pestilential bitches."

McQuaid swiftly emptied his goblet.

"I heartily agree with Mr Walton. But may I make a suggestion, sir?" he said.

Phillip had now returned to scanning the pages of the ship's log. He did not raise his head.

"Why not?"

"Two or three women in the advance party as cooks, seamstresses and laundresses would be useful."

Walton flung a withering glance at McQuaid.

"Useful? Only one use for women aboard this or any other ship. Twenty-five years at sea with never a woman aboard and never a moment of trouble. But now, twenty-five weeks out from England and Friendship's seething because of twenty whores in the 'tween decks."

Unnoticed, Henry Bellamy had come into the cuddy. He leaned over the table to pick up a bottle and fill a goblet.

"Did I hear you're planning to leave the women in Cape Town?" he said to Phillip.

Walton smiled.

"The captain's taking 'em all off, all of 'em, and putting 'em aboard the other transports," he said.

"But cooking, sewing, laundry?"

Phillip ran a finger down the crew list that lay alongside the log book.

"But there's already a cook in the ship's complement - and any one of a dozen seamen'd be capable of washing shirts."

McQuaid threw a covert glance in the direction of Bellamy and for once he had an ally in the marines officer.

"Not with the skill and care of a woman though. Our shirts'll have to last us a long, long time. And Dr. Arndell, it occurs to me, is going to suffer if he loses the woman who tends the sick in the hospital."

"I hope you go ahead with your plan, sir," Walton said.

Arthur Phillip sat back.

"Before we sail for Botany Bay the women will be removed to other ships," he said, striking the table.

McQuaid got to his feet.

"I hope you don't mind, sir, but I think you're making a great mistake," he said and, followed by a silent, grim-faced Bellamy, he left the cuddy.

It was dark when McQuaid crept from the companionway to a deck deserted except for the look-out who lay asleep and a solitary marine idly pacing up and down.

"The hospital," he whispered urgently, hoarsely, and, at the same time, thrusting a bottle into the man's hand.

The marine led the way to the trapdoor and quietly eased back the bolts.

McQuaid seized and shook Margaret by the shoulder, as she lay on a hospital bunk at the foot of the ladder.

"Wake up."

"Turnbull."

McQuaid glanced anxiously around the hospital and pressed an urgent finger to his lips.

"Quiet."

"Oh, he won't rouse," Margaret said, nodding in the direction of the only other occupant, the seaman who had undergone a flogging. "Rum. Dr. Arndell prescribed extremely generously. What d'you want?"

In the light of a lantern, McQuaid's face was pale and intense.

"I must do something. I need help. Strengthen my situation and assure yours."

"Assure mine?"

"Arthur Phillip's sending all Friendship's women to the other transports."

"Oh, no."

"Before we leave the Cape."

Margaret got to her feet.

"But how could I possibly help?"

"I - I beg you - again. Marry me."

"Impossible."

McQuaid's attempt to take Margaret's hand was half-hearted. She shrank from him at once.

"A business arrangement, nothing more. I can get the chaplain from Sirius. Husband and wife only in name. That's all."

"No, no, no."

"Separate bunks. I've already promised. For the sake of appearances, share my cabin just now and again. But sleep mostly here. Here with Pettifer if you like."

"No, Turnbull. A marriage mockery. I could never...."

McQuaid's pallid features suddenly hardened.

"Listen, girl. New South Wales is still months away, the worst of the voyage yet to come. 'Never' is a very, very long time."

Margaret raised her hands, fists clenched.

"I can't. I've thought and thought......"

McQuaid's tone was all malevolent.

"The Friendship's to be part of Arthur Phillip's advance squadron. Lose contact with Pettifer now and you risk never seeing him again. Only God knows if the slower transports'll ever make Botany Bay. I'll be back for your answer tomorrow night."

McQuaid swung up the ladder and in the darkness collided with the bulky figure of Henry Bellamy.

"Stuffy in the foc'sle, McQuaid?"

"Foc'sle?" McQuaid said with exaggerated innocence.

Bellamy glanced swiftly about him. The sentry, black against the night sky, was too far away to overhear.

Bellamy's broad hand thudded across McQuaid's shoulders, sending him sprawling.

"No business of mine. Thank God we're not all the same. Less competition. Another apprentice was it?"

McQuaid struggled to his feet, brushed himself down and said softly, "I intend to marry."

In spite of the sentry lolling on the ship's rail and well within earshot, Bellamy burst into laughter.

"You can't marry an apprentice seaman, McQuaid. Arthur Phillip isn't at all keen on sodomy."

"It's the convict girl who tends the sick."

Bellamy seized McQuaid by the shoulders and in the gloom scanned the pallid face.

"But I always imagined you were...."

McQuaid shook his head vigorously.

"An isolated instance," he said in a low voice. "It dogs and dogs me. We were both rather drunk...."

"I'd have to be bloody paralytic myself..... When's the joyful day?"

"If she doesn't turn me down - before we leave the Cape."

"You mean to tell me she prefers sleeping in the piss-sodden 'tween decks of the Charlotte rather than share your cabin aboard Friendship? Walton may be a crusty old devil but Tom Gilbert on the Charlotte's a real pitiless swine, tell her. Unless he happens to fancy one of the women himself, they're all battened down, day and night except when Phillip's poking around."

"Is that true?"

"How the hell should I know? I've never been aboard Charlotte. But the tale'd serve your purpose, wouldn't it?"

McQuaid thrust out a hand and winced as it was crushed in the iron grip of the marines captain.

"Thank you for your advice, Henry."

With a further thump across the shoulders, Bellamy sent McQuaid sprawling towards the companionway and, the moment he disappeared below, Bellamy made for the hatch coaming of the women's gaol deck. There was no sign of a sentry as he quietly eased back the bolts, raised the trapdoor and knelt over the opening.

While night on the open deck was airless and sultry, in the battened-down hold it was as if the women were suffering from high fever. Few were able to sleep and most lounged silent, listless, sweltering and half-naked in the narrow alleyways between the tiers of bunks.

In heavily disguised voice Bellamy growled, "The convict Dudgeon."

Charlotte's head emerged through the hatchway.

"You're to cook a meal for the cuddy," Bellamy dropped his voice to a whisper, "Promise them brandy later on."

Bellamy dragged the convict woman to her feet on deck, swiftly closed and bolted the trapdoor, then ushered her, barefoot and clad only in a shift, to his cabin.

"Foolish, foolish, Henry," Charlotte said, stretching and yawning as she settled on the edge of the bunk, "they know well enough I'm not wanted for cooking this time of night. They'll surge round me like wasps when I go back. Make sure it's brandy and more."

Bellamy enveloped the convict woman's hands in his own.

"You're not going back," he said.

"Not....?"

"We're getting married."

Charlotte shot to her feet and, head down to avoid striking the low ceiling, she stood over Bellamy, arms akimbo. Her tone was by no means unkindly.

"You must be mad," she said.

"Desperate."

"But we've gone over this time and time again."

The marines officer took the convict woman in his arms and, with infinite tenderness, he kissed her.

"Arthur Phillip's sending all the women to another transport before we sail from the Cape."

"Then I hope I find another marines officer just like you, Henry."

Bellamy shook her.

"Don't jest, woman. Parted for weeks, maybe months.... I'll go mad."

"Sit down," Charlotte said, propelling him to the edge of the bunk, "First, I couldn't marry you or anybody else because I already have a husband. And, even if I hadn't, I'd marry neither you nor any other man - ever!"

"Please, I beg you, Charlotte...."

"No - and that's my final answer. But.... I have an idea."

"Yes?"

"You change places with the marines captain on the other ship"

"Major Ross? As stubborn as yourself. Oh, my God...."

Bellamy buried his face deep in the straw-coloured hair.

Charlotte stroked the back of his neck.

"Y'know, Henry, for a captain-lieutenant of marines you demonstrate precious little aptitude in the way of battle."

A faint sob escaped from Bellamy's lips and Charlotte began to unbutton his shirt.

Chapter 47

His back to the window of a wide, richly carpeted room, a man, head down, was seated at a spacious desk. Behind him lay the vista of immaculately-tended lawns and flowerbeds ablaze with colour, the setting for Government House at the Cape of Good Hope.

Until Arthur Phillip and his companions were standing within inches of the desk, the man studiously ignored their presence then, apart from a curt nod as he raised his head, he responded neither to Phillip's salute nor to the naval captain's outstretched hand.

"Mynheer van der Graaf......"

The Dutchman's voice was guttural, harsh, his pronunciation impeccable.

"The Governor, Lieutenant-Colonel van der Graaf, is not available to visitors. I am Deputy Governor, Captain Jacob van der Heyden."

Phillip's tone of voice was incredulous.

"The Governor not available? Then, when may we have the privilege of meeting him, Captain?"

Van der Heyden straightened the papers in front of him with exaggerated precision, then sat back in his chair.

"You will not be meeting him, mynheer."

Arthur Phillip winced.

"Captain - Captain Arthur Phillip, His Britannic Majesty's navy."

The Dutchman responded with a tight-lipped and mirthless smile.

"You will not, as I have said, be meeting the Governor. But I have a message from him. Your fleet and its convict passengers are not in the least welcome here. You are urged to weigh anchor and be on your way."

Arthur Phillip, jaw muscles set tight, glanced swiftly at his companions, Walton, Shortland, the naval agent, and Turnbull McQuaid. Intently watching the Dutchman's delicately shaped hands as they resumed their straightening of the array of papers, McQuaid seemed to be not in the least perturbed.

Phillip's tightly controlled voice broke the silence.

"May I sit and explain, Captain van der Heyden?"

Van der Heyden jerked a finger towards a row of gilt chairs, crimson upholstered.

Phillip, the first to sit down, removed the tricorne hat and folded his arms.

"My fleet of eleven ships is in urgent need of stores for the rest of the voyage to -" the pause was momentary – "to the south seas. I'm seeking flour, fruit, livestock....."

"Enough, enough." Van der Heyden's lip curled. "Seek elsewhere. Our last wheat crop was a disaster. Because of drought there's scarce enough fruit for ourselves. And the last lambing season the worst within living memory."

"I'm authorised to pay whatever seems reasonable," Phillip said quickly.

"Pay with what? British navy credit?" van der Heyden said with a sneer. "Such goods as we are able to sell can be disposed of in far more lucrative markets - and for dollars."

Tight-lipped, pale, Phillip jerked to his feet.

"I much regret His Majesty's credit at the Cape stands so low and the welcome so chill. I can only hope that whenever you touch British shores you'll be accorded substantially better treatment, Mynheer Jacob van der Heyden," he said and, ramming the tricorne hat firmly over his bewigged head, he strode swiftly through the door and into the gardens.

Followed by Walton and Shortland, Phillip did not pause until he reached the high metal-scroll gates. There he turned and rasped, "Where's McQuaid?"

Walton shrugged.

"No idea."

"I thought he was following, sir," Shortland said.

"Well, he clearly wasn't. Fetch him. Mr Walton and I will wait."

An hour elapsed before Shortland returned. He was alone.

"Well?" Phillip said irascibly.

"He'll be here soon, sir," the naval agent said, swaying so perilously that he was compelled to grasp at a tall bush for support.

"Drinking?" Phillip said.

"Yes, sir."

"With.....?"

"McQuaid and van der Heyden, sir."

"Then where's McQuaid now?"

Still grasping the bush for support, Shortland turned uncertainly and pointed in the direction of the house.

"They left me with a bottle of geneva, sir."

Phillip's eyes narrowed.

"Left you, lieutenant?"

"And went upstairs - hand in hand."

"Oh, my God, that hell-begotten thing again. I'll - I'll speak to McQuaid when we're back aboard," Phillip said, unaware that the ship's chandler had sauntered up behind him.

"Why not speak to me now, Captain Phillip?"

Phillip swung round.

"On board," he rasped.

McQuaid smiled indulgently.

"Strike while the iron's hot, sir. Make plans at once."

"Plans for what?"

McQuaid was gleeful.

"Shipping stores, of course. Flour, vegetables, dried fruit, sugar, wine, honey and as many cows, sheep and poultry as we can accommodate."

Phillip eyed McQuaid with a look of distaste, mingled with deep suspicion.

"If our navy's credit's so low how precisely do we pay?"

"In dollars. I happen to have some, Captain Phillip. Dollars and other means of persuasion," McQuaid said.

* * * * *

The waiting longboat took Phillip and Shortland, with Walton and McQuaid as guests for dinner, aboard Sirius. Conversation beforehand was desultory and during the meal almost non-existent. They had barely finished eating when Walton got to his feet.

"Must be aboard Friendship," he said. "God knows what they've been getting up to all day."

He nodded to Phillip, gave Shortland a covert wink and, followed by McQuaid, left.

A distraught Arndell greeted Walton and McQuaid as they clambered over the ship's rail of the convict ship.

"The 'tween decks, Francis. I can do nothing, absolutely nothing."

Walton roughly elbowed the ship's surgeon aside and bounded to the hatch opening of the women's gaol deck. Ribald laughter interspersed with shrieks and screams surged from below. There was no sentry on duty. The wooden grating was securely bolted.

"The guards? Where the hell are they?"

Arndell pointed towards the grating.

"Down there. With the rest."

"But the bolts are firmly home."

Arndell shrugged.

"An opening from the store hold."

"Impossible. I had it iron-banded and riveted above."

"Another hole. Marines, seamen, everyone of them down there. And listen to the men convicts. Ever since mid-day going on like this, battering like madmen at the bulkhead. If they do manage to smash their way through there'll be....."

"Where's that Bellamy?"

Arndell threw up both hands.

"One guess," he said turning to leave.

"Wait, Mr Surgeon. Wait - how did you happen to know all of a sudden about the fresh opening in the floor of the women's 'tween deck?"

Arndell's smile was sardonic.

"Let me ask you something, Francis. When did you last inspect the women's gaol deck?" Arndell wagged a finger. "No, don't tell me. An entry in the log shows you made a thorough inspection only yesterday. And you discovered not a thing untoward."

Walton began to bluster.

"I know - I know exactly what I found."

"I'm not trying to drive you into a corner, Francis," Arndell said. "What I'm saying is, if you allowed all the convicts on deck all day, you'd have no difficulty with a thorough inspection of the 'tween decks - instead of one hurried peep through the wooden grating."

"Impossible. Since we left Brazil the weather's been....."

"Bad, I agree. But not all the time. He's a genius, Francis Walton, who can beat the drive of sex, his own or anybody else's."

Walton knelt to peer through the grating.

"They've got their hands on liquor. How?"

"A bumboat came alongside. Wines, spirits, honey, sugar, dried fruit, gew-gaws."

Walton stared at Arndell in disbelief.

"You telling me the bumboat handed over their stuff without payment? The convicts had no money, nothing to barter with."

"They paid. In gold."

Walton laughed.

"Gold? That scum? There was never a single gold piece among the lot of 'em."

"I thoroughly agree," Arndell said. "But there's a skilful coiner in the men's gaol deck who hasn't wasted a minute since we left, I assume, Portsmouth."

"What d'you mean?" Walton said irritably.

"I'd say there isn't a single brass buckle anywhere aboard Friendship today. In the hands of that coiner one buckle's enough to make four perfect-looking golden guineas."

Walton roared with laughter.

"Golden brass guineas. Serves those Dutchmen right."

The ship's master was serious once more, "But how did the women get their hands on the guineas?"

Arndell gave a wry smile.

"Something you'll have work out for....."

A fresh burst of ribaldry and screams drowned further words from Arndell. In a brief lull, he said,"Better call Bellamy?"

The commotion soared to new heights.

"No," Walton mouthed, beckoning Arndell towards the ship's rail, away from the shouts and screams and laughter. "Let 'em carry on. The liquor'll run out, they'll get hungry. Give 'em a final fling. Forty eight hours from now there won't be one woman left aboard Friendship."

There was ill-concealed anxiety in Arndell's tone.

"Sending every one of them ashore?" Arndell said.

"No, no, "Walton said smugly. "Some to the Lady Penrhyn and the rest to the Charlotte, thank God. Phillip's plan. And after a hot, sweaty night down there they'll be only too glad to get away."

"What d'you mean?"

"Give me a hand with that canvas and I'll show you."

Between them Arndell and Walton unrolled a bolt of canvas that had been lying in the scuppers and, under the latter's direction, they dragged it over the hatch grille, then the ship's master swiftly battened down.

"But it'll send them mad," Arndell said.

"Not much madder than they are now. Imagine a stinking hot, airless night in the women's gaol, Arndell. That'll cool their ardour. Rusty throats, empty bellies. Sweat and love-making don't mix for long. Now for the trapdoor beneath the 'tween deck."

The pair hurried below to the hold directly under the women's gaol deck. There they quickly discovered the newly-cut hole and, unnoticed by the men and women overhead, they sealed off not only the opening with heavy canvas and sacks of dried peas but also the alleyway which led to it.

"Let 'em try to escape from that," Walton said with a grin and, beckoning Arndell to follow, he went below to the cuddy where he poured wine.

"Every one of the women?" Arndell said, as he sipped at his goblet.

"Every one, thank God."

"My hospital woman?"

"With the rest of the whores. A toast, Arndell - to hell with all women."

"More like to hell with you, Francis."

Arndell knocked the goblet from Walton's grasp with his own goblet and stormed out of the cuddy. He made straight for the hospital hatch and, when the wooden grille refused to budge, he hammered it with his heel.

"Margaret, quick."

The grille moved. Arndell glimpsed Jonathan and behind him Margaret.

"Self-protection," Jonathan said. "Wedged from below."

"Bad news," Arndell said. "All the women are being sent to other ships."

Margaret sought and seized Jonathan's hand.

"I told you, darling," Jonathan said and at the same time he rounded on Arndell, "Surely something can be done."

Arndell, grim-faced, shrugged his shoulders.

"Wish to God it could."

"But I can do something, "Margaret said confidently.

Arndell slowly shook his head.

"Phillip's already made plans."

"And so have I," Margaret said, tightening the grasp on Jonathan's hand.

Chapter 48

In the punishing heat of the mid-day sun, the tar caulking between the boards turned to black rivulets which coursed sluggishly across the deck, but it was not until late afternoon that Walton finally relented.

With help from Arndell and Bellamy, he dragged aside the canvas from the hatch covers of the women's 'tween deck, kicked aside the bolts and raised the grille.

Sweating, gasping and cursing, seamen, marines and the convict women battled and clawed to clamber free of the gaol then collapse, exhausted, on the deck. When at length the gaol was empty, Walton leapt to the hatch coaming and surveyed, grim-faced, the panting men and women.

"On your feet. Women, line up over there." Walton pointed aft. "Men, stay where you are."

The convict women shuffled away and formed a ragged row athwart the ship in line with the mast. Walton quickly followed and counted.

"Two of the whores missing. Where?"

Detaching himself from the cluster of men, the mate had now unobtrusively joined Walton.

"Where, Mr Mate? Two missing women. Where are they, who are they?"

The mate stole a glance over his shoulder in the direction of Bellamy and Arndell.

"I -er - I don't know, sir. I'm - I'm not sure."

Arndell stepped forward.

"No great mystery, Francis," he said. "The seamstress in the hospital, sewing sheets and making bandages as usual."

"And the laundress doing her laundering - including some of your own shirts, I wouldn't be surprised," Bellamy said, leaning nonchalantly against the ship's rail.

Walton snorted and, turning to the mate, rasped, "Ship to be cleansed, top gallant to bilges. The women to tend their 'tween decks and make them fit for their successors!"

"Different women, sir?"

"Not ideal bedmates, if that's what you have in mind. Three score of Cape of Good Hope sheep."

Walton, Arndell and Bellamy had barely sat down at the cuddy table, when a beaming McQuaid appeared, a bottle of brandy in each hand.

"A celebration, gentlemen," he said as he filled four goblets with the spirits. "A toast to me," he went on, holding aloft his brandy.

Ignoring the invitation, Bellamy took a tentative sip, smacked his lips and smiled appreciatively.

"Not bad, not bad." He drained the goblet. "What are we supposed to be toasting?" he said, sliding the glass towards McQuaid to be re-filled.

"My marriage," McQuaid said brightly.

Bellamy guffawed, Walton and Arndell looked on, mystified.

"Ah, yes. I remember you did say something about it. But - well, I just couldn't believe.... You wouldn't know how," Bellamy said, his giggle obscene.

The ship owner's face was crimson.

"You're - you're being less than fair, Henry."

Walton was toying with the stem of his goblet.

"Who's the woman?"

McQuaid nodded in the direction of Arndell.

"He knows."

Arndell vigorously shook his head.

"I certainly do not."

"Oh, you must. Your seamstress." *seamstress!"*

For a moment Arndell stared at McQuaid, open-mouthed.

"Good God - never."

"Margaret Dunne, yes," McQuaid said, draining his goblet and, shaking, he replenished the glass.

Walton sat back and placed his hands, palms down, on the table.

"Marry a convict? A convict? You must be mad. One minute talk about a social round in the new colony and launching a trading empire, then it's getting wed to a convict whore."

Arndell, pale faced, his neck beginning to suffuse with pink, surged to his feet.

"Convict maybe, Francis, but certainly no whore."

Walton lifted his hands from the table.

"Now, now, Thomas," he said jocularly. "Don't let jealousy raise its nasty green head."

It was unusual for Arndell to raise his voice. Now he was bawling.

"Jealousy? I'm not jealous. It's the loss of the woman from my hospital. God only knows what sicknesses lie ahead. And the worst of the voyage yet to come."

Walton continued his jocular attitude.

"A loss either way. Either your convict woman moves to McQuaid's bunk or, in forty-eight hours, with the rest of the women to the Charlotte or the Lady Penrhyn."

Bellamy who, meantime, had been steadily emptying and refilling his goblet, struck the table with clenched fist.

"What d'you mean, Walton?"

"I was telling Arndell he couldn't win."

"Not that, not that. About the women going?"

"Phillip's brought forward the date. In two days, the lot of 'em leaving Friendship."

Bellamy shot to his feet with a ferocity that sent every goblet flying and he hurled himself out of the cuddy.

Slowly Walton's glance went to the door which Bellamy had slammed behind him.

"You've launched an epidemic, Turnbull," he said softly, cynically.

"Epidemic?"

"Not the sort that worries Arndell - in his professional capacity, I mean. Now, I wonder where Bellamy's gone? I want you and Arndell gone as well. I need peace. Enough paper work ahead to see me through 'til midnight."

McQuaid joined Arndell at the cuddy door, then turned.

"Captain Phillip's sending the chaplain from Sirius in the morning. I'd welcome use of the cuddy for the ceremony."

Walton fixed McQuaid with a baleful eye.

"So you've managed to buy Phillip as well. Who the hell am I to say, 'Sorry, no'?"

Jonathan had spent the morning at the apothecary's bench in the armoury, preparing ointments and potions and plaisters for what threatened to be a long and arduous voyage from the Cape of Good Hope to Botany Bay.

While the fleet anchored at the Cape, food and water for the convicts were fresh and plentiful, their spells on deck sunlit and generous. In spite of these, however, and in spite of the thorough cleansing of the gaol decks, the number of minor sicknesses among the convicts mounted daily.

It was early afternoon when Jonathan was at last free to join Margaret in the hospital. She was tending the only patient there, an elderly man whose eyes had been gouged out by a fellow convict because he had divulged to a marine the whereabouts in the 'tween decks of a stolen musket.

The man writhed and moaned as Margaret sought to bathe the festering empty sockets.

"Better if they'd killed him," Jonathan whispered.

"They will, I'm afraid, the moment he's back in the gaol deck," Margaret said.

"Then he'll have to stay here."

"Thomas Arndell would never agree."

"Leave Arndell to me," Jonathan said. "We'll give the old man this - laudanum. Make him sleep for a week, maybe longer. Imagine the poor wretch stumbling about the 'tween deck for the rest of the voyage, then a life of blindness in a convict settlement."

Jonathan slid an arm under the man's shoulders and raised him so that Margaret could administer the drug. Within minutes the convict lay in a deep sleep.

"I've done everything possible with Arndell, my love," Jonathan said, taking Margaret in his arms and kissing her. "He says he can't possibly intervene to keep you aboard Friendship."

"Turnbull McQuaid will help."

"That animal. How?"

"Didn't - didn't Thomas tell you anything?" Margaret said diffidently.

"No. What - what's the matter?"

Margaret's body stiffened in his arms. She burst into tears.

"Turnbull's persuaded Captain Phillip to let him marry me."

"Let him....? Good God. McQuaid's a monster You - you couldn't ....!"

"I can. I must."

"But not long ago the very idea of it sickened you."

"Even - even worse now. But it's the only way for you and me to stay together."

"Stay together? You sharing his bed?"

"No, no, no. Turnbull wants that even less than I do. I can stay here in the hospital. He's desperate to buy respectability, that's all."

Jonathan thrust Margaret to arms' length.

"I feel like vomiting."

"Please, please, dearest, I beg you, try to understand. I'm frantic. I'm doing this for you, for us. If we part now we may never see each other again. And I couldn't bear going back to a prison deck.... the stench, the filth, the rats, the women clawing, scratching, spitting - and you gone....

"I - I'd even rob that poor old man of his laudanum to kill myself.... I - will - not - leave - the - Friendship."

Jonathan enveloped her in his arms once more.

"Suppose - suppose, darling, we ever reach Botany Bay. What happens then? You living in style with McQuaid, I'm in some chain gang, digging pits, felling trees, sleeping in a cave. What hope of contact then?"

Margaret burst into tears.

"Please, please don't go on and on with questions. I'm playing for time to think. I haven't the faintest idea what miseries lie ahead. I'm doing what I think's best for us here and now…. Oh, Christ, why can't I die? I almost envy that poor old wretch," she said, pointing to the man with the empty eye sockets.

As the ship's carpenter drove home the final nail, Thomas Arndell, like some child for the first time seeing a new toy, clapped his hands.

"Splendid, chippie, splendid."

The new and solid bulkhead, replacing the wooden grille screening the 'tween deck hospital, was a further triumph in the surgeon's ongoing struggle for the wellbeing of the sick aboard the convict transport Friendship.

"Bad enough the smell seeping past the tarpaulin from a score of ragged, unwashed women herded together. But imagine the stench from sixty Cape sheep battened down for weeks, maybe months, on end. A solid bulkhead absolutely vital," Arndell had told Walton.

It was a uniquely propitious period to seek favours of the ship's master, almost wholly concerned about the Friendship which, after weeks lying at anchor, timbers heavily sea-water sodden, was little more than sluggish in her response to the helm.

Barely twenty four hours out from the Cape, yet the convict fleet was already locked in constant battle against the unpredictable and inhospitable waters of the southern ocean.

"That bloody hospital," Walton had snapped, anxious eyes on the topgallant. "There'll be a scream for silken sheets next. Oh, yes, yes. Tell chippie. And warn him not to upset the sheep."

Still in jubilant mood, Arndell made his way to the armoury.

"Pettifer. Oh, my God."

Jonathan lay slumped over the armoury bench. Blood from a gash beneath one eye had congealed. There were bloodstains on the rim of the stone pestle and on the bench boards. Arndell seized him by the hair and raised his head. His eyelids flickered. The surgeon gently lowered the head to rest once more on the bench top. Scanning the row of medicament jars, he picked up one of them. It was empty. Cautiously his nose sought the rim.

"Laudanum," he muttered. "How much, I wonder?"

Arndell hurried from the armoury and returned within minutes carrying a pannikin of water and a roll of muslin. He dragged the still-unconscious Jonathan to a seat on an upended keg and he bathed the wound.

Jonathan winced. His lids flickered. His eyes opened slowly.

"Pettifer?"

"Mm?"

"Laudanum?"

"Mm."

Jonathan's eyes lazily closed.

"Why, why, Pettifer?" Arndell's prompt arm prevented Jonathan from keeling over. "In heaven's name, why?"

"McQuaid," Jonathan muttered. "That bloody McQuaid."

"Go on. Get it all out."

"C-can you imagine Margaret in bed with McQuaid?"

"Bent on torturing myself, then, yes I could. But it wouldn't be true."

Jonathan groaned.

"Wouldn't?"

"Margaret already has her bed in the hospital."

"With McQuaid?"

"Not with McQuaid. Alone. In the hospital, I said. McQuaid's idea. Margaret's already told you, surely."

"But Walton?"

"Oh, forget about Walton. Delighted to be rid of the women. Besides, at the moment he's too obsessed with his ship and its tantrums."

Jonathan put a hand to his forehead and groaned.

"Next time, Pettifer, turn to rum. For a better sort of headache. Now, try plunging your head into this," Arndell said, guiding Jonathan towards the pannikin of water.

Chapter 49

Charlotte eased herself free of Henry Bellamy's arms and draped a blanket about her naked body.

"I'm going. I must."

Bellamy jerked upright.

"Going? Where?"

"On deck."

"Naked?"

"It's dark."

"You're not to leave this cabin."

"I must have fresh air."

"Somebody's sure to see you."

Charlotte raised one shoulder and the blanket slid to the cabin floor. The convict woman's palms glided sensuously over her breasts and down to her thighs.

"And would there be any complaints about the sight of me?"

"Enough of your tempting, woman," Bellamy said, hoarse-voiced, and, struggling to seize hold of Charlotte, he rolled helplessly out of the bunk.

"No, Henry. No more. I've had enough of you." The tone was calculated, coquettish. "I'll try the prison deck for a change."

Bellamy clambered back and sat on the edge of the bunk. There was whimsy in his eye.

"You're the first woman ...."

"To refuse you?"

"To choose a sheep in her bed instead of me."

"Sheep?"

"Cramming the 'tween deck. All the women have been sent to the other convict transports."

"When?"

"The day before we set sail from the Cape."

Charlotte was now all anxiety.

"Then - then what's to become of me?"

"Stay where you are."

"This tiny place? Day in, day out? No, never...."

"Why not? Good food, plenty of wine, a welcoming bed...."

"For a few days, maybe, but for weeks, months, oh, no, no.... Do something, Henry, do something."

As Charlotte voice soared to a crescendo, Bellamy clamped a hand over her mouth.

"Quiet woman, quiet. You'll have the whole ship's company beating a tattoo on my door."

Charlotte's teeth buried savagely into Bellamy's hand.

"Owch, you trollop."

Bellamy quickly withdrew his hand and she slapped his face.

"I said, 'do something'!"

Bellamy caressed a smarting cheek.

"Such as?"

Eyes blazing, Charlotte seized Bellamy's naked shoulders and her fingernails bit deep into his flesh.

"Do something, Henry Bellamy - or I will."

Bellamy slid a pacifying arm around her waist.

"I'll do what's best for...."

"Yourself?"

"And for you, Charlotte. I couldn't've let you go to another convict ship...."

"Or some other marines officer's bunk?"

"For God's sake, don't taunt, Charlotte. I'll never be able to do without you."

Charlotte thrust aside his arm.

"As a plaything?"

"No."

"To satisfy lust? When I was a prisoner in the 'tween decks there was at least sometimes fresh air and sunshine on deck. But now...."

Both of Bellamy's arms encircled her this time.

"I'll do something, I promise."

"What'll that be? And when?"

Bellamy appraised the convict woman for a moment, then his face lit up.

"Push your hair back. Right back," he said.

"Why?"

Bellamy's reply was to seize Charlotte's hair and drag it back to form a small pony tail. Like that of the other women in the convict ship, her hair had been cut short early in the voyage to control the spread of head lice in the 'tween decks.

"You're very beautiful," he said.

Charlotte was at once impatient.

"And now what's coming?"

Bellamy without ceremony planted a tricorne hat at a jaunty angle over Charlotte's flaxen hair.

"What's this all about?"

"The shirt, the tunic, the breeches," Bellamy said, pointing to a jumble of clothes. "Put 'em on."

* * * * *

"Strange sort of wedding feast," Walton said. "No bride turning up."

McQuaid's strained attempt at a smile did little to convince himself or Walton or Faddy.

"Margaret's in the hospital and'll join us later. Your goblet again, Francis. And yours, Faddy."

McQuaid was once more lavish with his brandy. Walton blundered to his feet and, swaying perilously, raised aloft the freshly charged goblet.

"No bride, no Bellamy, no Arndell," he said. "A toast, then - to absent friends."

Walton drained the goblet and glanced meaningfully at the bottle on the cuddy table.

"Help yourself, Francis."

In his drunken haste to to replenish, Walton splashed his tunic and the table with the brandy.

"Sorry, sorry, Turnbull."

"Plenty more, Francis," McQuaid said, sipping his own drink sparingly. "Plenty more. I didn't come aboard wholly unprepared for celebrations."

With unsteady hand, Walton placed his goblet on the table and, brows knitted, eyes battling to focus, he said, "I'll wager it wasn't wedding celebrations you had in mind."

Turnbull McQuaid purposefully rose to his feet.

"What precisely d'you mean, Francis?"

"To celebrate sharing your bed with a woman."

McQuaid gulped the contents of his goblet, filled it again then promptly drained it. He glanced in the direction of William Faddy. There was an expression of supreme contentment on the youthful features as, eyes closed, the sub-lieutenant slowly slid from his chair and disappeared under the cuddy table. Sweeping his own goblet aside, McQuaid put the brandy bottle to his lips and drank deep.

"I'll show you, Francis Walton," he bellowed banging the table with the emptied brandy bottle. "By God, I'll show you."

A savage lurch of the Friendship to larboard sent bottles and goblets crashing to the cuddy floor. In the instant Walton was cold sober.

"What in hell are the whore-spawn doing with my ship?" he roared and he dived for the door of the cuddy.

Alone now with William Faddy, Turnbull McQuaid dragged the marines sub-lieutenant back to his chair and urgently slapped his cheeks.

"Brandy, William?" he said.

The tightly closed eyes did not even flicker.

"Then to hell with you," McQuaid said, opening a further bottle.

As the Friendship bucked and juddered, there were hanging moments when the steps of the companionway approached almost the vertical.

Clutching the brandy bottle, McQuaid lurched up the steps and, the moment he stumbled into the open, he was pitched headlong across the deck into the scuppers.

"Walton," he roared, battling to regain his feet. His voice was lost in the hiss and clatter of hailstones. "Oh, to hell with you then."

Drenched by sea-spray, continually battered by hailstones, he slithered and crawled to the hatch opening of the hospital.

"I'll show you, Walton," he bellowed, as he kicked aside the bolts of the hatch. "I'll show you."

Wiping dry his eyes, he glanced drunkenly about him. The floor timbers were awash. Drenched by seawater, Margaret, grasping an iron ring set in a bulkhead, cowered in a corner. McQuaid splashed and blundered his way towards her.

"You. Come!"

The breath from his wide-open mouth was heavily spirits-laden. She cringed.

"On deck?" she said weakly. "I daren't."

McQuaid's hitherto tipsy expression hardened.

"Not on deck. Here."

Thrusting a hand into his tunic McQuaid drew out a slim dagger. As if unsure of himself, he paused for a moment, then he dragged Margaret roughly to her feet and slashed her skirt and underwear. Naked from the waist down she stood aghast and shivering.

"No, no!" She screamed in abject terror. "Please,no, no…. I - I thought….."

McQuaid pitched the dagger aside and, seizing Margaret by the throat, he flung her to the floor inches deep in swirling water then he threw himself on top of her.

"You - you thought," he muttered through clenched teeth. "They all thought." He turned to tear open the front of his cream breeches. "We're man and wife, don't forget." Momentarily he raised his head to shout towards to the trapdoor. "Watch this Walton, watch me now!"

A seaman at each side adding their weight, Walton, grim-faced was grappling with the ship's helm. Above the roar of the South Atlantic storm and the clatter of hailstones, there was not the faintest chance of Walton's hearing McQuaid's words but, in any case, the sight of a man, even a man like McQuaid, raping his wife was of no interest whatsoever to the ship's master. At that moment, Walton's sole concern was to save the Friendship.

McQuaid rolled aside, leaving Margaret gasping and sobbing on floor boards awash with sea water.

"But you - you told me...." she said, sobbing.

McQuaid grabbed the edge of a bunk for support, scrambled to his feet, struggling meantime to drag on and fasten his breeches.

"Woman, I loathe you," "he rasped as he clambered through the hatch opening.

Slithering across a deck ankle-deep in hailstones and water, he tumbled down the companionway. In the cuddy William Faddy, eyes closed, was still in the chair where McQuaid had sat him earlier. McQuaid filled two goblets with wine and put one of them to the sub-lieutenant's lips.

"Drink and congratulate, William."

Faddy's eyes opened for an instant.

"No - no more."

Again McQuaid pressed the goblet to Faddy's mouth.

"Just a sip."

The tip of Faddy's tongue emerged to moisten his lips. He grimaced.

"Couldn't."

Shrugging, McQuaid swiftly emptied both goblets.

"Ever - ever had a woman, William?"

Faddy nodded and an inane tipsy smile spread over his face as his eyes grudgingly opened.

"Mm - soft, yielding, y-e-s."

McQuaid's mouth twisted.

"Foul, foul. Got to get rid of the taste," he said filling and promptly draining one more goblet of brandy.

Towards midnight, the storm showed signs of abating and Francis Walton, shivering, drenched, was able to hand over the wheel to a seaman. As he crossed the deck to hurry below, he was buffeted aside by a pair of marines, arms firmly about each other.

"Clumsy oafs."

The taller of the pair turned, giving Walton a broad wink, and in the feeble light of a mast-lantern, the ship's master recognised the face of Henry Bellamy, but he did not recognise Bellamy's companion. He could not fail to notice, however, the ill-fitting uniform of the stranger. The sleeves of the tunic were too long and the tricorne hat, hiding much of the face, was perched at much too jaunty an angle. In the shadow cast by the head of the companionway, Walton paused to glance again at the two marines leaning close together over the ship's rail, their backs to him. The pair turned to face each other then lock in a tight embrace. A tricorne fell to the deck and Walton caught a glimpse of cascading straw-coloured hair.

An hour later Bellamy strode nonchalantly into the cuddy. Faddy and McQuaid, heads resting on the table in the midst of empty bottles and empty goblets, were in a deep sleep.

Laboriously penning in the ship's log, Walton glanced up.

"Marines, they seem to come in all shapes and sizes these days, Henry," Walton said.

Bellamy flung an anxious glance in the direction of McQuaid and Faddy. Neither stirred.

Walton, smiling, slowly shook his head.

"True," Bellamy said.

"Strange but some marines never look like marines," Walton said.

Bellamy began a search for a bottle that was not already empty.

"True again."

"Disguise intended to fool Phillip?"

Bellamy's face crumpled mischievously.

"And everybody else - in a poor light."

"If you don't happen to fool Phillip - or somebody tells him - he'll have you fed to the Indians in Botany Bay," Walton said.

Bellamy, guffawing, patted the head of the sleeping McQuaid.

"Nonsense. What about our pretty McQuaid here? The man at the Cape, remember. What's Phillip done about that?"

Walton gave a sage nod.

"Marrying the convict woman thoroughly confused Phillip. In any case, though, McQuaid's rich, influential. What have you got in the way of dollars - and wiles with foreign governors - that could measure up to McQuaid?"

Bellamy shrugged.

"Not much. Phillip likely to come aboard?"

"In a day or two. Discussion about his flying squadron."

"Damn."

"So make certain her uniform fits. Epaulettes, Henry, rest on the shoulders, never half-way down the arms," Walton said dryly. "Best keep her out of sight for the next few days. For the next few months would suit me."

Chapter 50

"Balsam," Jonathan said, as he clambered down the hospital ladder.

Margaret stared straight ahead.

"Balsam for the man's eyes, d'you hear?"

Margaret, nodding, burst into tears. Grasping the jar of ointment, Jonathan joined her on the edge of a bunk.

"Tell me, dearest."

"Turnbull came."

"And....?"

"The smell of his breath, his hands.... Oh, my God."

She turned and buried her face in Jonathan's chest.

"McQuaid. Did he...."

"Yes, yes."

"But he detests women - as women."

Margaret began to beat her temples with the heels of her fists.

"I'm going mad, mad."

Jonathan took her gently by the shoulders.

"What - what did he say?"

"'See what I'm made of' - over and over and over again."

Jonathan's embrace made her gasp.

"Not ever again. Not ever. I promise," he whispered hoarsely.

"But when he's drunk...."

"I've told you - never, never again."

He kissed Margaret lightly on the brow and leapt up the ladder.

The door of the cuddy was ajar. Jonathan kicked it wide open and hurled himself inside.

McQuaid, his back to the doorway, turned, abject terror at once seizing his pale face.

"Wh - what d'you ......?"

Jonathan lunged at the shipowner, but a blow to the back of his own head sent him sprawling over McQuaid, now spreadeagled on the floor of the cuddy. Walton, aiming a pistol at Jonathan's head, stood over him.

"Up. Outside," Walton rasped.

Ramming the muzzle of the gun into Jonathan's neck, he marched him up the companion way and across the deck to the barricade.

"Cable locker," he barked at the marine sentry. "Shackled to the floor. Bread and water, not much, no light, no blanket. Take him."

In the cuddy McQuaid was inspecting his cut lip in the mirror.

"Lucky escape, McQuaid. Strong as a gorilla, that convict."

McQuaid, blood on his face, turned.

"String him up."

Walton steered McQuaid to a chair and filled a goblet with brandy.

"Here, drink this."

Spurning the proffered liquor McQuaid snarled, "Listen, Francis Walton...."

"I can spare a couple of minutes."

"You'll spare - as you put it - all the minutes I require."

"Shortland'll be aboard any minute with orders from Phillip."

McQuaid dabbed his blood-flecked mouth with a silk handkerchief and grimaced, face fury-white.

"To hell with Shortland."

"Neither wise nor practical. Nor is a hanging."

Again McQuaid dabbed his mouth.

"I insist. String him up."

Walton pursed his lips.

"If you'd been a crew-member or a marine we might've made the ruffian rope-fodder. But you're not. Only a passenger."

"And part-owner."

Smiling ruefully Walton shook his head.

"Meaning precisely nothing. But even if I agreed to a hanging, how would I get it past Phillip?"

"What's it to do with Phillip?"

"A hanging'd have to be logged and striking a passenger's no hanging matter."

"Swing the brute and forget to record it."

Walton folded his arms and at back.

"Tck, tck, a shipowner suggesting false records?"

"Not false, merely deficient." McQuaid leaned confidentially forward. "I'd make it worth your while."

"You'd never manage that, McQuaid," Walton said, shaking his head. "If I stooped to your suggestion would you ever trust my logs again?"

"Oh, come on, Francis. What's your price?"

"Go to hell."

Turnbull McQuaid shot to his feet.

"Condoning the act of a scoundrel, a cut-throat, then."

"No, no. He'll be punished. A starving in the chain locker, then flogging."

McQuaid's face lit up.

"A thousand lashes," he said with glee.

"Twenty-five."

McQuaid's fists thumped the table.

"Twenty-five? Twenty-five? Never, never again will you get command of any ship of mine, Walton."

With scant ceremony Walton thrust McQuaid back to his chair.

"Don't threaten me, Turnbull McQuaid. Phillip may have conveniently overlooked that business of you and the deputy governor at the Cape. But he mightn't be so lenient over the young apprentice you filled with brandy and wild promises, then dragged into the spare sail locker. Lucky for you I made no log entry about the poor lad's mutilations."

"M-mutilations"

"You know what I mean. You'll be interested to learn he'll be supernumerary for the rest of the voyage - if he manages to survive. I'd be quite prepared to admit the log omission to Phillip...."

There was a knock on the door of the cuddy and the mate, followed by a man in naval officer's uniform, came in.

"Lieutenant Shortland from Sirius," the mate said.

McQuaid and Walton acknowledged Shortland's salute with a curt nod.

"Captain Phillip's boarding the Supply to lead his advance squadron. The Friendship's part of it. So every square inch of canvas, Mr Walton."

Walton's tone was caustic.

"Every square inch? Has Arthur Phillip given up all thought of putting live convicts ashore in Botany Bay?"

The expression on Shortland's face hardened.

"Captain Phillip has the convicts' interests very much at heart."

"Then remind him," Walton said, "Friendship, hard pushed, sails like a whale - under water as often as over it."

"You'll carry out Captain Phillip's orders."

"Not if my ship's safety's at risk."

"Captain Phillip's orders."

Walton, face thunderous, turned to the mate.

"All hands on deck. Every inch of canvas - and God help us."

In spite of crowding on more and more sail for greater speed as the advance squadron penetrated ever deeper into the southern reaches of the Indian Ocean, progress grew increasingly sluggish. In gales that were incessant day and night, decks were constantly awash and, battened down below, the convicts huddled desperately together, cold and drenched and terrified, in an atmosphere growing fouler by the hour.

Preoccupied with problems of navigation and handling the Friendship which, he was convinced, carried too much sail, Francis showed little or no interest in Jonathan's fate, in spite of constant pleas by Thomas Arndell.

When, at length, the gales showed signs of slackening, Arndell found Walton, grey-faced and hollow-eyed, alone in the cuddy, snatching a rare hour of freedom from the helm.

"The convict Pettifer?" Arndell said.

"Enough on my plate without worrying about convicts," Walton muttered.

"He'll freeze and starve to death."

"And rid me of at least one problem."

"And create a hell of a problem for me. - and everybody else."

"What d'you mean?"

"D'you realise he's the only apothecary in the whole of the fleet?"

"Well?"

"He knows more about medicines than White and Considine and Balmain and myself all rolled into one. Let this one man die and you've signed the death warrant of a hundred - maybe including yourself."

A hand to his head Walton rose wearily from his chair.

"Oh, do - do what you like. But the flogging goes ahead."

After six days shackled to the floor of the sail locker, Jonathan, cold and stiff and starved, was dragged to the open deck and, blinking against the unaccustomed light, he was propelled to the barricade. There his wrists were lashed to iron hoops and an empty puncheon set between his bare feet and the base of the barricade.

Arndell emerged from the companionway as the trussing was nearing completion.

"Rum?" the surgeon whispered urgently.

Jonathan shook his head and his smile was sufficient to reveal the gap where once a naval agent had smashed a front tooth.

"Laudanum afterwards perhaps?"

"I promise," Arndell said.

"Margaret?"

"Going frantic for you," Arndell said, as he thrust a rolled handkerchief between Jonathan's teeth. "Bite on it when...."

"Now if you've finished the medical examination we'll get down to business," Walton said roughly, dragging Arndell aside.

Gripped by the bos'n's mate, the cat-o'-nine-tails was poised high for the tenth stroke when Arndell leapt forward.

"Enough."

Walton's head jerked in the direction of the bo's'n.

"Tell him to carry on."

Arndell seized Walton's arm.

"I could make you die, Walton," he muttered through clenched teeth. "Slowly, surely, secretly. And, by God's teeth, the moment the opportunity arrives I'm going to snatch it...."

Again the blood-stained leather thongs hissed through the air and, spewing forth the rolled-up handkerchief drenched in blood, Jonathan gave a piercing scream.

"Stop, stop."

Charging Walton to one side, Arndell seized the bos'n's mate and hurled him against the barricade.

McQuaid, who had been watching the flogging with undisguised relish, snatched the cat from the seaman now lying on the deck.

"If your man can't, I will," he said to Walton with a snarl.

Walton's immediate response was a punch which sent the shipowner stumbling across the deck. Then he picked up the cat, briefly contemplated the thongs, dripping with blood, and said quietly, "Unfasten." And, as he walked away, "A sack soaked in sea-water over his back then down to the 'tween decks."

Already Arndell was on his knees examining the wounds of the prostrate Jonathan.

"To the hospital, you mean," he said to Walton.

"I said 'tween decks."

"I knew you were mad. I didn't realise you were vicious, sadistic as well."

About to disappear through the opening in the barricade, Walton paused and turned.

"What was that?"

"Mad, vicious, sadistic. Have you seen the 'tween decks? Ankle deep in bilge water, blankets and palliasses sodden and stinking, the consumptives coughing their lungs up, lice living on the living, rats waiting hungrily for the dead."

"Who the hell, d'you imagine, runs this ship?" Walton roared.

"You. That's why you ought to know about conditions in your 'tween decks," Arndell said.

"Oh, bloody hospital then," Walton said as he stalked away.

Two marines leisurely unfastened Jonathan's bonds and, as they hauled him, face down and feet first, through the barricade, one of them flung a wet sack over him. Arndell, leaping forward, snatched it away.

"Leave him to me," he said.

Drawing one of Jonathan's arms over his shoulder, Arndell dragged the barely conscious apothecary across the deck, through a hatch and down the hospital ladder. With Margaret's help he laid him gently in a deeply-blanketed bunk.

"How - how long?" she asked Arndell anxiously.

Arndell's shakes of the head were slow.

"Days, weeks....."

"But if Turnbull...."

"Drunk or sober, Turnbull McQuaid's not likely to trouble you again in here," Arndell said with a confident smile.

Jonathan stirred. His head moved to one side.

"If McQuaid so much as lays a finger on you, I'll...."

"You'll do precisely nothing," Arndell said quickly. "Aim to survive the voyage, nothing else. I'll do all I can to keep you here until Botany Bay."

Margaret continued to bathe the mutilated flesh. Groaning, Jonathan struggled to sit upright.

"I'll garrotte the animal," he said, miming the act with stiff, crooked fingers.

"Then it'll be the rope for you. Think, Margaret on her own, myself with no apothecary," Arndell said, lightly patting Jonathan's matted hair. "Aim to survive, I tell you. Nothing more. You may well have need of McQuaid - if not during the voyage, then later."

"Need of that- that....?"

"Even the mighty Arthur Phillip found McQuaid useful, remember."

Chapter 51

A powerful south-easter surged between the headlands, whipping to cream the tops of the Pacific rollers as they pursued the advance squadron of the convict fleet to its anchorage in Botany Bay.

Francis Walton eased his grasp on the spokes of Friendship's wheel and allowed his eyes to idle across a vast expanse of sand dunes and waving sword grass. Hitherto, he had been so intensely preoccupied with navigating his ship through uncharted, potentially dangerous, coastal waters that he was unaware of Arndell's presence until the surgeon said, very quietly, "Paradise."

Hollow-eyed, grey-faced, Walton turned.

"Oh, it's you," he said. "Paradise? Paradise?"

"If they can summon up enough strength to crawl out of the 'tween decks, the convicts should revel in the sight of dry land, any sort of land."

Walton rubbed both eyes and yawned.

"Twenty hours at the helm, so maybe I'm not seeing all that well. Paradise, you say? More like some godforsaken hell."

Arndell shot the ship's master a quizzical look.

"When was your last cooked meal, Francis?"

"Can't remember."

"I'll remind you. The cuddy, night before last. Roast chicken with spices and almonds and wine. When did your 'tween deck passengers last have a cooked meal?"

Walton shrugged.

"Don't know."

"Nor care," Arndell said brusquely."I can tell you when those miserable wretches last ate hot food and had warm drinks. Since fuel for the stove in the caboose ran out four weeks ago, they've had neither."

"But they've still had food."

"Yes, Francis, live food. Warm food some might call it. Maggots in the biscuits."

"There was still the salt pork."

"That nobody could chew."

Walton summoned a passing deckhand to the helm.

"Yours 'til the anchors take hold and the canvas furled," he said, then turned to Arndell. "Couldn't chew?"

"Some with hardly a tooth left in their heads."

"Why?"

"Scurvy. Scurvy not only snatches teeth away, it leaves gums soft as pap."

Walton gave a yawn.

"Well, they'll find chewing grass easy enough - but not just yet."

"The sooner you get 'em ashore the better, Francis."

"Up to the naval agent, not me. But he's not likely to waste much time. The sooner he's rid of Friendship and the rest of the transports, the better his prospects for promotion. A signal, look."

Shading his eyes, Walton peered across the bay and then pointed to the sloop, Supply, anchored alongside the Alexander and the Scarborough.

"From Phillip - 'Disembarkation forbidden'. Sorry, Thomas, your friends in the 'tween decks carry on with their salty pork a bit longer." Walton stretched wearily and made for the companionway.

About to go below, he paused, "What's the date, Thomas?"

Arndell was thoughtful.

"January eighteenth - nineteenth? Not sure."

"Assume the nineteenth and join me in the cuddy. I didn't expect to survive to celebrate my fortieth birthday in Botany Bay or, looking back over the past 15,000 miles, any other bloody bay."

"Congratulations. Didn't you think Friendship'd make it?"

"Aboard a ship built for nothing more than quick profit, any moment can be your last. We'll invite Bellamy and the rest."

It was late afternoon when Thomas Arndell roused Walton, sprawled across the cuddy table, from a deep sleep.

"Arthur Phillip," he whispered urgently into the ear of the ship's master.

Walton shifted his head to a more comfortable position on the table and muttered, "He can go to hell."

Arthur Phillip, Governor-Designate of New South Wales, standing less than half a pace behind the Friendship's master, gave a frosty smile.

"Not before he can find a haven superior to this Botany Bay for the settlement," he said, taking a chair.

Walton, bleary-eyed, sat up with a jerk.

"I'm - er - I'm sorry....."

"I very much hope so. Problems, Mr Walton. To Joseph Banks the bay and its wild flowers seemed like Canaan. To me, with fifteen hundred souls to feed, and house it looks more like a parched wilderness."

Walton put a weary hand to his head.

"Don't tell me it's 'Up anchor and sail on'."

"Very little fresh water, so we can't stay long. I'll take boats to the north and inspect Port Jackson. According to James Cook, an excellent anchorage."

The mate, excited, agitated, burst into the cuddy.

"The rest of the fleet, sir. Here and dropping anchor. Captain Hunter from Sirius is asking for orders."

Rarely given to strong language, Arthur Phillip muttered a curse. Then repeated it.

The mate laughed.

"Tell him that, Captain Phillip?"

"No, no."

"More problems?" Walton said.

"I'd planned to be a week ahead of Sirius and the rest, with a site for the settlement well under way. A very bad sailer, that Supply. I'll wager my Lords Commissioners were only too pleased to be rid of her."

"Her and the convicts," Arndell said. "Talking of convicts, sir, the sooner they're all on dry land the better."

"First things first, Mr Surgeon," Phillip said testily. "A good well-drained site, plentiful water, sound tents then sound roofs."

"And a hospital," Arndell said quickly.

Phillip shook his head.

"The sick stay on board for the time being."

"To die, Captain Phillip?"

"Sadly, maybe."

Walton swiftly moved into the conversation.

"Leave the sick to Lieutenant Shortland," he said drily. "He'll soon have 'em dumped ashore."

Arndell's expression was grim.

"Care of the sick's the province of surgeons, not naval agents."

"We're not talking about the care of the sick, simply their -er - disposal," Walton said. "The job of the naval agent's to save the Admiralty money. For him - and for me - the sooner Friendship's rid of convicts the better. I'd prefer tea from China in my holds to sheep from the Cape and scum from Newgate."

Phillip leapt to his feet. He was paler than usual. The hawk-like nose, lips, firm and precisely shaped, gave a supercilious air.

"No ship, no seaman, no marine, no convict will be released to anybody for any purpose, until I consider the moment opportune."

Bowing faintly to Walton and then Arndell, he beckoned the mate to follow him up the companionway.

Walton spat.

"A pox on the arrogant whore-spawn."

"That'd not be much help to the miserable souls below hatches. Even with Phillip, they've got a future unmatched since the days of the Roman galley slaves," Arndell said and immediately followed Arthur Phillip to the upper deck.

Phillip was about to straddle the ship's rail and clamber down to a waiting pinnace, when the surgeon caught up with him.

"A word, sir?"

Phillip, frowning, stepped back on deck. His manner was brusque, irritable.

"No time for trivialities."

"Scurvy, consumption, gangrene, ulcers and various complaints so far unknown to medicine I can't regard as trivialities, Captain Phillip. We need a hospital on shore at once."

"I've already told you. First things first."

"Health has to be the first thing, sir."

"In my scheme of things, establishing a settlement and legality take precedence over everything else."

"Then if you'll forgive me saying so, sir, the whole expedition's been a waste of government money and a calculated exercise in cruelty."

Phillip's tiny eyes blazed.

"I'll have you know Mr Surgeon - Mr Assistant-Surgeon to be precise -it is I who command the project. To my mind an entirely worthy one. Waste of money? Cruel? Explain."

Arndell began to shuffle uneasily.

"I - er - I ...."

"Explain, explain."

The words began to tumble from Arndell's quivering lips.

"If our object was killing convicts, it seems pointless dragging them fifteen thousand miles before delivering the coup de grace."

Phillip's expression slowly softened. He placed a hand on Arndell's shoulder.

"I'll see you get your hospital somehow, Arndell," he said quietly.

"Thank you, sir."

Arndell stood and watched as Arthur Phillip swung a leg once more over the ship's rail. Phillip winced and, for a fleeting moment, the thin, pale features were contorted in pain. Arndell's eyebrows rose. He seemed about to speak but instead he turned on his heel and hastened to the trapdoor leading to Friendship's hospital.

Margaret, bent over the bunk of a sick convict, straightened up at the surgeon's approach, eyes bright with anticipation. Her tone was eager, nervous.

"We've arrived?"

"Almost," Arndell said.

"Ashore soon?"

"When there's a suitable site. Where's convict Pettifer?"

Margaret pointed to the man in the bunk whom she had been tending.

"His wounds are desperately slow to heal," she said in a voice loud enough for the rest of the hospital's occupants to hear.

"Let me see."

Glancing first in the direction of the other convicts, all of whom appeared to be sleeping, Arndell covertly clasped Jonathan's hand and put a warning finger to his lips, as Margaret unwound the linen bandage for him to examine the confusion of partly-healed slashes crowding the skin from waist to neck on Jonathan's back.

"Enchusa ointment," Arndell said in a loud voice, winking secretly at Margaret. "If he fails to respond over the side with him."

Arndell moved to the adjacent bunk where a man lay asleep, lips agape revealing gums toothless and bleeding. He drew aside the blanket and surveyed the emaciated and bruised body. He looked to Margaret.

"Been here two weeks, hm?"

"Three. Eyes gouged out, remember." Margaret dropped her voice. "I couldn't possibly let him go back to the gaol deck. He sleeps much of the time. Laudanum."

Arndell's voice was equally soft.

"Tonight - be over-generous."

"I - er - couldn't."

"Much kinder."

"But where there's life there's....."

"Ten times the normal dose. I insist," Arndell whispered before quickly moving to other sick convicts.

As he was about to climb the ladder for the upper deck, Arndell turned and said to Margaret softly, "Not exactly ideal for courtship but the best I could arrange."

Margaret's lips lightly touched his cheek.

"Thank you. Thank you and God bless you, Thomas."

* * * * *

Morning had idled into afternoon and afternoon into evening. Charlotte Dudgeon was growing increasingly restive.

The heat in Henry Bellamy's tiny cabin had grown more and more oppressive, the atmosphere almost as foetid as that of the women's gaol yet she could not venture on deck.

There was not even a semblance of warmth in Charlotte's kiss when at last Bellamy returned, grim-faced and dishevelled, to fling himself on the bunk.

"Why so chill?" he said as the convict woman shrank from him. "After sand and thirst and sweat - and a possible spear in my back - I'd hoped for a warmer homecoming."

Charlotte maintained her distance as best she could in the frugal space of the bunk.

"Spear in the back?"

"Filthy naked Indians brandishing clubs and spears."

"But your muskets."

"Arthur Phillip's orders - 'Don't fire on the natives'."

"So what was the point in an armed guard? Stay aboard with me tomorrow."

"Witch." Bellamy struggled to embrace Charlotte. Her arms firmly protecting her breasts, she crossed her legs and stiffened. "Witch! - If only I could stay.... Phillip'll be back in twenty-four hours to inspect the clearing. In any case a pair of frigates standing off. If they're Dutchmen there could be trouble."

"Trouble?"

"The first nation to establish a settlement here captures a whole new land."

"Lucky the Bow Street magistrates don't know."

"What d'you mean?"

"Well, for stealing a horse they'd cheerfully have a man hanged, drawn and quartered. What'd be the penalty for stealing a whole country?"

Bellamy parted the protective arms.

"I know what I'd like to steal from you, woman."

And, this time, Charlotte offered no more than a token, light-hearted resistance to Bellamy's urgent lusting body.

Chapter 52

In spite of earnest and persistent pleading by Arndell throughout the closing stages of the voyage to Botany Bay, Francis Walton had steadfastly refused the convicts access to the open deck.

"Too dangerous," he'd said. "I've heard the mutterings in the guardroom and the fo'c'sle. Thanks to Bellamy, discipline began sliding down the scuppers soon after the Cape. Believe me, Medicine Man, we're as close to mutiny as ever I've seen - and you keep pestering me to let seventy drawlatches and horse thieves loose to roam the ship."

But one sunny morning in late January 1788, Walton finally relented. Friendship had been lying at anchor now for two days when seventy ragged and emaciated men crawled out of their noisome quarters in the 'tween decks and, goaded by musket muzzles, they stumbled round and round the cluttered decks of the convict transport.

Arndell, tight-lipped, and the grimacing Walton looked on.

"Should've had 'em shackled," Walton said.

Arndell was scornful.

"Shackled? Good God, man, put 'em in irons and they won't have the strength even to crawl, never mind stumble. If you can't be humane, be sensible, Francis. There'll be no thanks from Phillip if he hasn't enough men left alive to wield his shovels and axes."

Walton surveyed his filthy, skeletal passengers.

"A week or two ashore and they'll be well enough," he said with a laugh.

"Wish I had even one tenth of your faith, Francis Walton. Tell 'em, will you? Explain how they'll be coughing up no more blood, how scurvy-rotten gums grow strong white teeth again, how elbows and knees fat as cannon balls'll soon become strong and graceful. Tell 'em."

Choking with emotion, the tears welling up, Arndell paused, "Tell 'em, Francis, for Christ's sake, tell 'em."

Walton, gaunt and almost as pale as the convicts, was leaning against the deck barricade.

"Yes, I'll tell 'em," he said. "Get 'em lined up."

Arndell leapt to a hatch coaming and held wide his arms.

"The ship's master has something to tell you."

"Out with his guts."

"This up his arse."

"Let's see him swing."

"Overboard with 'im."

Arndell battled to maintain composure.

"Listen."

"We want Walton, we want Walton."

"Fools, he brought you safely...."

"His guts. We want 'em."

An agitated Faddy appeared at the barricade opening.

"Fire!" he barked.

There was a crackle of musket and one of the convicts stiffened, flung high his arms then slumped to the deck.

Without so much as a glance at the dead man, Walton leapt to the coaming.

"A few more miles and the voyage over. And you'll be rid of me...."

The convicts burst into cheers.

"And I'll be rid of you," Walton went on. "The minute this wind slackens we lift anchor for Port Jackson. Make a dash for freedom if you like. But this is Botany Bay - no food, very little water. You'd survive long enough to die with an Indian's spear in your belly. I make you a promise" - there was renewed cheering from the convicts - "if you decide to swim ashore not one of the marines will waste a single bullet on you."

Stepping from the coaming, Walton stumbled and would have fallen but for Arndell.

"I suggest sleep, Francis. Indeed, as ship's surgeon I order it."

Walton wearily shook his head.

"Impossible. When the wind slackens, we follow Sirius and the rest to Port Jackson." He pointed to the mouth of the bay. "Supply's already gone."

Arndell wagged an admonishing finger.

"The mate's well able to handle Friendship."

The ghost of a smile flitted across Walton's lined features.

"After bringing a ship fifteen thousand difficult miles, don't you think I'm entitled to the last easy ten?"

"A light sleeping potion, Francis. I promise to rouse you in good time…. Convicts to remain on deck?"

"Till noon," Walton said peremptorily as he turned to the barricade opening. "I'll be waiting for your potion in my cabin."

Ten minutes later, carrying a brimming beaker, Arndell tapped on Walton's cabin door and stepped inside. He was greeted by a series of rhythmic snores.

Fully dressed, Henry Bellamy gently stroked the cheek of the sleeping Charlotte Dudgeon. To inspect his marines he had been astir since six o' clock that Sunday morning. The wind had now slackened and the fleet would shortly leave its anchorage in Botany Bay for the final and very short leg of the voyage.

Charlotte stirred briefly, turned over and drifted off to sleep once more.

"Time to get up," Bellamy whispered, gently slipping away her blankets.

Charlotte stirred and shuddered.

"No, no."

"We're sailing in two hours. Better get dressed - just in case."

Clutching a blanket about her naked body, Charlotte sat up.

"Sailing?" she said sleepily.

"To Port Jackson. Leave this wilderness to the Frenchies."

Charlotte's eyes opened wide.

"Did you say 'Frenchies'?"

"The Dutchmen, remember, last night. French frigates, not Dutch. Anchored in the bay now. Commanded by Jean-Francois de Galaup de la Perouse - a French count no less."

Charlotte's lips slowly savoured the name.

"Jean-Francois de Galaup de la Perouse."

Bellamy smiled.

"Quite a mouthful. But it rolls quite readily off your tongue. Don't tell me you know..."

Charlotte's brow puckered.

"De la Perouse. There was a Francois and - er - Marianne, I think, de la Perouse. They visited the manor house. Francois, a young naval lieutenant. She looked old enough to be his mother. Costly jewellery and expensive perfume are no substitute for love he very soon discovered, after a late evening stroll with me round the lake."

"Doing something like this?" Bellamy said as he attempted embrace her.

She wriggled free.

Bellamy's tone was peevish.

"So that's why the name came tripping off your tongue so lightly. Well, it's hardly likely Jean-Francois Whatsit is your French navy lover.

"I'll find out," Charlotte said, tightening her bodice.

"How?"

"I'll think of some way. Jealous, Henry?"

"Me, jealous? You're a captive, my captive. Not the remotest chance of leaving the Friendship without me."

Charlotte leaned forward to tweak the marines officer's nose.

"Then not one but two British marines officers will pay a social visit to the French frigates."

"No time for social visits once we get to Port Jackson."

"Then what will there be time for?"

Bellamy responded with a crushing embrace.

"This - and much more," he said, kissing her savagely.

"I'll get you some breakfast."

Alone in Bellamy's cabin Charlotte finished dressing and picked up a hand mirror. She pouted then smiled.

"Newgate and 'tween decks and a marine officer's cabin. Amazing. Not a sign of them," she whispered to her reflection as she began to comb her hair.

As Bellamy, bearing a plate of cold chicken and a jug filled with porter, kicked open the cabin door, Friendship creaked then shuddered. There was a savage lurch to starboard. Pieces of chicken scattered over the cabin and Charlotte was drenched in porter.

"Clumsy oaf," she shrieked.

"I - I'm sorry, love."

A bottle of perfume hurtled through the air, narrowly missing Bellamy's ear, and crashed to the floor.

"Gerrout."

Slamming the cabin door behind him, Bellamy fled up the companionway. Once more the timbers of Friendship shuddered. Her anchor had been weighed, her sails trembled then began to fill.

"Good morning, Francis," Bellamy said.

Walton, eyes to the stem, gripping the helm of Friendship as she slowly got under way, responded with a curt nod.

Bellamy smirked.

"Oh, please your bloody self," he said and sauntered towards the stern.

Ahead of Friendship, another convict transport, Prince of Wales, also was under way. Prone to even more rolling than Friendship she was substantially slower than the brig so that the gap between the two vessels, initially a prescribed cable's length minimum, began to narrow as they approached the northern headland of the bay's mouth.

Bellamy glanced questingly in the direction of Walton, still hunched over the ship's wheel. He turned to watch one of the store ships, Borrowdale, coming up steadily astern. None of the ships' masters had experience of the waters of Botany Bay, but they had been warned by John Hunter, commander of the warship Sirius, about possible shoals and shallows. Soundings taken by James Cook's ship, Endeavour, some years earlier pointed to certain disaster for a vessel that veered even marginally from the narrow charted channel either to larboard or starboard.

As the bows of Prince of Wales nosed tentatively into the Pacific, a stiff south-easter grabbed savagely at her canvas. She yawed and, momentarily out of her helmsman's control, she pitched directly across the path of Friendship.

"Oh, Christ."

Walton flung every ounce of his weight against the wheel but, in the lee of the Prince of Wales, there was little help from the south-easter which had seized the sails of that vessel. Friendship lazed grudgingly to starboard.

Eyes wide, teeth clenched, Bellamy, gripping the rail, braced himself for the inevitable collision.

The tip of Friendship's jib boom struck the Prince of Wales to larboard and, with a noise like the crack of a dozen muskets, the spar snapped. For seconds, the two convict transports ran together, larboard to starboard and then Friendship, the faster sailer, nudged herself free and scurried ahead alone before the lively south-easter.

Walton, intense grasp still on the wheel, flung back his head. Bellamy leapt to his side.

"Well done, Francis. Bloody well done."

The ship's master shoulders went slack.

"Lucky, you mean. Bloody lucky."

Arndell emerged from the companionway as Bellamy, giving a cursory nod, was on his way below.

"Close, Francis, close," Arndell said to Walton, hands still on the wheel and shaking.

"Nonsense," Walton said.

"You must get some sleep, I warned you, Francis. Any more errors of judgment and....."

"Go to hell."

Following the man o' war Sirius in line astern and hugging the coast, the fleet of convict transports and store ships made the calm waters of Port Jackson shortly after noon on Saturday the twenty sixth day of January in the year 1788.

At a mid-point of the entrance to a cove on the south side of the port, Sirius dropped anchor and the rest of the fleet sailed on to the head of the cove.

Anchored now fore and aft, the convict transports Friendship and Scarborough lay so close, larboard to starboard, that they rode the gentle swell as one.

Francis Walton rubbed bloodshot eyes. Discernible through the Scarborough's rigging was a stream running into the head of the cove and, to its left, a flag raised high. All around, tall trees marched almost to the edge of the steep, craggy sides of the anchorage. It was a bland summer's day, quiet except for the screech of parrots in the trees and the gentle slap of water against the hull of the Friendship.

Walton's eyes were suddenly moist.

"Thank God that's all over," he murmured, unaware that Arndell stood immediately beside him.

"Only just about to begin," the surgeon said.

Chapter 53

Margaret and Jonathan were urgently swathing the corpse of the blinded convict, when Arndell joined them in the hospital. Jonathan, grim-faced, glanced up.

"When are we sailing?"

"No more sailing, Pettifer."

"But this corpse? We must get rid quickly. The stench ......"

Arndell drew aside the canvas winding sheet, glanced at the body then swiftly covered it again.

"Yes, yes. Give me a few minutes," he said, clambering out of the hospital.

Arndell found Bellamy alone in the cuddy.

"Where's Walton?" he said urgently.

"Out like a snuffed candle. Enough of your sleeping potion to float the Friendship. Why d'you want him?"

"I need a longboat for shore."

Bellamy laughed.

"Help yourself. You'll get no help from the crew. They're celebrating, the lot of 'em." Bellamy filled and drained a goblet of brandy. "We're there, we've arrived, leech-man. Walton failed to drag us to the bottom of the ocean after all."

"Sober up, be serious. There's a corpse and the sooner it's buried the better."

Bellamy hunted for a bottle, found one, drank deeply from it and hiccupped.

"Easy. Best maritime tradition. Over the side."

"To turn up on the beach a few yards away? Even drunker than I thought, Henry. But prove you're not - help me. I must have a boat."

"I said, 'help your bloody self'."

"But your marines....."

"Every one of 'em off duty." Bellamy threw wide his arms. "The whole ship's company, all the world's off duty."

"As well as a boat I want shovels."

"Whaffor?"

"To dig a grave for the corpse, you fool. Shovels, where?"

"Arm - arm - arm ....."

"Armoury?"

Bellamy gave Arndell a tipsy, exaggerated nod then collapsed over the cuddy table.

* * * * *

On the west side of the cove, Arndell and Jonathan gently nosed the longboat towards a tiny inlet and there, out of sight of the anchored fleet, they dragged the corpse ashore and, digging into a sandy crevice between rocks, they buried it. Beckoning to Margaret, hunched anxiously in the bows of the longboat, the three scaled the rocks to reach the tall gum trees.

"Your home from now on," Arndell said.

On the far side of the stream running into the cove a string of fires dotted the water's edge. Groups of uniformed figures moved from one to another. There were cheers and occasional outburst of singing and laughter.

"They all seem to be happy about it even if you aren't," Arndell added.

Beyond the towering trunks of the gums, blue changed rapidly to deep purple. Then, as if a black curtain had been suddenly flung across the sky, it was night.

"Back." Arndell whispered and, following him, Margaret and Jonathan returned to the rocky inlet and the waiting longboat.

* * * * *

Dawn was slashing the night sky when Lieutenant Faddy roused the sprawled Henry Bellamy in the cuddy.

"The convicts're going ashore, sir."

Bellamy slowly raised his head and opened one eye.

"Wh - a - a - t?"

"Convicts, sir. Walton's putting 'em ashore."

Bellamy opened the other eye. His brow creased in heavy concentration.

"Ashore? Walton? He can't."

"Captain Phillip's orders. Mount guard on shore, he says."

Elbow on table, Bellamy rubbed his eyes.

"Guard? Why the hell a guard? If they want to escape, let 'em."

Faddy took a chair on the opposite side of the table.

"He's putting the convicts to work. Landing stores, digging, felling trees."

Bellamy lurched to his feet only to collapse on his chair.

"Tell Phillip my men're marines not turnkeys." Bellamy seized a brandy bottle, put it to his lips, found it empty and hurled it at a bulkhead. "Yes, go tell Phillip just that."

Neither Bellamy nor Faddy was aware that the door had opened.

"And what, precisely, must sub-lieutenant Faddy tell me?" Arthur Phillip said, as he stepped briskly into the cuddy.

Faddy jerked to attention. Bellamy, brows heavily furrowed, continued to loll in the chair.

"My - my marines are no turnkeys," he said to the bulkhead facing him.

"Your marines are also my marines. They take orders from me through you. Twenty men on guard duties within the hour, Captain Bellamy - if you please."

The marines captain grimaced and nodded to William Faddy.

"Hear that, Faddy? Tipsy or sober get 'em ashore."

Faddy, saluting crisply, left the cuddy.

Pale, thin face firmly set, Arthur Phillip tapped the table with an index finger. His tone was contemptuous.

"You fail to appreciate the importance of the occasion."

Bellamy picked up a bottle, also empty.

"Damn."

"Did you hear what I said?"

"Shit."

"Do you hear me, Henry Bellamy? This very morning we are founding a city, a new country. I am...." Phillip's face contorted in pain as his hand went urgently to his side. He drew in breath sharply. "A - vast new country - and you loll there in your usual drunken stupor."

Bleary-eyed, unkempt, Bellamy stumbled into his cabin where Charlotte Dudgeon lay asleep. He shook her shoulder.

"Going ashore," he said.

Charlotte, fully roused, sat up.

"My breakfast."

Bellamy was struggling to fasten the buttons of his shirt.

"I'm in a hurry. Lunatic Phillip's breathing fire. Wants me on shore."

"And I want my breakfast."

"But Arthur Phillip...."

"To hell with Arthur Phillip."

Still fumbling with shirt buttons Bellamy hurried out of the cabin and very shortly re-appeared with biscuits, cooked rice, some chicken and a pannikin of water.

"Nothing else in the galley. The cook's ashore setting up a kitchen for the working parties," he said.

Charlotte eyed Bellamy's offering with contempt.

"Make sure there's better - a lot better - for supper," she said, seizing Bellamy by the hair. "Or no more favours from me, Henry Bellamy."

Bellamy struggled free and kissed her.

"I'll have to go," he said.

"Walton's agreed to extra rations this morning," Arndell whispered to Jonathan as the latter emerged from the hospital to collect breakfast, alongside the men of the gaol-deck, from the forward caboose.

"A change of heart?" Jonathan whispered in reply as he joined the other convicts jostling each other on the cluttered deck.

"For a very hard day ahead," Arndell managed to say quickly as Francis Walton stepped through the barricade opening.

"We'll inspect," Walton said, beckoning the surgeon to join him on a hatch coaming.

"So Phillip's planning to establish a mighty empire with this mob." Walton's eye ranged over the ragged, scrawny prisoners. "More life in St. Paul's churchyard. And a hell of a lot less stench."

Walton leapt from the coaming and, with Arndell at his side, strode past the men, hunched in ragged lines. He paused as he reached Jonathan.

"Plenty of scope here for your fancy pills and potions, scarface," he said, then turned to retrace his steps to the barricade.

When the pair were out of the convicts' earshot, Arndell said, "Careful, Francis. Any one of those convicts, given a tenth of a chance, would cheerfully garrotte you. I saw signs in every face - and there's no way of battening down once they're ashore."

Walton guffawed.

"Garrotte? Me? The whole mob together couldn't muster enough strength to garrotte a chicken," he said as he summoned the mate.

"Felling axes, saws, scythes, shovels and spades. Load up a longboat and see 'em ashore. But not in any boat taking convicts. If killings are in the air, we'll have 'em on Arthur Phillip's sandy shore not aboard any of my boats."

Two seamen, the Friendship's carpenter, the blacksmith and a pair of marines ferried the tools to a rocky, natural wharf on the east side of the cove. Arthur

Phillip was there, feverishly pacing up and down a narrow strip of sand.

"Tools a-plenty but where are the prisoners?" he said testily.

"Waiting on deck. sir."

"Waiting? Waiting for what? Get 'em ashore at once."

The longboat was quickly unloaded and the tools, under armed guard, were stacked on the rocks.

Hectored, cursed and clubbed by marines, the convicts were driven to the ship's rail and made to clamber down knotted ropes to the waiting longboats.

"Bayonets, bayonets, if they won't move fast enough," Walton bellowed.

Arndell grasped Walton by the elbow.

"I think you'd be better below," he said, voice quivering with emotion, then he leapt at a marine belabouring a convict who cowered in terror at the rail.

"Stop it, stop it, you bloody monster."

Arndell kicked the guard deep in the groin and the man, dropping his musket, crumpled in agony on the deck. Arndell then hauled the convict to his rag-bound feet and led him to Walton standing at the barricade opening. He drew a gentle hand across the matted hair, now drenched in blood.

"No, no, don't turn your head away, Francis. Take a look, a good, long look."

Walton threw a perfunctory glance.

"Not all that bad."

"Not.....? Wielding a spade over there, "Arndell said, pointing to the shore, "he won't last ten minutes."

Walton glanced again at the pale, emaciated creature now slumped on the planking.

"Blood all over the holystoning. Oh, look at him, he's a goner. Damn. Why the hell couldn't he snuff it on shore and let Phillip take over? All yours, Arndell. And remember, not over the side."

Chapter 54

From the vantage point of a rocky promontory, Captain Arthur Phillip faced the convicts who stood in ragged lines, their backs to the edge of the waters of the cove.

"His Majesty King George has been pleased to appoint me governor of this new colony. The appropriate ceremony later. Meantime, work. No work, no food. The marines have strict orders. Musket bullets are precious, so would-be escapers will be treated to the bayonet. There are three abominations - theft, murder, sodomy. Steal or kill and you hang. Be caught in sodomy and you will be hacked up and fed to the cannibals. Clear?"

The convicts remained sullen, silent.

"Sawyers, smiths, brickmakers, builders, fishermen, one step forward!"

Not one of the assembled convicts made a move. Phillip's eyes scanned a sea of faces all devoid of expression. He snapped his fingers.

"Then you will learn to be sawyers, builders and the rest....

Mess captains forward."

A dozen convicts resentfully took a step towards Phillip who, leaping from the rock strode swiftly past, jerking an index finger at each man.

"You eight, with six men apiece, take cross-cut saws. In the marked area, by dusk, not a single tree to be left standing. You two, with your men, will level the ground as marked out for marquees and tents. And you, clear a site to build a forge."

Phillip had now reached Jonathan, last in the line. He eyed him intently.

"Seen you somewhere before?"

"No, sir."

"Hm. What d'you know about fishing?"

"Not a thing, sir."

"Then learn."

Phillip stepped back to the high rock. His voice was deep, vibrant, "You will all learn. Learn or perish."

He pointed to Jonathan.

"Take your six men and haul up the nets already in the harbour. No fish - no food for any of you today."

The nets, laid by seamen across the cove at first light, were so crammed with struggling fish that, by the time Jonathan and his convict team had managed to drag them to the rocky shore, many hundreds of the creatures had made good their escape through the coarse mesh.

On a rocky escarpment, a group of copper-coloured men had been steadily gathering to watch the battle of the convicts with their overwhelming catch and, when their numbers had risen to about a score, they swooped down to the beach.

One of them, brandishing a club and a spear, ran ahead of the rest then jerked to a halt as he came face to face with Jonathan. Naked, a fish bone thrust through the gristle between his nostrils, black, tousled head, he came no higher than Jonathan's shoulder.

Plunging his spear into the wet sand but still grasping his club, the man raised a hand and with grimy finger traced the lengthy scar on Jonathan's cheek. This seemed to please him. He smiled broadly and revealed strong yellow teeth, one front tooth missing.

Struggling to maintain composure, Jonathan smiled too and the gap in his own teeth was revealed. The man let out a whoop of delight, poked his finger into the gap and at once the rest of the coloured strangers surrounded Jonathan, frantically vying with each other to fondle Jonathan's scar and inspect his mouth.

"Buggeri-gai, buggeri-gai," they chanted. "Magra, magra."

Stepping back, Jonathan indicated by frantic signs that their help in hauling in the rest of the fish would be warmly welcomed. Very soon, piled high with their catch, the nets lay on the beach while the strangers, now joined by women and children were clambering away over the rocks, arms full of squirming fish.

The last to leave was the man with the spear and the club. Once more, eyes wide with admiration, he fondled Jonathan's scar.

"Parrebuga," he said then darted off in pursuit of the other strangers.

"Parrebuga," Jonathan called after him.

"What the hell does that mean?" a convict said as he ripped a fish apart and rammed the raw flesh into his mouth

Jonathan shrugged.

"Haven't the faintest idea. But he seemed happy saying it."

* * * * *

Margaret was alone when Turnbull McQuaid joined her. The mid-day sun beat relentlessly down on the upper deck of the *Friendship* as the vessel idled at anchor in the cove. The heat inside the tiny hospital in the 'tween decks resembled that of a bakehouse.

"What brings you here?" Margaret said.

McQuaid mopped his brow with a silk handkerchief.

"I'd like to talk," he said.

"There's nothing to talk about."

"I insist."

The hatch lay open. Margaret leapt for the ladder but McQuaid, moving swiftly, seized her by the ankles and, dragging her back, flung her on a bunk.

"Go - go away," Margaret said, panic-stricken.

"Listen, stupid bitch. I want to talk. Talk, nothing else. Ever."

"You foul, filthy...."

The slap on Margaret's cheek was unduly savage.

"You're my wife. We are going to talk."

Margaret, comforting hand on her face, regarded McQuaid with undisguised loathing.

"About what?"

"Me and you. A proposition. An outward appearance of a loving wife and there'll be a house for you ashore in a few weeks. Phillip's promise. Or you go on and on tending sores and gangrene."

"Never, never."

"Listen. A semblance, an appearance, that's all I want. Nothing more. I could stand nothing more. The stench of a woman, any woman, makes me want to vomit."

McQuaid paused and, before continuing, took a deep breath.

"As the months go by, I'll establish greater and greater influence over Arthur Phillip. Your convict

Pettifer could be virtually free and, if you're both discreet, you'll meet whenever you please."

"I could never, never trust you."

McQuaid's hand slid inside his embroidered jerkin.

"Remember the days at St Catherine's? The perfumes, the elegant gowns, the dainty footwear? Remember your pink and white complexion, perfectly groomed auburn hair, the maid who pandered to every whim?"

From his jerkin, McQuaid dragged out a silver framed looking-glass, "Remember? Well, take a look at yourself now."

Margaret gasped as McQuaid thrust the mirror to her face.

"Oh, no, no."

Withdrawing the glass, McQuaid sneered.

"Oh, yes, yes. Neither your maid nor your own father would recognise you. How much longer d'you imagine your convict lover'll feel the same about you? Food for thought, hm?"

He flung the looking-glass on a nearby bunk. "Food for a lot of thought," he said as he clambered to the upper deck.

* * * * *

Although, for Henry Bellamy, by no means a day of unremitting and backbreaking labour, it had been, nevertheless, an extremely trying one. His close-fitting and substantial uniform, so often a boon in the icy reaches of the south Atlantic, was now sweat-drenched from its long day in the unremitting heat of a South Pacific sun.

Since early morning, Governor Phillip had stumped the settlement area, haranguing the convict mess-captains and ceaselessly instructing the marines and their officers. He specifically ordered Henry Bellamy to inspect, at half-hourly intervals, every guard on the settlement's wide perimeter.

"And your men will keep a watchful eye on the work of the prisoners," Phillip said.

Tunic and shirt unbuttoned, hands on hips, Henry Bellamy glowered at the immaculate and apparently cool Arthur Phillip.

"You expect my marines to be overseers?"

Phillip, lip curled, eyed the slovenly Bellamy.

"Yes."

"I'll remind you the marines are here to protect the settlement and preserve order - nothing more," Bellamy said.

The dark eyes of Phillip narrowed.

"And I will remind you that, in an emergency, orders from me take precedence. It is I who identifies the emergency. And we are in the midst of an emergency now."

Face thunderous, Bellamy turned and stalked away.

"Captain-lieutenant Bellamy!"

Henry Bellamy paused.

"What?"

"Something more."

"Carry on."

"Subject to maintenance of good order aboard the transports, all officers will live ashore in tents. Male convicts will also be tented ashore. The animals may be landed immediately safe pens are created. No women to leave the transports until their tents are up and stores landed. The Indians will be treated like civilised creatures. No brutality, no bullets. Understood?"

Bellamy, smirking, jerked his head.

"Arrogant sod," he muttered under his breath as he began to walk away.

"Captain Bellamy!"

"Yes?"

"Did I hear you use the word 'arrogant'? Well, maybe.... but 'sod'? Me? Never. If I hear you describing me that way again, I'll have you court-martialled."

It was late evening when the convicts, blistered and bleeding, staggered to the longboats and rowed back to the transports. Then goaded by the marines' bayonets, they struggled up the knotted ropes hanging overside and collapsed on the open decks.

"Up, up, scum-boys." The bayonets continued to jab the gasping, prostrate men. "Back to your stinking hell-hole."

Musket butts urged the weary, sweating convicts down to the 'tween decks once more.

Jonathan and his mess team who had dragged the fishing nets ashore were the last to struggle aboard the Friendship. As he straddled the ship's rail, Jonathan glanced back at the rocky shore. Where, only that morning, tall gum trees had marched almost to the rocky edges of the cove, there was now a wide clearing, dotted here and there with fires. A tall flagstaff dominated the scene.

The butt of a musket thudded between Jonathan's shoulder blades and sent him careering across the deck.

"Homesick already, scarface? On your way."

Jonathan made a dive for the opening in the barricade, but a second blow knocked him flat. As he struggled to his feet, a savage kick drove him in the direction of the coaming of the men's prison deck.

"Wrong way, hell-spawn. None of your hospital whoring tonight."

* * * * *

At midnight, McQuaid stumbled out of the cuddy where he had spent much of the evening drinking and alone. Arndell had earlier left to seek the cool air of the open deck, after consuming considerably more brandy than usual. At the same time, Francis Walton, still weary following the long storm-tossed voyage, had long since sought his bunk. And Henry Bellamy, seething from his encounter with Arthur Phillip, had gone to his cabin immediately after supper bent on solace in brandy and the arms of Charlotte Dudgeon.

McQuaid's hands reluctantly abandoned their grasp of the ship's rail and with uncertain step he made his way to the hospital hatch.

"An empire," he muttered to the night air. "A vast commercial empire. So I must have you again, woman. Damn your stinking body. Must have you to - to show ...."

The ship's chandler landed with a thud on the floor of the hospital.

Arndell stepped into the pool of light shed by a lantern.

"To show what, Turnbull?"

McQuaid struggled to his feet.

"Who's that?" he said peering tipsily about him.

"Me, Arndell."

"Arndell? Arndell? What - what the hell're you doing here with - with my wife?"

Chapter 55

Clad in marine officer's uniform, Charlotte was sitting on the edge of the bunk when Bellamy came into the cabin.

"Celebrate my first day on dry land," he said, handing Charlotte a bottle of brandy.

As he sought to embrace the convict woman, she knocked his arms aside.

"And when will my first shore day be?"

"Soon, my sweet, soon," Bellamy said, patting her buttocks.

She slapped his face.

"Why - why that?" he said, putting a hand to his smarting cheek.

"You're making a fool of me. I'm not staying a minute longer in this - this stinking little hen-coop," she said.

"Listen, my love. I'll get food. We'll drink brandy, then take a stroll on deck."

"On deck?" Charlotte snorted. "A stroll on deck? Don't you think I've had enough dressing up like a tin soldier, stumbling over pig-sties and ropes and water casks, dodging into shadows at the sound of every cough, every footstep?"

"Please, Charlotte, please listen." Bellamy took the convict woman's hand. "At the moment, all I can do is keep you here. When the other women are landed, I'll smuggle you ashore to join them."

"And so the parting."

"Not for long, I hope to God."

"What are our plans then?"

"We get married."

"But I've told you. I've already got a husband."

"Not in New South Wales."

"But I'm still married."

The marines captain dropped to his knees.

"Look, I'm begging. I can't do without you, woman."

Charlotte kissed the tips of her fingers and pressed them to Bellamy's lips.

"Don't you understand? I can't go on and on like this." She spoke more gently now and she pointed to the ill-fitting uniform. "This - this outfit fools nobody. Francis Walton knows, Thomas Arndell knows...."

"Oh, what the hell does that matter? It's us, us, us."

Bellamy buried his face deep in Charlotte's lap.

"....and most of your marines know as well," Charlotte went on.

"My brandy and my rum keep that lot blind."

"Henry, can't you understand? I'm frantic for a change."

"I'll do all I possibly can, I've told you. I promise."

Charlotte raised Bellamy's iron-grey head.

"Are the Frenchies still in Botany Bay?"

"I think so. Why?"

"Take me to see them."

"I couldn't."

"Couldn't, Henry? You said you'd do everything. "

"That uniform, even your tattered blouse and skirt from the 'tween decks - we couldn't possibly board the French frigates."

The tip of Charlotte's tongue lightly caressed the end of Bellamy's nose, a pleasurable experience for him, Charlotte well knew.

"Find me a gown, Henry, a becoming one," she whispered. "Then we board the Frenchies to pay our compliments as man and wife."

Bellamy scrambled to his feet.

"And where could I possibly find a gown for you?"

Charlotte winked.

"The chaplain on Sirius has a wife with him...."

Bellamy eyed her with amused astonishment.

"What, tell her I want a gown for the convict woman tucked away in my cabin so she can visit in style the French naval officers at Botany Bay?"

Charlotte's smile was indulgent.

"No, no, I don't think an explanation like that'd appeal to the worthy woman. But if you told her the gown was for the poor girl who ceaselessly tends the sick in the Friendship's hospital .. .. But I'm sure your manly charms could well take care of the finer details, Henry Bellamy."

Bellamy shook his head.

"Impossible."

Charlotte rose to her feet and easing herself out of the ill-fitting uniform, she stood naked before her lover.

"I'm sure you'll find....."she began and the rest of her words were smothered as Bellamy, locking her in a breathtaking embrace, drew her down to the bunk.

A gurgle of ecstasy escaped the lips of the marines officer as they sought and found Charlotte's nipples.

"A beautiful, becoming gown, nothing less - in exchange, Henry," she whispered thrusting him away.

* * * * *

Although dazed from striking his head against the coaming, Jonathan was sufficiently alert to grab the guard's ankle. For one frantic moment the man battled to keep his balance, then he plunged headlong into the 'tween decks. There was a scream followed by an outburst of cheering from the eager reception committee of convicts waiting below.

Jonathan hurled himself across the deck then, crouching between the foot of the mast and the galley-caboose, he waited. When no second marine appeared in search of the first, he crept inside the tiny shack and there fell asleep.

It was dark when, at the sound of the ship's bell clanging the hour, Jonathan jerked awake. He struggled to his feet and cautiously pushed the caboose door ajar. The deck was still deserted and there was silence except for muffled sounds of roistering seamen in the foc'sle.

He eased himself out of the caboose and, clambering overside, he swung hand over hand using the knotted boarding ropes until he came to a spot abaft the deck barricade. Out of sight of the marine on sentry duty, he swung back over the ship's rail.

Scattered about the deck were scores of wooden chocks, used for battening down hatches. He grabbed three of them and hurled one at the larboard end of the barricade. Immediately, the sentry rushed to investigate the noise and Jonathan, bent low, dived for the hospital hatch.

McQuaid had left the grating open. Jonathan flung another wooden chock at the extreme end of the barricade then dropped into the hospital. McQuaid, standing at the foot of the ladder, was sent sprawling across a bunk.

Cursing, the shipowner scrambled to his feet.

"You?" he growled, rubbing an elbow.

In the background, Arndell, with Margaret close behind him, stood, hand on hips, and laughed.

"The place is more popular than the cuddy," Arndell said.

"Shurrup, sawbones."

McQuaid turned to Jonathan again. "What do you want? As if I didn't know."

Margaret thrust her way into the midst of the three men.

"Please, please, Turnbull."

McQuaid flung her aside.

"What're you doing here, convict?"

"I prepare the medicine," Jonathan said.

"Medicine?" McQuaid snorted. "The only medicine you prepare is in your breeches. You still haven't learnt to keep away from my wife. I'm going to prepare some medicine of my own for you, convict. The rope."

Arndell placed a restraining hand on McQuaid's sleeve.

"Don't be a fool, McQuaid," he whispered with urgency. "We must have an apothecary."

McQuaid rounded savagely on the surgeon.

"Keep your mouth shut, sawbones."

Jonathan lunged at Turnbull McQuaid who, attempting to parry the blow, stumbled. Seizing the shipowner by the throat, he shook him until the man's pink features turned purple.

"And now I'm going to tell Thomas Arndell something," Jonathan said. "Margaret's aboard this stinking ship because of you, you hell-spawn. There were trumped-up charges against her. You knew. And you didn't so much as raise a finger. Why? Because your filthy profits might be in danger."

The purple face of the gasping McQuaid was slowly turning dark grey.

"Stop, stop. You're killing him." Margaret slapped Jonathan's face. "Please, love, please let him go. They'll - they'll hang you."

Like a discarded shoe, Jonathan flung the spluttering semi-conscious McQuaid to the floor.

"Next time, McQuaid, ..." he said and then glanced up at two lanterns dangling through the hatch opening.

A pair of marines leapt into the hospital. One drove a savage foot into Jonathan's groin and, as he doubled up in agony, the other man crashed a musket butt to his head. Now unconscious, Jonathan was seized by the ankles and dragged feet first up the ladder.

McQuaid, still frantic for breath, stuttered, "Over the side with him. I'll - I'll make it well worth your while."

A protective arm around the sobbing Margaret's waist, Arndell waited, grim-faced, until the guards had left with their captive, then he turned to McQuaid.

"You struggle to buy and foul everybody and everything that comes your way, McQuaid. Get out of my hospital."

"I want my wife."

Arndell's face went deathly pale and a pinkness began to suffuse the side of his neck. His measured tones wholly belied his seething rage.

"See this, McQuaid?"

Arndell plunged a hand inside his jerkin, dragged forth a scalpel and flung aside the leather sheath that concealed its slim and shining blade.

"Get out, get out. Or I won't hesitate. It'll be your testicles - for what they're worth. And I make no promises of careful surgery, you bloody, evil bilge-rat."

Chapter 56

"Phillip'll give your convict the rope," Walton said, as he laid aside the quill pen and contemplated his entry in the ship's log.

"Hang?" Arndell said.

"Not for attempting to garrotte McQuaid. That sod can take his own action."

Arndell's smile was faint.

"If he can find witnesses."

"If, as you say, he can find witnesses. Or buy some, of course. Striking the marine's different. Discipline. Phillip worships discipline. Nothing like a knotted rope round a neck, he says, as a warning to the rest."

Breakfast scarcely touched, Arndell bounced from his chair.

"A liberty boat, Francis. Spare it?"

"What for?"

"I've got to see Arthur Phillip at once."

"A fair distance with only one pair of oars. He's not on shore today. Aboard Sirius. Yeh, take a longboat. A waste of time and breath, though."

Henry Bellamy, also aiming to board HMS Sirius riding at anchor in the mouth of Sydney Cove, had already commandeered the remaining boat.

"Room for one more?" Arndell said as he let go the overside rope and joined the marines captain.

The only reply from Bellamy was an ill-natured grunt.

"No strutting up and down a sandy beach cracking a whip this morning, Henry?"

Bellamy repeated the grunt. This time it was more forceful.

"Not looking all that happy this sunny morning, Henry. Big problems, hm?" Arndell, teasing, went on.

"No."

"What is it then?"

"Stick to your pills and leeches, sawbones. Security of the settlement's my affair."

"Security? Is - er - is the settlement in grave danger?"

Bellamy snorted but stayed silent and, for the remainder of the voyage across the cove, no further word passed between the two men.

As the marines captain clambered aboard Sirius, a guard stood stiffly to attention and saluted. The barrel of a musket, however, barred the way of Thomas Arndell following Bellamy.

"What do you want?" the guard snarled.

"I'd like to see Captain Phillip," Arndell said.

"You'll be lucky."

The muscles of Arndell's face tensed.

"Every second you carry on playing soldiers, the grip of the cholera gets tighter and tighter."

"Who the hell are you?"

"Surgeon from the Friendship."

The marine, a red-faced ox of a man, stood head and shoulders above Arndell. The latter was forced to stand on tiptoe to peer closely at the man's eyes.

"You're not very well," Arndell continued.

"What d'you mean?"

Arndell peered again at the eyes.

"Maybe something, maybe nothing. But I don't much like.... I'll have to discuss with the Governor.

Summon you later possibly. I wouldn't say it's got a hold yet - although...."

The marine led Arndell swiftly down the companionway and pointed to a door.

"Better see Captain Collins first," he said and, tapping on the door, he hurried away.

"In."

David Collins, Arthur Phillip's secretary and the settlement's judge advocate, raised his glance briefly from the array of papers on the desk which rested across his bunk.

He frowned.

"Arndell from the Friendship, isn't it?"

Arndell nodded. Collins, a bluff-faced, dour-looking man, indicated that Arndell should clear enough space at the foot of the bunk for sitting.

"If it's medical matters, you're on the wrong ship. John White's your man and he's aboard the Charlotte, anchored inshore from the Supply."

"It's not medicine, it's discipline," Arndell said wryly.

"Why can't the Friendship handle her own affairs?"

"Extremely delicate now we're in port. The ship's master, Walton, wants the governor to take over, I feel. In any case, Captain Phillip will have a hand in the final decision."

Collin thumped the desk top.

"Come on, come on. What is it?"

"A hanging."

"For what?"

"We think....."

"'We'?"

"Francis Walton and I. We think Arthur Phillip'll demand the rope. A convict striking a marine."

Collins sat back and guffawed.

"You come here when we're completely overwhelmed, landing stores and hundreds of men, directing labour, hunting for timber and water - to discuss one Newgate ruffian? You must be crazy. In any case, Phillip's sick. White's tending him - not that that makes a lot of difference."

Arndell's face broke into a smile.

"Good, good."

"What the hell does that mean - 'good, good'?"

"Precisely that - good, good. Can I see the governor in my capacity as a surgeon?"

Collins' frown was followed by a faint twinkle in his eyes.

"Cunning - but suppose White objects?"

"Well, you said yourself, White isn't making much headway. Glad of a second opinion, maybe."

Collins swept aside the welter of papers and stood up.

"On your own head then. When he's not well, Arthur Phillip tends to throw things around. And his aim's bloody deadly. I'll show you in."

The governor was seated at a desk.

"Assistant surgeon Arndell from the Friendship, sir," Collins said, then at once withdrew.

Arthur Phillip's face was chalk-white but yellow around his eyes which were little more than slits. Arndell glanced at the governor's feet. The flesh of both ankles bulged over the sides of the buckled shoes.

Phillip motioned feebly towards a chair, then picked up a bottle to fill a goblet. His voice was weak and tremulous.

"Problems aboard Friendship, Dr Arndell?"

"Only one, sir. A convict."

Phillip gave a weary shrug.

"They're all problems, Dr Arndell."

"This is a special case, sir."

"How special?"

"The convict struck a marine."

Arthur Phillip sat bolt upright.

"A hanging then?"

"There are special circumstances, sir."

"The ship's master and I would be...."

"Discipline's the deciding factor. More necessary than ever. Tough discipline. Now we're getting everything ashore, our control grows steadily weaker and -" Phillip gasped and pressed an urgent hand to his side "- and no longer can we manacle the convicts to bulkheads or batten them down under hatches. Chain-gangs are poor substitutes. We'll make a special example of this man. Set up gallows overlooking the cove -" Phillip gasped again, pressing a hand even more urgently to his side, "and assemble the rest of the convicts."

Face tight-muscled in pain, Phillip sipped from a goblet and grimaced.

"I - I'd like you to re-consider, sir," Arndell said quietly.

"No justification."

"The convict was brutally provoked."

"Any witnesses?"

"Other convicts."

Phillip's lips curled, he shook his head.

"Midnight ruffians, pickpockets, confidence tricksters, pimps...."

"And scores of wrongly convicted wretches," Arndell said with some heat.

"Maybe, maybe, Dr Arndell. But it's no part of my duties to question magistrates' decisions. I'll not have authority flouted."

Arndell rose reluctantly from his chair.

"Thank you for listening, sir. May I add one more thing?"

Phillip, face again contorted by pain, was testy.

"Yes, yes."

"I'm surprised so many marines survived the voyage from Portsmouth."

"What d'you mean?"

"Forbearance on the part of the convicts. Compared with some of those brutes in the King's uniform, the turnkeys of the Thames prison hulks and Newgate gaol were ministering angels."

The Governor's mouth was firm.

"The marines were not recruited to serve strawberries and cream on June lawns in England, Dr Arndell."

"Nor, I imagine, was it the government's intention to flog and starve and humiliate convicts in addition to plunging them into a life of exile, misery and slavery - sir."

Arthur Phillip with a gesture of hopelessness pointed to the chair which Arndell had vacated.

"Sit down again. I know you take your duties seriously. But there's more to your visit than that."

"I assure you, sir...."

"Your interest in this one convict goes deep. What is it? - Are you and the ruffian...?"

"Good God, no, sir."

"Then what is it?"

"Pettifer's a brilliant apothecary. Hang him and you throw away irreplaceable skills and knowledge."

Phillip changed posture and winced.

"Yes, yes - I recall the man. But discipline, Arndell, discipline."

Arndell viewed Phillip calmly.

"He might well prescribe for your malady, sir."

Phillip gave a sudden gasp and once more his hand jabbed at his side. He took a second draught from a goblet.

"With - with more success than Dr White, possibly, sir," Arndell added softly as he made for the door.

Phillip's features slowly regained their composure.

"Wait."

Arndell's hand was resting on the handle of the door already open.

"To what purpose, sir?"

"Sit down."

"I've said all there is to say, sir. You've already seen the settlement's dire shortage of skills. Barely a handful of carpenters, brickmakers, smiths, farmers, no more than maybe twenty of the convicts capable of signing their own names. If you plan a colony of idleness, ignorance and bitterness, I couldn't imagine a better beginning. If you feel you must, then by all means consign to oblivion the finest brain in the settlement."

Flinging back the door, Arndell left it wide open and hurried along the alleyway.

"Arndell, come back." The surgeon paused and turned. Arthur Phillip was standing in the open doorway of his cabin, holding on to the jamb for support. "Come back - please."

Thomas Arndell, grimacing, followed Phillip slowly into the cabin and closed the door behind him.

"I think you're wrong, Arndell," Phillip said in measured tones.

"I know I'm right, sir."

"Wrong, wrong," Phillip barked. "The convict apothecary's by no means the cleverest man in the settlement. You are. I abominate blackmail nearly as much as sodomy. But I admire your skill in applying it. Your convict apothecary will not hang."

"Oh, thank you, sir."

"But I'll teach him a lesson. We'll go on deck."

Arthur Phillip struggled into his tunic and donned his tricorne hat. From the poop of HMS Sirius, he pointed east across Port Jackson.

"A tiny island, see? Rock and little else, Captain Hunter tells me. Fourteen days and nights there, on not much bread and water, should gripe and pinch your convict's guts enough to teach him never again to strike one of His Majesty's marines, no matter what the provocation."

"Thank you, sir. Thank you."

Phillip made to go below then paused, thumb and forefinger grasping his lip.

"D'you - d'you think your apothecary could produce a suitable potion before Dr White....."

"I'm sure he'd be delighted, sir."

Anxious to tell Margaret about Jonathan's coming exile to the tiny barren island in the middle of Port

Jackson, and also struggling to think of some way to reach Jonathan himself with the news, Thomas Arndell was in no mood for conversation as he and Bellamy rowed back across the calm waters of Sydney Cove to the Friendship.

Occasionally smiling in secret to himself, Bellamy also seemed content with the silence as he contemplated the canvas-wrapped bundle resting across his knees.

Walton was pacing Friendship's deck as Arndell and Bellamy clambered over the ship's rail.

"Where in hell have you two been? China, the Cape? I've been waiting hours for my longboat."

It was clearly not a suitable occasion for Arndell to be seeking permission from Walton to see Jonathan in his prison.

"Sorry, Francis," he said and hurried to the hatch of the hospital.

Smiling hugely, Bellamy said nothing and disappeared below. Bursting through the door of his cabin, the marines captain flung the canvas package on the bunk.

"She hopes it fits," he said in a hoarse whisper. "Try it on. I'll be with you in an hour."

Accustomed to the sight of Charlotte Dudgeon in tattered convict garb or borrowed uniform or even in the nude, Henry Bellamy was wholly unprepared for the sight which greeted him when he went back to his cabin.

He gaped open-mouthed at the convict woman, gowned in black-cherry velvet, bodice holding high and firm the ample bosom, toes of matching morocco shoes peeping from below the hem of the gown. On the bunk lay a cloak, fashioned in similar velvet and lined with silk. There was jewellery too. Pendant ear-rings, necklace and bracelet, set with precious stones of deep crimson, sparkled in the light of the cabin's lanterns.

"The chaplain's wife's been more than generous," Charlotte said.

Bellamy gulped, for the moment tongue-tied.

"As - as indeed Mother Nature was with you."

Charlotte gaily tossed her head and the ear-rings, dancing, sparkled even more.

"When do we leave, Henry?"

"Leave?"

She came close. Bellamy held back.

"For the Frenchies."

"Oh - er - later, later."

Charlotte's full lips pouted.

"I want to go right away."

Bellamy, traced with forefinger from her chin to her breasts.

"Later, later," he breathed between her parted lips.

With impatient hand she thrust his face aside.

"We go now - or you never touch me again."

"It's - it's not all that easy. We need a boat."

"Tell Walton then."

"He's ashore. So are the longboats."

"When's he back?"

"Not until they bring the convicts aboard for the night."

"But it'll be dark."

"Exactly. And it's not the easiest of walks in the night from here to Botany Bay. Woods and swamps, they say. But early tomorrow, before the first convict work party goes ashore we'll....."

Charlotte's response was to drag off her ear-rings and necklace.

"Here, take 'em back."

"Charlotte, my sweet, please be reasonable. I have to make precise plans. Arrange with Walton, not only for the boat, but two seamen to take us ashore."

Bellamy reeled from the unexpected slap on the cheek.

"One more chance, Henry Bellamy. Your last, your very last. Promise for tomorrow." She artfully avoided his attempt to kiss her. "Promise, I said."

"Oh, God, woman, I'd promise you anything," Bellamy murmured as he drew her down with him to the bunk.

"My gown. Do be careful."

"To hell with your gown."

At dawn the following day, two figures in scarlet tunics carrying knapsacks, one much taller than the other, threaded their way between the gum trees south of Sydney Cove.

The early morning air was warm, humid. When the pair finally emerged from the woods to cross a sandy heath where the ground was soft and yielding, Charlotte stopped. She discarded her knapsack and sank, exhausted, on a grassy tussock.

"You sure we're on the right path, Henry?"

Bellamy, who had discarded not only his knapsack but also his tunic, mopped his brow.

"Unless the sun rises in the west, yes."

"You seem displeased, Henry."

Bellamy once more wiped his brow and stared at the sodden handkerchief.

"I thought my marching days were over and now you drag me into this," he growled, pointing across the heath to a further expanse of trees. "It could be evening by the time we reach Botany Bay - only to find your Frenchies have disappeared."

"Well worth the effort, soldier-boy."

"Unless Collins or Phillip happen to be looking for me."

Charlotte kissed him lightly.

"A man who wheedles velvet and jewels from a woman can find a ready explanation for anything," she said, scrambling to her feet. "Now, shall we press on?"

Beyond the woods there lay a swamp and for some distance it became easier and safer for the couple to make their way on hands and knees until at length the terrain began to slope away revealing a sandy beach, then an expanse of sparkling water where two frigates lay at anchor.

Their hands, their faces, their uniforms, their shoes so caked in sand and mud that they were almost unrecognisable, the marines captain and the convict woman embraced each other.

Half an hour later they lay sprawled on a sundrenched sandy beach, eating biscuits and hunks of chicken washed down with copious draughts of fresh water which spouted from a nearby rocky cleft. There they fell asleep and did not stir until late afternoon.

Charlotte dragged herself free of the marines uniform, kicked away the buckled shoes and leather chaps and, straw-coloured hair streaming behind her, she ran naked into the waters of Botany Bay. The shoeless Bellamy, less venturesome, stood at the edge of the lapping tide hungrily watching the naked Charlotte plunging again and again into the limpid waters. At length, body glistening, Charlotte ran splashing back to the beach where she snatched up her knapsack, then sought refuge behind a rock. Bellamy followed.

"No, Henry. Leave me. I want to get ready for meeting our Frenchie friends," she said, pointing in the direction of the frigates, and with only trifling effort her wet, naked body wriggled free of his embrace.

Bellamy frowned and, seeking the far side of the rock, he sat and jabbed viciously into the soft sand with a piece of wood.

Charlotte emerged from behind the rock.

"What d'you think?"

Bellamy gasped. In the afternoon sun Charlotte's flaxen hair bore a tinge of bronze, her hitherto pale face was now aglow. She wore the velvet gown, the morocco shoes, the ear-rings, the necklace and the bracelet once more.

"I - er - I think we'll go back," he murmured not for a single moment taking his eyes off the convict woman.

"Back, Henry?"

"To the Friendship."

"Before paying our respects to the Frenchie gallants? Before tasting their choice wines and brandy? Come, Henry."

Charlotte took firm hold of Bellamy's arm and directed his steps along the beach towards the three-masted French warships, Astrolabe and Boussole.

A longboat was heading for shore. Two men leapt from the bows into the shallows. Bellamy straightened his tunic and donned his hat. Charlotte quickened pace.

Chapter 57

Fettered and manacled, Jonathan was dragged on deck by a marine and, momentarily blinded by brilliant sunshine after days of darkness in the cable locker, he stumbled then collided with the base of the mainmast. Arndell leapt forward and hauled Jonathan to his feet. He pressed a handkerchief to the wound where Jonathan's head had struck the mast.

"I've done everything possible. No hanging, thank God," he whispered urgently.

He turned to Walton, emerging from the barricade opening.

"Hold on to your boat for a while, Francis. A wound like this calls for hospital."

Walton glanced at the injury.

"Hospital for that? Crazy as Phillip. Bloody lucky convict scum. Rocky island instead of the rope. Overside with him. I'll want the longboat back in an hour."

"I'm going with him," Arndell said as he continued to stem the flow of blood.

Walton looked on impatiently.

"Your affair," he snapped and strode away.

While the smith was striking off Jonathan's chains, Arndell hurried below and returned carrying a jar, a phial and a package wrapped in canvas.

An hour later, the boat nosed into a small inlet of the banishment island. Arndell continued to treat Jonathan's wound and the flow of blood had now almost ceased.

The pair leapt ashore and, when they were out of sight and beyond earshot of the seamen waiting in the longboat, the surgeon opened a parcel and said, smiling, "Gifts from Walton, although he doesn't know it. Sorry about the mould on the bread but the chicken's fresh roasted. McQuaid doesn't know either but this is from him."

He held up a bottle of brandy and then from a slim leather case he drew forth a scalpel. "This from me. Less obtrusive than a knife but a hell of a lot more effective."

Jonathan put a hand to his head.

"Thank you, Thomas. I can't think straight...."

Arndell smiled ruefully.

"Stay like that for a fortnight - the easiest way to survive this lot," he said, pointing to their surroundings of bare rock. "I'll come whenever possible. But getting hold of a boat...."

Jonathan silenced him with a wave of the hand.

"Nine months aboard that stinking Friendship, endless days in the filthy blackness of the cable locker - heaven."

"You might just need this in your heaven," Arndell said giving him the jar and the phial.

"What?"

"A balsam for your cracked head and peace for your mind."

"Balsam?"

"Of benzoin and balsam of Peru and hepatic aloes and - well, I'm the one prescribing, not you."

"And the peace?"

"Laudanum, when McQuaid's brandy runs dry."

"Thank you. Tell Margaret...."

"I will."

The pair shook hands warmly and Arndell hurried away to board the waiting longboat.

As Jonathan lay comfortably sprawled on a flat rock, warm in the morning sun, strange fingers touched his cheek. He struggled to his feet and came face to face with a copper-coloured man, naked and filthy, clutching the remains of the bread left by Arndell. Behind him were more copper-coloured men, each bearing a spear and a club.

Once more, the man's fingers went to Jonathan's scarred cheek, then to Jonathan's lips and the gap between his teeth. The stranger's face broke into a broad smile, revealing the absence of one front tooth. At once, his followers burst out laughing and Jonathan now saw that all of them had gaps in their upper jaws.

"Magra, magra," they began to murmur, a word used by the other coloured men in Sydney Cove when they had been helping to haul ashore the nets brimming with fish.

Jonathan shook his head.

"No magra," he said.

"Now-ee?" the leader of the aborigines said and, realising that Jonathan had not understood, with a finger-tip he outlined the shape of a boat on the flat rock and its progress through water.

"Boat," Jonathan said with a laugh.

The yellow-toothed mouth savoured the word again and again.

"Boat, boat, boat."

Jonathan pointed in the direction of Friendship's longboat, at that moment disappearing between the eastern headland and the naval vessel Sirius which rode at anchor in the mouth of the cove.

The wind from the Pacific, gentle and warm since dawn, was now blowing fresh. Jonathan in ragged cotton shirt and threadbare serge breeches shivered.

"Fire?" he said.

The aborigines glanced from one to the other. With his hands, as best he could, Jonathan demonstrated flames and warmth and the leader, taking him by the hand, hurried him to the far side of the island and the sight of five waiting canoes, each with a woman aboard tending a flickering fire.

In the shelter of the high rocks, the men lit a fire of dry seaweed and driftwood, then they took to their canoes and returned with fish impaled on their spears.

Before sitting down to cook and eat the catch, they demanded by signs that Jonathan remove his shirt and breeches so that he sat as naked as they.

It was evening when the aborigines finally left Jonathan, but not before gathering a further supply of fuel for the fire.

"Parrebuga," the head man said, pointing to the east and making a wide semi-circle with his arm.

"Parrebuga? Tomorrow?" Jonathan said.

When the aborigines visited Jonathan next morning, they were led by another man who by signs indicated that the leader of the previous day was suffering from stomach pains and had remained aboard his canoe. Grasping the phial of laudanum, Jonathan, followed by the man, scrambled over rocks to the inlet where the canoe was lying.

There he found the sick man, hunched in its bows, one hand pressed to his distended stomach, the other clutching a hollowed-out piece of wood containing a syrup similar to pine-tree sap except that it was red.

Jonathan dipped a cautious finger into the fluid and tasted. In the air, he drew a picture of a tall tree. The man nodded. Jonathan mixed laudanum with the syrup and put it to the lips of the aborigine.

On his haunches in the stern of the canoe, Jonathan waited until the man had fallen into a drugged sleep, then he scrambled back to his rocky shelter.

Before dawn next day, Jonathan awoke to find himself surrounded by aborigines once more and, in spite of his protestations, he was lifted bodily, taken to a canoe and paddled swiftly across Port Jackson to a deserted bay.

There he was bundled ashore and led across a narrow spit of sand to the entrance of a cave. He paused and turned. A whimper escaped from the depths of the cave and immediately a score of hands sent him stumbling headlong into the darkness.

He retched at the stench and, hand firmly clamped over his nose and mouth, he blundered back, motioning the aborigines to bring the sick man into the daylight. Three of the men dived into the cave and two of them emerged, carrying a naked young woman.

Deep copper-coloured and thick-lipped like the men, she was covered in evil-smelling grease. One side of her face was so savagely swollen that her eye was almost totally hidden.

Jonathan edged gingerly forward. In the middle of the girl's cheek the tip of a fish-bone projected. Jonathan touched it lightly and the girl screamed.

Then the third aborigine stepped out of the cave holding aloft a partly-consumed fish. The expression on his face made it clear that it was a variety of fish which must never be eaten and, to emphasise this, he began to belabour the sick girl's head with the creature.

Jonathan glanced quickly over his shoulder. Standing firm on their right legs, their left legs bent so that the soles of their feet pressed hard against their right knees, the men had formed a tight, expectant circle on the sand around him and the prostrate girl.

Ripping away part of his ragged shirt-sleeve, Jonathan soaked it in laudanum and, in spite of the girl's frantic screams, he cleansed as best he could the swollen cheek of its grime and foul-smelling grease.

Motioning the onlookers to take firm hold of the girl's head and arms and legs, he made swift cross-incisions with Arndell's scalpel. Yellow pus at once spurted wide over the sand. He plunged fingertips deep into the raw flesh and dragged free the offending fish-bone. He wiped clean the wounded cheek with a further strip of his shirt-sleeve and pressed the phial of laudanum to the lips of his sobbing patient.

Chapter 58

Thomas Arndell made straight for the hospital.

"Is he free?" Margaret said, seizing Arndell's arm as he clambered down the ladder.

"Almost," Arndell said.

"Almost?"

"A fortnight's exile."

"Where?"

"A rocky islet beyond the mouth of the cove. Don't worry. Fortunate it all happened. A chance to tell Phillip about him"

"But he'll starve."

"No, no. I'll be taking food."

"How?"

"Jonathan has a cut on his head and wounds must be tended by a surgeon."

Margaret took Arndell's face between her hands and her lips lightly touched his forehead.

"Bless you, Thomas, bless you," she said.

* * * * *

The hammering on the door of Arndell's cabin grew increasingly impatient.

"Arndell.!

Once more, the surgeon buried his head even deeper in the bedclothes.

"Arndell."

"Oh, go to hell."

"Arndell, you idle sod, the Governor."

"I said 'Go to hell'"

"He's waiting."

Wearily, Arndell rolled out of his bunk and dragged wide the door. Walton stood in the alleyway.

"Phillip wants you."

"Why?"

"How the hell should I know? There's a boat alongside," Walton snapped and hurried away.

John Hunter, commander of Sirius, David Collins, the settlement's judge-advocate, and John White, its surgeon-general, were restlessly pacing the quarter deck as Arndell boarded the naval vessel.

White leapt down to greet him. "The governor - I've been battling all night."

"Kidneys?" Arndell said.

"Without doubt. But diagnosis one thing, treatment another," White said wryly. "Will you look at him?"

"I'd feel more competent with breakfast inside me."

"Later, later," White said testily, steering Thomas Arndell to the governor's cabin.

A muffled groan acknowledged John White's diffident knock. He opened the door and, beckoning Arndell to follow, he went inside.

"Dr Arndell, sir," he said to Phillip, lying in his bunk, covered in blankets.

"Show me where the pain is, sir," Arndell said, dragging aside the bedding.

Phillip winced as he rolled on to his stomach and placed a hand immediately below his ribs, between his side and backbone.

"It's there."

"Taking plenty of fluids, sir?"

"Yes."

"The pain constant?"

"Sometimes worse than others."

Arndell turned to White.

"A stone, you think?" he said quietly.

"Without doubt."

"Extremely flattering - but why call on me?"

"Suggestions about medicine."

Arndell glanced briefly at Phillip.

"You've tried the obvious?"

"Dyers' madder, parsley piert, chervil, even rupture-wort."

There was more than a hint of whimsy in Thomas Arndell's shake of the head.

"I know nothing better," he said then, raising his voice, he went on, "If, though, we could get hold of Pettifer...." He looked to Arthur Phillip, but from the recumbent figure there was no evident response.

White frowned.

"Pettifer, Pettifer. Ah, yes. But...."

"But what?" Arndell said.

White slowly shook his head.

"A convict treating the Governor?"

Arndell eyed the chief surgeon askance.

"You were confident enough taking him ashore to buy medicines."

"Vastly different," White said. "Imagine the whispers end to end of the fleet. A convicted felon arranging medicine for the governor."

Arndell pursed his lips.

"Let Captain Phillip decide. It's his body after all."

"There's Ross, there's Collins, to be consulted," White said.

"Well, if saving face," Arndell said, "is more important than saving the governor of New South Wales...."

"Oh, get your convict here," White said testily.

"Easier said than done, Dr White. Pettifer was sent to an island out there."

"Who sent him?"

Arndell silently pointed to the sleeping Arthur Phillip.

"Oh, hell, it would have to be. First things first though. Get him here at once."

Phillip, who had been dozing, began to writhe. Raising the governor's head, John White administered medicine from a goblet.

"What is it?" Arndell said.

"A little red bearberry in a lot of Rio wine. Very soothing."

"I'd heard bearberry was marvellous for tanning leather or dyeing woollens," Arndell said caustically. "I'm extremely interested to know it soothes agonised bellies. The sooner we get hold of my apothecary, the better."

White hard on his heels, Thomas Arndell leapt from the boat and clambered up an escarpment to the circle of rocks in the middle of the banishment island

"Enough gut-pinching?" he shouted.

Apart from a lone seabird, battling with a hunk of mouldy bread, the place was deserted. Arndell knelt to touch the dead embers of a fire.

"It looks as though you'll have to continue the red bearberry treatment," he said to White as he scanned the rocky islet and the surrounding waters.

"What d'you imagine happened?"

Arndell shook his head.

"No boat, long swim. Better ask the sharks, Dr White," he said abruptly, turning in the direction of the longboat.

Sharper eyes than those of Arndell or White might have discerned a wisp of smoke rising from a fire on the edge of a bay eastward of Sydney Cove.

Inside a cave overlooking the bay, a girl with a cross-shaped wound on her cheek lay asleep. At the mouth of the cave, a bent and wrinkled crone sat on guard, her tiny brown eyes beneath beetling brows rarely shifting from Jonathan, as he carefully turned a crayfish over and over on the smoky fire.

With little relish, Jonathan quickly consumed the crayfish then he got up and strolled towards the cave mouth.

The old woman, shaking her head and muttering, barred his way. In dumb show Jonathan pointed to her cheek and then into the cave, but the crone continued to shake her head.

"The girl, her cheek, you wizened old stick."

The woman opened wide her toothless mouth and, waving frantic arms, she screeched.

The girl, roused from her drugged sleep by the commotion outside, appeared at the mouth of the cave. She leapt at the crone, seized and bit her ankle. With a squeal the old woman hobbled away.

Grimacing at the smell of greasy, grime-encrusted skin, Jonathan examined the girl's cheek. The swelling had subsided and the girl did not flinch as his fingers explored the surrounding flesh.

She raised a filthy hand to trace the scar on Jonathan's cheek. Gently he thrust her aside.

"Even bathed and perfumed, wench, I couldn't fancy you," he said with a laugh.

The girl's face broke into a smile which, as the pain of the knitting flesh seized her, was gone in an instant.

Jonathan drew out his phial of laudanum and pressed it to the ugly lips.

"I hope it's no love philtre, my beauty," he said and the girl managed to muster a further brief smile.

* * * * *

As the longboat made for Sirius, Thomas Arndell glanced back at Pinchgut Island.

"I - I wonder?" he murmured.

"You wonder what?" White said.

"If the Indians have captured him. And if the marines would launch a search."

"For one missing convict?" White said icily.

"For the only man in the fleet who is likely to find Governor Phillip some relief," Arndell said.

Chapter 59

Roast chicken in choicest wine sauces, pastries with fresh cream from cows kept aboard Astrolabe, bananas from Samoa and sweetmeats from Paris were only a small part of the hospitality afforded by Count Jean-Francois de Galaup de la Perouse to his visitors from Sydney Cove.

Rarely had Henry Bellamy tasted such exquisite brandies, scarcely ever had he reclined in chairs of such comfort and splendour.

It was breaking dawn when Bellamy, deep in drunken stupor, was gently lowered over the side of the French frigate and ferried to the beach on the northern shore of Botany Bay.

He failed to stir even when two French sailors carried him over the sand and laid him down beside the rock where Charlotte Dudgeon had changed into her velvet gown the previous afternoon. They made a pillow for him from a marine's discarded uniform and they left a flask of water, a roast chicken wrapped in linen and two bottles of brandy. Between the bottles, was wedged a sheet of paper.

The sun was riding high when at last Bellamy opened his eyes. His hand struck one of the bottles and he sat up. He took the water flask and drank deep, then he glimpsed the sheet of paper. The sunlight dazzled him. He eased himself into the shade of the rock and there, haltingly, he read aloud.

'Count de la Perouse promises me silks and satins and fine brocades, all far more becoming than convict tatters, ill-fitting marine's uniform and a solitary velvet gown, methinks. So, please don't pursue me. Your ever grateful C.D.'

Hands groping up the face of the rock, Bellamy scrambled to his feet. Swaying, he shaded his eyes to peer in the direction of the French frigates.

"Bloody, Frenchies," he muttered and, slumping to his knees in the sand, he seized a brandy bottle. He dragged free the cork and gulped madly. "Bloody, bloody Frenchies."

It was midnight when Bellamy, grasping a brandy bottle, reached the perimeter of the settlement and blundered into one of his marines on sentry duty.

"Halt."

The man's bayonet jabbed savagely into Bellamy's mud-bespattered tunic. Seizing the naked blade, he sent the guard staggering against a tree.

"Whore-spawn," he snarled "get me a boat to Friendship."

Francis Walton and William Faddy were deep in conversation when Bellamy stumbled into the cuddy at midday.

"You wake up sometimes, then," Walton said. "We've been hammering on your door loud enough to rouse the dead. Surprised your convict whore didn't hear, even if you didn't."

"Any food?" Bellamy demanded.

"For her?"

"For me."

"Why not her?"

"Gone."

"Where?"

"Dunno."

"Good - missing convicts in fashion," Walton said cynically.

Bellamy looked to Faddy.

"What's he babbling about?"

"There's a man missing, sir."

"A convict?"

"Yes, sir."

"Why worry? Haven't we more than enough?"

"Captain Phillip's wanting this particular one," Faddy said sheepishly. "He insisted on a search party."

Bellamy flopped on a chair.

"My marines?"

Faddy nervously nodded.

"I'm not having it. Wasting time and energy hunting for lost pickpockets and footpads. Did you authorise?"

"Yes, sir."

"He was ordered to," Walton snapped. "If you hadn't disappeared you'd've had to do the same. Bloody absurd. Four surgeons - and none of 'em can cure Phillip's bellyache. So they scream for the pills-and-potions con."

"Recall my men," Bellamy barked.

Faddy leapt at once to his feet.

"Calm yourself, Henry," Walton said. "If your marines come across him in all that salt water, swamp, rocks and sand, it'll be a feather in your cap. Take my advice - keep your mouth shut."

Faddy remained nervously at attention.

"Recall them, sir?"

"No, no," Bellamy said irritably. "Take yourself for a walk."

When the door closed behind Faddy, Walton said, "Sense at last. That lad deserves promotion for the cover-up work he's been doing for you in the last couple of days."

"Well, I went to....."

"Look. Henry. I don't want to know - but if you ever take a boat from my ship again without permission, I'll have you for theft. So.... she didn't come back with you, hm?"

"Who?"

"Your convict whore."

Bellamy buried his head in his hands and it was minutes before he spoke.

"No whore, Francis, no whore.... God, but I'm going through hell."

* * * * *

Alone with Margaret in the hospital, Turnbull McQuaid, arms folded, surveyed his new wife icily.

"You'll have to get accustomed to the idea," he said.

Her expression was stony, resolute.

"Not yet."

He seized her by the elbows.

"Listen, I didn't travel half-way round the world to have my plans upset by you or anybody else. Thoughts of sharing my bedchamber with you makes me want to vomit. But if it guarantees so-called respectability, by God, I'm prepared to suffer it."

Margaret struggled free.

"Why, why me? Surely there were other women?"

"With a father who runs the sort of chandlery your father runs?"

Margaret stared at him, incredulous.

"You - you mean you've put up with months and months of this rat-infested, floating hell, you seek a woman's body that sickens you....."

"To gain respectability and get my hands on that Wapping chandlery business - yes, yes."

"And it's worth all that to you?"

"Every sea-sodden mile, every whiff of your body, every maggot in the pork - because it spells power, woman, power. Your father's trade combined with mine - in five years, a monopoly nobody in Europe could ever assail."

McQuaid's eyes were wide. He pointed to the larboard bulwark,

"Out there, vast new lands for development. Soon, a hundred ships of mine, fetching and carrying. A trade empire second to none. And then even King George himself wouldn't dare spit on me."

Determinedly Margaret shook her head.

"My father would never, never hand over his business."

"Ask him, if ever you see him again - but by the way you react any family reunion seems very much in doubt. Ask him about the night he came sneaking to my house in Well Close Square. Ask him what he was prepared to do for you then."

"I can't believe....."

"Your father's very words - 'I'll pay to my very last penny'. How much more willing he'd be now, parting with his last penny to his new son-in-law."

"I-I'd never, never let him," Margaret shrieked.

McQuaid smiled tolerantly.

"But, if he accepted the idea that his grandchild...."

"What grandchild? Two things are certain. I carry no child - and I'll never, never carry yours."

"I don't think you fully understand, woman. I'd offer you to some of my - er, my more masculine acquaintances."

"God, no."

"But, within reason, I'd accept any preferences you may have, of course."

"I'd kill myself first."

"No, you would not. Now prepare for moving ashore in a day or two."

"I'm staying here."

"As soon as there's a suitable habitation in the settlement, we go ashore - together."

Margaret made a frantic dive for the ladder but McQuaid seized her by the hair and hauled her back.

"Where d'you think you're going?"

"To Francis Walton."

"Why?"

"Permission to stay on board."

"Refused."

"Nothing to do with you. You're not the ship's master."

"No - part-owner."

"There's little you could do."

"Except cancel Walton's contract."

"But the voyage is over."

"Surely there's honour between owners and masters - you wouldn't dare."

McQuaid stepped aside and pointed to the ladder.

"Try me. Go see Walton."

Margaret hesitated.

"No," she said slowly. "No, I'll come ashore with you - on one condition."

"Well?"

"There'll be a hospital tent?"

"One of Phillip's priorities."

"I'll tend the sick on shore."

"Oh, no."

"I've tended them on board, I can surely tend them ashore."

"Fool. You cringe at the thought of my attentions. You'd do well to ponder on the attentions of drunken marines and seamen - and, no doubt, the occasional convict."

"There was rarely trouble aboard Friendship - except with you."

"Only because of shipboard discipline, deck barricades, strong bulkheads, convicts battened down, the wildest of 'em in irons. But, on shore, thirteen hundred men separated from two hundred women by rotting canvas. In a month, the gleets and sores more rife than the scrofula and the scurvy. If you survived the attentions, you'd never survive the tending."

* * * * *

To the west lay a mountain range, one moment indigo and deep violet, and the next, as the sun sank behind it, an impenetrable coal-black.

Jonathan inched closer to the fire near the cave's mouth and listened. Inside his patient was snoring peacefully. Stabbing fingers to his mouth, he indicated to the crone, who earlier had crept back, that he was hungry.

She disappeared into the cave, then emerged to offer him a piece of curved bark containing a ball of squirming maggots. Taking one of the tiny, white creatures, she thrust it between his lips. He recoiled at the smell of her filthy hands but he took the squirming maggot and impaling it on the tip of his scalpel he held it close to hot embers then cautiously began to chew the brown, frizzled body.

The old woman, eyes wide, clapped her hands. She seized the scalpel and following Jonathan's example she gurgled with delight as her toothless gums masticated the roasted creature. Not until she had consumed the rest of the maggots did she hand back the scalpel and resume her cave-mouth vigil.

The sun was already high when a feather-like touch on his cheek roused Jonathan. The crone had gone. The aboriginal girl leaning over him was gently fondling his scar but, the moment he stirred, she darted back to the entrance of the cave. He sat up and, smiling, beckoned her. Briefly she was hesitant, then, as she began to creep nervously back, a crude spear landed quivering in the sand, inches ahead of her.

A party of shrieking aborigines, brandishing clubs, descended on the pair. At once the girl was a virago, scratching, spitting, butting the men. One of them wrenched the spear from the ground. She snatched it from him, broke it across her knee and tossed it aside.

"Whurra-whutta, whurra-whutta," she screeched at him and his gesticulating companions.

The men, huddled in a tight circle, chattered and gesticulated excitedly, then seemingly they decided that the girl, far from being anxious to escape from the thrall of this huge and strange creature with skin like a white maggot, was in fact frantic to be alone with him once more.

The man who had flung the spear advanced with exaggerated mincing tread, on feet splayed like those of a camel and, seizing the girl by the shoulders, he hauled her upright and thrust her into Jonathan's arms. Then he and his companions, yelling derisively at the couple, disappeared over the rising rocky land behind the cave.

Although Jonathan was a heavy man, the aboriginal girl displayed no great difficulty in dragging him across the soft sand and into the cave.

From beneath lowered lids, she eyed him with an expression of utter rapture. She smiled slowly, revealing firm but dingy yellow teeth. Mouth now wide open, she cupped her bare breasts, then slid her hands down her body to her groin.

"No," Jonathan said, holding himself rigid. "No."

She took his hands and drew them to her thighs. Repeatedly, her lips closed and parted, her brown eyes beseeched him and, whimpering in ecstasy, she forced his unwilling fingers deep inside her. Then Jonathan landed spreadeagled across the cave mouth. The girl, screaming, fled.

"On your feet, convict."

A marine seized Jonathan by the hair and, helped by another, dragged him out of the cave.

Chapter 60

Face pallid and drawn, shoulders hunched, yet resplendent in full dress uniform, Arthur Phillip had been pacing the deck of HMS Sirius in silence for an hour when he suddenly announced, "A longboat. I shall be ashore at midday."

John Hunter, second-captain of the warship, and John White, chief surgeon of the fleet, exchanged covert glances.

"My medical instructions...." White began.

"Your medical <u>advice</u>, Dr White...." Phillip swiftly interrupted.

"My medical advice, sir, was 'stay in your cot for three more days'."

Phillip glared.

"I considered the advice and decided to reject it. My house at the head of the cove is ready for occupation."

Hunter slowly shook his head

"But there's mounting danger to your health, Arthur," he said, anxiety in his voice. "The past months have been nothing but worry, pressure. You can't endure much more."

"I'm waiting," Phillip said. "And don't shrug those shoulders again, John Hunter - I find it extremely irritating,"

Contemptuously brushing aside assistance, Phillip clambered overside and leapt into the waiting longboat.

It was a day of leaden skies, the threat of imminent thunderstorms hung on the still air.

At the head of the cove, sweating and cursing, the scrawny convicts chained together in teams of six, battled with felled gum trees whose size and weight would have presented a challenge to a dozen circus strongmen.

On the beach, Phillip paused to mop his brow.

"When do the convicts eat?" he said to Andrew Willer, provisions commissary.

"The end of the day, I suppose, sir."

"Supposition won't sustain men who labour like farm- horses," Phillip said, pointing to a convict team desperately struggling with a forty-foot gum tree. "They must have food at midday."

Miller shook his head dubiously.

"I'm afraid, sir, fed before evening they'd become idle and refuse to work."

"Then the overseers must use whips."

"Impossible, sir. The overseers are convicts themselves. They'd never whip one of their own kind."

"Instruct the guards, then."

"If you remember, sir," Miller said wryly, "Major Ross insisted marines were protectors of the settlement not turnkeys."

Arthur Phillip grunted his displeasure and hastened towards a clearing where his canvas house had been erected earlier in the day. Here and there, convicts were listlessly grubbing out tree stumps.

Phillip turned to Miller and rasped, "To be fed at noon."

"Not easy, sir. We keep scarcely any food ashore."

"For what reason?"

"Theft, sir. Store tents aren't secure enough."

"Then sawyers will erect gallows this afternoon. Tomorrow, all convicts will muster ashore and I'll explain a handful of stolen rice means the rope. Now - go find some food for the wretched creatures."

A man in a tricorne hat, heavily-brocaded tailcoat, light buckskin breeches and gold-buckled shoes, picked his way with infinite care over the rough ground towards Phillip. He was followed by a bonneted woman of pale, delicate features and rich auburn hair.

"Governor Phillip," Turnbull McQuaid said, with an exaggerated flourish of his tricorne hat, "I beg you to meet my wife."

Studiously avoiding McQuaid, Phillip smiled at Margaret and held out a hand, then moved on.

Apart from Andrew Miller, the other members of Phillip's landing party had gone their separate ways after stepping ashore, but they had now begun to gather in the governor's canvas house.

Phillip took the sleeve of David Collins, his judge-advocate, and whispered, "Did you see McQuaid's wife?"

"Yes, briefly."

"She and McQuaid - extraordinary."

"But you knew, sir, surely?"

"Oh, I vaguely recall approving a marriage to some convict woman or other aboard the Friendship. A few days out from the Cape, I think. Didn't give it a second thought. But McQuaid and a beautiful woman like that. Can't for the life of me understand how she...."

The approach of Andrew Miller brought the whispered conversation to a sudden halt.

"I've arranged to land more food, sir," Miller saluted briskly. "May I say something?"

"You mean 'say something more'."

"Yes, sir."

"Well?"

"They're saying....."

"Who?"

"The marines, sir."

"What are they saying?"

"All work in the settlement ceases from today for a week at least."

"Why?"

"Food at noon today and then, tomorrow, the women convicts are being landed."

"So?"

"More distraction from work."

A blandness crept across Phillip's pale face.

"Are you a religious man, Andrew Miller?"

"Officially, yes, sir."

"Then you'll know it's unwise to muzzle the ox that treads out the corn."

"But the women, sir. It'll be all hell let loose."

Arthur Phillip's face contorted with pain and, ramming a hand to the small of his back, he stumbled to a chair where Collins helped him out of his tunic.

"I hadn't realised you were allowing the women ashore so soon," Collins said.

Phillip, hand still to his back, groaned.

"The sooner I face up to the problem, the sooner I get the measure of it," he said. He beckoned to Miller, "My desk in that corner, dining table and chairs over there. My cot here. Oh, and a flag, don't forget."

Miller saluted.

"By tomorrow evening, sir."

"By this afternoon."

John White, the surgeon, who had been prospecting possible sites for a hospital tent on the west side of the cove, burst through the flap which served as a door to Phillip's canvas house. Drenched by the rain, he dragged off his tricorne hat. Water from its brim sluiced to the rocky floor.

He wiped his eyes and said, "Madness to think of staying ashore in this, Arthur Phillip. It'll kill....."

A deafening thunderclap drowned the rest of White's words.

"I'm waiting," Phillip said.

"Look at that." White pointed to rain trickling down the canvas walls. "You're not strong enough to withstand conditions like this."

Arthur Phillip lurched to his feet.

"My place is in the settlement. I'm staying ashore."

"I beg you, Arthur. It's - it's suicidal."

Phillip's eye was on one of a score of rivulets coursing down a wall. "And did you hit on a possible site for the hospital?" he said, turning to the surgeon.

"Yes."

"Put your hat on and we'll inspect."

"But - but it's pouring down, Arthur."

"Precisely why I said 'Put your hat on'."

* * * * *

Turnbull McQuaid peered through the flap of a store tent where he and Margaret had sought shelter from the storm. There was now only the occasional and distant grumble of thunder, the rain had ceased and the clearing, dust-dry an hour earlier, had now become a steaming quagmire.

McQuaid glanced at his gold-buckled shoes and white silk stockings.

"Wet they'll get, but we must go," he said ruefully.

"Through the mud?" Margaret said.

"I'm not staying here," McQuaid rasped.

She pointed to sacks and boxes piled high in the middle of the tent.

"We're not likely to run short of food."

"We're going."

"Madness."

Together they peered through the opening. The convicts, who had stumbled back to the clearing from the giant gums where they had been crouching in a desperate attempt to shelter from the deluge, were now resuming their labours. Nearby, three gangs of them, slithering and cursing, battled to drag one enormous trunk over rocks and mud to the sawpits established close to the mouth of the stream.

All of a sudden, the men stopped and began to jeer. Margaret craned forward. Over the rise beyond the governor's marquee, a man was being dragged and frogmarched by two marines in the direction of a guard tent, pitched close by the sawpits.

The captive, barefoot and naked to the waist, stumbled. The marines released their hold and the wretched man collapsed face down in the yellow mud.

Margaret, swiftly gathering up her skirts, plunged across the quagmire. She dropped to her knees and cradled the captive's head on her lap. The two marines stood by and laughed. The watching convicts continued to jeer.

"Get up, woman, get up," McQuaid snarled and, seizing her shoulder, he dragged her aside.

"Margaret," the captive muttered, then a marine's foot drove him into the mud once more. The two marines hauled their captive to his feet and propelled him towards the guard tent.

Chapter 61

When there was no response to his knock on the door of Henry Bellamy's cabin, Arndell pushed it open. The smell of spirits lay heavy in the atmosphere of the tiny cabin.

"Henry."

A grunt escaped from the huddle of blankets.

Arndell drew aside the coverings to reveal Bellamy, his back to the surgeon, hands pressed hard over his ears.

"Go to hell."

Arndell lightly tapped Bellamy's bare shoulder.

"Did your men find the apothecary?"

"Dunno."

"Can you find out?"

"If I go ashore, yes."

"Please go, then. If your men've found him, it'll sweeten Phillip's temper."

"To hell with you and Phillip as well.""

"Oh, come on, Henry. Phillip's storming up and down, demanding this, ordering that. He's insisting on everybody - marines, sailors, settlers and convicts - mustered early tomorrow morning. Better get yourself ashore and make plans."

Bellamy turned reluctantly and opened one eye.

"Hand me that bottle."

Arndell leaned over the bunk to lift a bottle from a shelf and his feet tangled with a garment on the floor. He handed the bottle to Bellamy and picked up a woman's skirt.

"Where is she, Henry?"

Bellamy gulped at the bottle.

"If any other sod asks that again," he said thickly, wiping his lips with the back of his hand, "I'll stick 'em."

And he mimed the act of thrusting a dagger deep into the pit of Arndell's stomach.

"Well, how can I help?"

"Get her back from the Frenchies."

"Escaped to them, has she?"

Bellamy hurled the empty bottle at the bulkhead.

"Escaped? I'm a bloody fool, I took her. Yes, I took her." Bellamy gulped. "Took her, handed her over, gowned and perfumed, to that powdered and periwigged Perouse."

"Intentionally?"

"No, you fool. The alternative for her was this - this rat-box. He's offering Parisian silks and satins and furs."

Sitting up, Bellamy buried his face in his hands.

"There's maybe one way of getting her back. A message to the Frenchies. Tell 'em she's an escaped convict, a murderer. Phillip might help."

Bellamy swung his legs to the floor and struggled into his breeches.

"What's that to de la Perouse? What's Arthur Phillip to a French count? Head of a mob of pickpockets, thieves and forgers. If he has any taste for Charlotte and, by God, from what I saw, he couldn't get her to his cabin fast enough -" Again, Bellamy buried his face in his hands. "He'll hide her away 'til the frigates set sail. I daren't think..."

"I'm truly sorry, Henry."

Bellamy thrust his arms into the sleeves of his tunic. His eyes were red and wild and he was so unsteady that Arndell had to support him.

"I'm - I'm going, Arndell," he said with a sob, "I'm going."

The surgeon helped to button and smooth the red tunic, then he straightened the marines captain's hair.

Arndell's voice was gentle, persuasive.

"If you'll help me, I'll help <u>you</u>, Henry."

Bellamy regarded the surgeon dully.

"You're - you're patronising me, leechman. You think I'm - I'm drunk."

"No, Henry. If I thought you were drunk, I wouldn't be asking you, would I? When the time's ripe, I'll help, I promise - if you'll help me right away."

Bellamy thrust his feet into his shoes, fumbled for the door-handle and stepped into the alleyway. Arndell followed and, quickly ramming a hat over the iron-grey hair, he steered the captain to Friendship's deck. As he was about to help him overside, he said urgently, "You will do something for me, won't you, Henry?"

Bellamy grunted non-committally.

"I want - I must see the convict apothecary," Arndell said.

When the longboat reached the shore, the oarsmen had to carry Bellamy to a guard tent, pitched midway between the governor's marquee and the smithy. A marine on duty outside the tent saluted the tottering Bellamy.

"Your uniform, a bloody disgrace," Bellamy said thickly, stabbing a finger at the marine's tunic.

"Yesterday's mud, sir, after the hunt for a convict."

Arndell brushed Bellamy aside.

"Where is he?"

"Over there."

"Show me."

Bellamy nodded.

"Yes, show him, show him."

The man led Arndell to some tree trunks lying close together and dragged one of them aside, revealing a sawpit. Arndell dropped to his knees and peered into the depths. At once he leapt into the pit and uncovered a body huddled deep in woodchips. He thrust his hands into the armpits and dragged the discovery, a man, to his feet.

"Quick, help me lift him."

Arndell pushing from below, the marine hauling from above, Jonathan was brought to the surface.

"Get me water," Arndell said, scrambling out of the pit.

The marine made no move.

"Henry."

Bellamy stumbled across the clearing.

"What?"

"Order him to get food, water and dry clothes."

Bellamy's brow puckered.

"Henry, d'you hear?"

The marines captain nodded stupidly.

"Don't just nod your head. Order food, water, clothes, for God's sake," Arndell said.

Bellamy lunged at the marine.

"Get 'em, get 'em," he said thickly.

"All night in mud and sawdust - a wonder he's still alive."

Bellamy sneered drunkenly.

"Hundreds more convicts, hundreds."

"But only one apothecary. John White's searching. Phillip's in desperate need of the man."

Arndell glanced up from tending Jonathan and glimpsed Bellamy weaving his way towards the beach and the longboat.

"Hie, Henry," he bellowed.

The marines captain paused and turned his head.

"What?"

"Take him back to Friendship?"

Bellamy pondered.

"Does he smell?" he shouted.

"Of mud and wood shavings, yes."

Bellamy pointed uncertainly towards the boat.

"Bring him."

Arndell slung Jonathan over his shoulder and stumbled with him to the longboat.

Later, Bellamy and Arndell met in the cuddy. Because all the marines and crew had gone ashore to hear the Governor's proclamation, Friendship was deserted.

Spruce in fresh uniform, the marines captain now appeared to be sober.

"Where's your convict?"

"Hospital. Fed and washed. I'm grateful to you, Henry, very grateful. Hadn't you better go ashore and listen to Phillip's harangue, drink his porter?"

Bellamy's fingers gave an extra gleam to an already sparkling button of his uniform.

"D'you imagine I cleaned up to drink Phillip's bilge-water?" Bellamy gave a broad wink. "I've a mind to taste de la Perouse's best brandy."

"A long, long march. You'll be in need of more than brandy. I hope it's all worthwhile. Now, I'll gladly get Phillip's help...."

Bellamy shook his head.

"I'll go it alone," he said, moving to the cuddy door. "If I'm not back in a day or two, Phillip can send a search party."

Chapter 62

Arthur Phillip peeped behind the arras which curtained off one end of McQuaid's tent and glimpsed a four-poster bed, sumptuous in embroidered woollens and silks. At the foot of the four-poster there was a cot similar to Phillip's own austere bed.

"Three sleepers?" Phillip said. "I didn't imagine newlyweds required help or supervision."

"Lest one of us takes ill," McQuaid said quickly and, closing the curtains, he steered the governor towards a gilded side-table laden with bottles and silver goblets.

"Your husband came from England well-prepared, Mrs McQuaid," Phillip said to Margaret.

McQuaid laughed.

"I see no reason for depriving myself, Governor," he said as he motioned Arthur Phillip to a chair. "Brandy?"

"I've already overstepped the mark, thank you," Phillip said, shaking his head.

"Oh, come, sir. Your first visit to my new abode. A light French wine,perhaps?"

"I said, thank you, no." Phillip turned to Margaret. "Would you think me impertinent if I asked a question - of a personal nature?"

Margaret eyed the governor blandly.

"Convicts are not permitted to think, Captain Phillip."

"Mrs McQuaid, please...."

"I know what you're going to ask. Why was I flung into the Friendship's 'tween decks."

"Well, yes."

"Then I'll tell you."

Swiftly McQuaid intervened.

"You'll understand, sir, my wife's somewhat - er - sensitive."

Margaret glanced irritably at McQuaid.

"Sensitive about being a convict, my husband means. He's wrong, of course. Sensitive about false convictions, that's all."

"Oh, well, I have no records," Phillip said lamely.

"No records?" McQuaid said.

"Like so much else, they weren't shipped." Phillip moved his chair closer to Margaret's chair. "So - so, if I assumed your wife was sentenced to seven years' transportation, I could arrange for immediate pardon."

Margaret, stately in a gown of emerald green velvet, rose to her feet.

"A pardon, Captain Phillip? Pardon for what? For some crime I didn't commit?"

Nervously, McQuaid cleared his throat.

"A - a mere legal term, my dear. The governor must assume the decision of the magistrates was correct."

Arthur Phillip's hand settled lightly on the sleeve of Margaret's gown. McQuaid saw. He smiled covertly. And, when Margaret quickly withdrew her arm, a deep scowl at once seized his features.

"I apologise, Mrs McQuaid," Phillip said. "Distressing for you, painful and infinitely embarrassing to myself."

"'Distress' is hardly the right word, Captain Phillip," Margaret said icily. "'Pardon' as you term it would be arrant nonsense. I'd accept nothing less than abject apology."

Phillip sat open-mouthed,

"Apology?"

Face like thunder, McQuaid said swiftly, "I think you've said quite enough, my dear."

"Quiet, Turnbull. Why make an exception of me, Arthur Phillip, when scores of innocent folk out there're struggling, sweating and dying, poverty their only crime? It's little they ask for. Only a return to an existence in London's filthy alleyways. Where at least they were never driven to eating maggots and fern roots for survival."

McQuaid seized his wife's wrist.

"Governor Phillip," he said, "my wife has suffered considerably. I beg you excuse....."

"I need no excusing," Margaret said, roughly pushing aside McQuaid's hand.

"I'm - I'm sorry, Mrs....." Phillip began, then his face contorted in agony. He pressed a hand to his side. "See - see me to my tent. Find White, Arndell - please, please."

* * * * *

"Pettifer!" Arndell shook Jonathan. "A chance to show your mettle."

Jonathan stirred in his hospital bunk.

"What?"

"Quick. The armoury. Every medicament for kidneys you can think of. Phillip's going berserk."

Jonathan put a hand to his head and a low whistle escaped from his pursed lips.

"What - what ever was the potion you gave me last night?" he said.

"Your favourite. Laudanum. I wanted you to sleep. Here, dress."

Arndell threw clean shirt and breeches, stockings and shoes on the bunk.

"Cure Phillip and......" Arndell began.

"Work a miracle, you mean."

"Possible."

"The miracle?"

"A cure."

"Hardly likely Phillip'd let a filthy convict examine his exalted body. And what about White and Considen and the other surgeon? Why can't they treat him?"

"Short of medicines."

"Well, if they are short, so are you."

"You are the only man with the ample stocks."

Jonathan looked puzzled.

"I have ample, you haven't?"

"Put it this way. I may have stocks but I wouldn't identify any as specifics for kidney trouble. Except perhaps rupture wort and White's tried that already...."

Jonathan smiled.

"But you weren't aware of the efficacy of wall pellitory or eringo?"

"Oh, yes, I was."

"Cunning. And you'd forgotten all about oil of flaxseed?"

"Exactly."

"Cunning again. Thanks. Does Arthur Phillip take wine?"

"Sparingly."

"Then shall we prescribe a decoction of eringo in wine for fifteen days?" Jonathan said.

Arndell opened the jar of eringo root.

"Barely enough here for seven days."

"Well, eringo favours sandy coastal areas, so possibly it could grow hereabouts. If not, then a combination of eringo and flaxseed - maybe better in any case. Balsamic, diuretic and clearing stone and gravel all at the same time."

Arndell burst into laughter.

"Pettifer's Nostrum. You'd make your fortune at St Bartholomew's Fair."

Smiling, Jonathan tipped the contents of the eringo jar into a mortar.

"Now, if you could find me something to eat and drink, I'll carry on with the preparation."

"No risks, please," Arndell said with a wry smile.

"Only to the stone in Phillip's kidney."

John White's assistants, Considen and Balmain, were emerging from Phillip's tent as Arndell arrived with Jonathan. They gave the surgeon a peremptory nod but ignored the convict. Inside the tent, however, the greeting from White was warm though brief. Phillip lay on his right side, his back to the three men. Jonathan glanced in the direction of Arndell then White.

"I'd prefer you to stay while we examine the governor, sir, if you wouldn't mind," Arndell said.

John White drew himself up to his full height, towering over Arndell and rivalling Jonathan.

"I'd no intention of leaving," he said acidly.

"Would you mind giving me your present findings - and any advice you deem necessary?" Arndell said.

"It's up to you to make up your mind. Then I can question you on diagnosis and treatment."

Chapter 63

"You must answer it," Charlotte whispered, slowly easing herself from the count's embrace.

Open-mouthed, they lingered long over the kiss, then de la Perouse dragged himself away from the English woman and, rolling out of bed, he thrust his legs into silken breeches, drew on a cambrai shirt and at a leisured pace buttoned the frilled cuffs.

The hammering on the cabin door grew more insistent.

"M'sieur le Comte."

"Confound you." De la Perouse opened the cabin door barely an inch. "My instructions were 'not to be disturbed'. What is it?"

"An English soldier," the midshipman in the alleyway said. "He insists, demands to speak to you, m'sieur le Comte."

"Where?"

"He's on deck, m'sieur le Comte."

"Tell him - tell him to go to hell."

The midshipman stood, silent, ill at ease.

"You heard my instructions. Go."

"He - he has a pistol, M'sieur le Conte."

"The English pig. Tell him - tell him to wait. And tell him I'll not see him until he surrenders the firearm. Bring it to me."

The count firmly closed the cabin door and turned once more to Charlotte, now sitting up and wriggling into a silk shirt.

"Did you hear, did you understand? They're pursuing you, my Charlotte," he said, appraising a naked breast escaping from the shirt as she raised an arm to adjust the garment. "And no great surprise with temptations like that."

"He pursues, not <u>they.</u>"

"The captain?" de la Perouse said.

"Who else?"

"I shan't let you leave - ever."

De la Perouse leaned over the bed to fondle the now concealed breast.

"A secret, Jean-Francois," Charlotte murmured, drawing closer, "I've no intention of leaving."

"How do we treat this anxious suitor then?"

"A meal, Paris style, much wine, much brandy. Then send him reeling home."

The midshipman was once more hammering at the cabin door.

"His firearm, sir."

"Well done. Wait for me in the alleyway. No, no, go back and tell him I'll see him in due course. Offer cognac."

De la Perouse closed the cabin door and feverishly dragged off his breeches. It was the work of a moment for Charlotte to remove the silk shirt that she had donned only minutes earlier.

* * * * *

After struggling for miles through woods, over swamps and rock-strewn sand, Bellamy, mud-bespattered and weary, was in no mood to exchange pleasantries in spite of the bottle of cognac already half-empty. He halted his restless pacing as de la Perouse emerged from below.

"Good morning, Captain Bellamy."

Ignoring both salute and outstretched hand, Bellamy barked, "Where is she?"

"I do not understand," the Frenchman said.

"You bloody well understand all right, Frenchie - where is she?"

De la Perouse surveyed Bellamy's grimy face, the shoes and stockings and breeches plastered with mud.

"The captain will wish to wash and change his clothes, then we can talk."

"Talk now, wash later," Bellamy snarled.

The count slowly shook his head.

"For the moment, sir, I have pressing matters of ship's business to attend to."

He clapped his hands and a seaman appeared. He spoke rapidly then turned back to Bellamy.

"My crew will attend to your needs. You and I will meet later for talk and a meal," he said, then left Bellamy on the deck.

An hour elapsed before Bellamy was conducted to the count's table. De la Perouse, who was alone, rose and bowed stiffly to his guest, spruce now in silken shirt, white breeches and new shoes.

The food was of a quality and range superior even to the meal de la Perouse had given Bellamy when he had originally arrived with Charlotte. The count made sure that Bellamy's brandy goblet was never empty. Whenever the marines captain attempted to launch a conversation, the French count pretended difficulty in making sense of the Englishman's halting French. At length replete, Bellamy sat back and belched appreciatively.

"Good."

De la Perouse winced.

"I'm delighted to know you enjoyed the meal, captain."

Bellamy nodded.

"Now, what about Charlotte," he said.

"The woman?"

"Yes."

"As far as I am aware, she followed you ashore two days ago."

"And came back?"

De la Perouse shook his head, "Came back?"

"You swore you'd never take convicts aboard."

"Yes, indeed."

"Then, why did you take Charlotte?"

Once more, the count filled Bellamy's goblet.

"That begowned and bejewelled English lady, a convict? A convict dining at my table and you did not tell me?"

He rose, and circling the table, he seized the back of Bellamy's chair.

"Please leave my ship."

Bellamy jerked to his feet, swayed and grabbed the table edge for support. His eyes were glazed, his speech slurred. He thrust forward his brandy goblet for replenishment.

"A - a mistake, count, all a - a mistake. Of course, you couldn't believe the lady was a convict. When they told me at the Sydney Cove settlement, I couldn't believe it either. My - my instructions are to escort her back."

"I've told you. The woman followed you ashore two days ago. Again, I ask you to leave my ship."

Bellamy, swaying, made to sit down again. De laPerouse promptly moved the chair to one side and, as the marines captain strove to sit, he collapsed on the floor. Cursing, he grasped a table leg and scrambled to his feet.

"You're trying to make a fool of me, Frenchie."

The muscles in the count's face went taut.

"Leave my ship immediately and I'm prepared to overlook your rudeness, your outrageous abuse of my hospitality. A boat is waiting."

Bellamy stood, one hand desperately seeking the table edge, the other pressed hard over his eyes.

"Oh, I - er - I'm sorry. So frantic for Charlotte, I - I forgot....."

De la Perouse beckoned to a seaman.

"The captain wishes to go ashore."

"No, no," Bellamy muttered drunkenly.

"My compliments to Captain Phillip," de la Perouse said and, with a covert wink, to the seaman, "By no means a pleasant route back to the English settlement. See that the captain carries a loaded pistol for his safety and ample brandy for his comfort."

Then, as the door closed behind Bellamy and the seaman, the count added, "And to ensure he gets even more drunk and shoots himself, the greedy English pig."

Bellamy was no more than a remote dark figure weaving an uncertain way northwards over sandy hillocks and between rocky outcrops, when de la Perouse, his arm firmly around the waist of Charlotte Dudgeon, appeared on the deck of the frigate Astrolabe.

For a while the pair watched the receding figure in silence then Charlotte said, "Please, Jean-Francois - please leave me."

"You'll not try to follow him?"

Charlotte shook her head with vehemence.

"Of course not."

With some reluctance, the Frenchman freed the convict woman from his embrace. Alone now at the ship's rail, she kept her eyes on the dark speck that was Henry Bellamy until at last it disappeared into the distant woods. She glanced about her and, swallowing hard, she brushed away a tear.

At the head of the companionway, about to follow her French lover below she paused and turned for a lingering glance shorewards. The tears welled up. Swiftly wiping her eyes she went below.

* * * * *

Jonathan tiptoed to the four-poster bed. McQuaid was snoring rhythmically. Margaret lay in the cot at the foot of the four-poster.

"Margaret," he whispered.

Margaret stirred.

"Jonathan. How ever....."

He placed a gentle hand over her mouth.

"Quiet, my love, quiet."

He pointed to the arras which separated the bedchamber from the main body of the marquee.

"I'll be waiting," he said.

Dressing swiftly, she joined him. Clasped in his arms, she whispered, "Outside?"

"Too dangerous."

"Where did you sleep?"

"A tent - close to the governor's house."

"My love, I can't believe......"

"I'm treating the governor. Thomas Arndell arranged it." Jonathan's gentle hands caressed her face, her breasts, her thighs. "Don't waste precious moments."

"But if Turnbull wakes up?"

Jonathan laughed softly.

"Does it matter? Part of the marriage bargain. Besides, he's not looking for any trouble. He desperately needs support from Phillip. And Phillip can't do without my medicine."

"Please, dearest. An escape - if only for an hour."

Arms close about each other, they moved to the wall of the marquee. Jonathan gingerly drew aside the canvas flap. The night air was soft, balmy. Moonlight flooded the settlement.

"Dangerous, passing the guards' tent," Jonathan whispered.

Shrieks and laughter came from the convicts' quarters.

"Listen, - those women must've passed it successfully," Margaret said softly.

"But, if the guards.... They know you're McQuaid's wife...."

Once more, Jonathan enveloped Margaret in his arms then, momentarily freeing her, he gently drew off her gown to leave her standing naked in the moonlight.

"God, how beautiful. And how I want you."

"Not - not here, my love. Please, I beg you."

His mouth sought the lobe of her ear, her neck, her breasts.

"Why - why not?"

"It's hateful. Not - not here. That man..."

Jonathan knelt down and picked up the velvet gown.

"Put it on - we'll go."

Jonathan lifted the barefoot Margaret and carried her in his arms swiftly over the rough ground to his own tent. He was about to raise the flap, when a dozen pairs of copper-coloured hands laid hold of him. Margaret was flung aside.

Hustled across the freshly-turned earth of the governor's garden, Jonathan was dragged through a belt of trees, then over a rocky ridge to the mouth of a cave overlooking a sandy bay. Flung to the ground, he scrambled to his feet and was confronted by a crowd of naked aborigines, daubed in white. In the moonlight, they resembled skeletons. Two of them leaping forward tore off his clothing and performed a dance round him, repeatedly falling to their knees, their arms and heads raised to the moon. They took it in turn to daub Jonathan's naked body from head to foot with red and white pastes, pausing from time to time to fondle his scarred cheek and to inspect the gap in his front teeth.

Then, as swiftly as they had fallen upon Jonathan, the men disappeared into the night and from behind him a pair of thin hands, oily and stinking, began to caress his neck and his face.

He turned. The body of the aboriginal girl, no more than a black outline against the shimmering waters of the bay, began to writhe. Crossing her arms again and again, her palms slapped the flesh of her sparse breasts.

"Boodjeree, boodjeree," she moaned. "Wileemaring, wileemaring."

Edging closer, she placed her hands finger-tip to finger-tip, thumb-tip to thumb-tip, so that her groin was framed in a square. Then she raised her hands to strike her temples.

"Boodjeree, boodjeree."

Comprehension crept slowly across Jonathan's face.

"Boodjeree," he repeated clumsily. Then he lay flat on the sand, arms firmly to his side, eyes closed, and said, "Dead, dead."

The girl clapped her hands with excitement.

"Boodjeree, boodjeree."

Patently, the girl's husband had died and she had now discovered an acceptable substitute. Although with skin like that of a white maggot and mouth thin like that of a fish, this creature was skilled in magic medicines and, gap-toothed, as handsomely scarred as any of her own kind.

Her mood was at once coquettish. Earnestly she beckoned Jonathan to follow her into the cave. He ignored the invitation and began to dress. He failed to hear the sound of approaching feet, muffled by the soft sand.

"Arms high in the air," a voice growled tipsily.

Jonathan spun round and came face to face with a marines officer pointing an uncertain pistol at him.

"Good God," Bellamy muttered, "you, a convict?"

There was a cry from the cave and, backing to its entrance, Bellamy staggered inside. He emerged dragging the screaming aboriginal girl by the hair. He flung her to the ground. Putting a hand to his nose, he grimaced and wiped his palm on the back of his tunic.

"The - the stench," he growled. "You convicts, you'd take anything - anything."

Arms flailing drunkenly, Bellamy stumbled. There was an explosion and the girl slumped to the ground and lay still. Swaying, Bellamy stared dully at his smoking pistol and then at the blood spurting from a wound in his victim's breast.

Hurling the marines captain aside, Jonathan dropped to his knees beside the aboriginal girl. Her eyes were half closed, her eyelids were still and, even as he watched, the flow of blood had become no more than a lazy trickle. He eyed the copper-coloured face for a moment, hesitated, then he planted a kiss on its brow.

He bounced to his feet and swung round on the marines captain.

"You - you drink-sodden, bloody savage."

The blow to Bellamy's chin sent the captain staggering to the water's edge. Jonathan leapt to drag him back.

"Now, start digging, you uniformed ape. Dig as if our lives depended on it - because, by God, they well might."

Ten minutes later, the girl lay buried deep in the sand and the ill-assorted pair were hastening towards the settlement.

Not a word was exchanged between them until they came within sight of the string of fires and the sentries.

Jonathan paused to whisper, "On your own. Tell 'em to double, treble the guard."

"Don't you instruct me, convict," Bellamy hissed.

"If you want to save your skin and the skin of the rest..."

"What d'you mean?"

"You drink-sodden oaf. Believe me, those Indians'll have their revenge for the dead girl. No amount of Arthur Phillip's red baize and glass beads are likely to win 'em over now."

"I - I can handle the safety of the settlement."

"I doubt it - even when you're sober."

Bellamy was not only very drunk, he was also exhausted. He dropped to his knees.

"I- I can't...."

Jonathan dragged the marines officer to his feet, slung him over his shoulder, sprinted the last hundred yards and dumped him outside the guards' tent, then he fled.

At the entrance to McQuaid's marquee, Arndell pounced on Jonathan.

"Where the hell have you been?"

Jonathan brushed the surgeon's question aside.

"Where's Margaret?"

"In there."

"I must see her."

"Later, later - please. Phillip's in agony. I'm at my wits' end - so's White if only he'd admit it. Good God - look at your state! Get that filth washed off - and find a clean shirt. Then to Phillip."

Chapter 64

Jonathan at his heels, Arndell thrust through the curtain which separated Arthur Phillip's bedchamber from the rest of the canvas house.

"I've found Pettifer," he said softly to John White, silent and pensive, at the side of Phillip's cot.

White gave a curt nod and pointed to the twitching, restless Phillip.

"The result of your ministrations," he said caustically. "Look, worse, much worse."

Arndell took a closer look.

"Only to be expected. A stone never dissolves without discomfort for the host. May I?"

Arndell deftly turned Arthur Phillip so that the governor lay on his back. He pressed his fingers deep into the sick man's stomach. He checked the pulse rate, peered into his eyes, then turned for a whispered conversation with Jonathan.

"Well?" demanded White impatiently.

"Pettifer will look at his range of medicaments, sir," Arndell said.

White, expression thunderous, drew Arndell to one side.

"I fail to understand, Arndell - a convict with his own private stock of medicines?"

"Don't forget he's a qualified apothecary."

White swung round on Jonathan.

"You wait outside," he rasped. When Jonathan had withdrawn, he went on, "Kindly explain how your convict comes by his own specifics."

"I took him ashore in Rio to replenish stocks. We - er - we had a disagreement over various medicaments, so I chose mine and he got his own."

"Who paid?" White snarled.

"I did."

"You must be mad, Arndell. Your own apprenticeship taught you sufficient about medicines, surely, to gainsay this - this convict."

"Uses, maybe, but not detailed preparation."

"And you've every confidence in this felon's purported knowledge?"

"Every confidence, sir."

"Why, in God's name, didn't you impound all his medicaments the moment you stepped back aboard the transport?"

"Can you identify ingredients, Dr White?"

"I read as well as anybody," White said loftily.

"When jars carry no labels?"

"What the hell d'you mean?"

"The convict Pettifer's...."

A brief groan escaped from Arthur Phillip.

Arndell continued in an urgent whisper, "The convict Pettifer's exceptionally skilled. Label or no label, he identifies substances at a glance - and I cannot."

"D'you see the implications, Arndell?" White's tone was malevolent. "Unknown ingredients...."

"Pettifer knows them well enough, sir."

"The absurdity, the enormity, the - the blind madness. A governor's life, a colony's future in the hands of a footpad."

Arndell raised a calming hand.

"Two things I beg, Dr White."

"Well?" John White snapped.

"That you hang both Pettifer and myself if Arthur Phillip dies from our treatment."

"Not only hang, Arndell - I'll have you both drawn and quartered face to face with each other. Now - what's your further request?"

"I'd like Pettifer here for private discussion."

White, a tall man, drew himself up to his full height.

"Why private?"

"He might be somewhat diffident, discussing symptoms and medicines in the hearing of the chief surgeon, sir."

"Oh, very well. Ten minutes, then," White said smugly.

Arndell disappeared through the curtain and returned with Jonathan. White gave a peremptory nod, then left them alone with the sick governor.

Arndell was brusque.

"So much for your eringo and flaxseed. He's worse. Why?" he said.

"The proportion of flaxseed may be too high. - Such as remains inside him," Jonathan nodded in the direction of Phillip, "should carry on dissolving stone."

He pursed his lips.

"Eringo on its own, I think. A touch of your laudanum wouldn't go amiss."

Arndell eyed Jonathan uncertainly.

"I hope to God you're right. Back to your tent - I'll call you if necessary. But don't disappear this time."

"You mean - don't get kidnapped."

"Kidnapped?"

"I'll explain when I've had some sleep."

Jonathan's sleep was short-lived. At midnight, Arndell burst into his tent.

"Indians," he hissed into Jonathan's ear.

Jonathan stirred and would have settled down to sleep again but the surgeon whipped away the bedding.

"Clubbing and spearing."

Jonathan stumbled into the moonlight. The guards' tent, pitched close by the smithy, was burning like a torch. He plunged back inside and struggled into his breeches. Then, grasping his shirt, he followed Arndell.

Jonathan found Arndell striving to withdraw a spear from the chest of a screaming marine. Another guard lay spreadeagled, skull smashed open. A third, moaning and gasping, a spear embedded in his back, his hair and tunic ablaze, clawed at the rough earth in a frantic attempt to escape from the burning canvas.

Jonathan wrenched the weapon free and, with his shirt, he smothered the flames engulfing the wretched man.

"The hospital?" he called urgently to Arndell, striving to pacify the gibbering, injured marine. The hospital, a marquee, had been set up on the west side of Sydney Cove. The path to it round the head of the cove and across the stream was rough and tortuous.

"Too far. Take him to your own tent," Arndell said.

Arndell's words had scarcely died away when the man lurched to his feet, flung his arms wide to the sky then, screaming, he collapsed face down on the ground. For a moment his body twitched and then lay still.

"You can thank your gallant Captain-lieutenant Bellamy for this," Jonathan said to the dead man.

"Bellamy you mean?"

Jonathan spun round. It was Arndell.

"The drunken beast. Indians' revenge," Jonathan pointed to the corpse. "Bellamy shot one of their women."

"Deliberately?"

"Drunk as usual. Not much idea what he was doing."

"How d'you know?"

Jonathan smiled wryly.

"Unwilling spectator," he said.

He told Arndell the story of the old aborigine cured of stomach pains, of the girl with a fishbone embedded in her cheek and the kidnapping.

"Husband dead, so she wanted me."

"You didn't....?"

"What? Body drenched in grease, smelling like a midden?"

"Well, at least Bellamy saved you from that."

"Wanton, stupid, cold-blooded murder. A gentle, likeable creature in spite of her filth. And, persuading the men to kidnap me, a woman of some influence among the Indians, I'd say."

Jonathan contemplated the smouldering remains of the guard tent.

"We've not yet heard the last of Bellamy's tipsy madness."

Preparing medicines on the bench in Friendship's armoury, Arndell was unaware that Francis Walton had been watching him until the ship's master spoke.

"I thought you'd left us for the delights of life ashore," Walton said, his voice unusually subdued and weak.

Pestle in hand, Arndell turned.

Walton's face was grey, beads of sweat stood on his brow and, in spite of the warmth of the morning and the heavy blanket clutched to his shoulders, he was shivering uncontrollably.

"Less chance of Indian spears in my back. But - you're ill. What is it?"

"The African disease," Walton said flatly.

"Slaver's curse?"

"From the bloody blackbirds, yes."

Arndell grimaced.

"You sailed in the slave ships, then?"

Drawing the blankets even closer about him, Walton nodded.

"Accounts for your callousness," Arndell said. "Strange I've never noticed earlier attacks."

"I've had 'em - and kept out of the way. The mate knows - he's the same. Stood in for each other."

"But you should have had medicine."

"We needed no bloodsucker to make up Jesuit's bark decoction."

"Why come to me now, then?"

A minute elapsed before his wildly-chattering teeth would permit Walton to reply.

"No - no medicine left," he blurted out.

Arndell continued with the pestle.

"It must've taken a lot of courage," he said, smiling at the bulkhead.

"What?"

"Coming to me like this."

Walton began to bluster.

"Not another word, Francis. Tell the mate Virginian snakeroot, in the opinion of some surgeons, heightens the efficacy of the Jesuit's bark. Now, if you'll go back to your bunk, I'll prepare a decoction."

His brow dry, a faint colour now back in his cheeks, Walton lay sprawled and exhausted in his bunk.

"A better pills-and-potions man than I imagined," he said gruffly.

Arndell smiled.

"Thank you."

Walton raised himself to one elbow.

"I need a surgeon for the voyage home. Interested?"

"When d'you sail?" Arndell said with caution.

"The day we've unloaded the last of the stores. Could be some little time. Phillip and his commissary insist on secure store buildings - and the work's sluggish."

"Make it twelve months and I'd think about it."

"Twelve months? I hope to up-anchor in weeks. The longer we idle here, the more barnacles on the timbers, the more desertions from the crew."

"Your men anxious to stay?" Arndell said, incredulously.

"Well, what's ahead for them? Six months of scurvy in this - this floating rat-and-lice box, rotten as an over-ripe pear. And no women. Here, it's women all day - and all night, if they keep on bribing the guards.... I've no idea what plans Phillip has for the future but, at the moment, he's nothing more than governor of the biggest whore-house in history."

"Phillip's a sick man," Arndell said. "When he's on his feet again, there'll be wholesale changes, mark my words. Is - er - is Turnbull McQuaid planning a return to England with you?"

Walton pursed his lips.

"Very unlikely. I see him here for a year or two, setting up a trading empire, a monopoly selling to the settlement and buying whatever it produces."

"Oh, Arthur Phillip'd never let private hands take over, never," Arndell said, shaking his head.

"I've seen stranger things," Walton scoffed. "Did you ever imagine sodomite McQuaid would marry a woman? Did you ever imagine Phillip'd entertain a sodomite at his table? And you, Arndell, did you ever, in your wildest dreams, see yourself treating the high and the mighty - after that string of medical blunders back in London?"

The side of Arndell's neck suffused with pink, then turned crimson.

"You're a rat," he said, snatching at the door handle.

"No, don't go, Arndell."

Walton quickly struggled to a sitting position in his bunk and attempted to grasp the surgeon's sleeve.

"I meant no insult. Maybe Jesuit's bark and Virginian snakeroot act on the tongue the same way as McQuaid's brandy. Believe me, I'm damned grateful. I'll do something for you some day, I promise."

Arndell slackened his grasp on the door handle.

"You mean that?" he said.

"Yes."

"You'll let me know the minute you have a sailing date?"

"Is that all you want?" Walton said.

"The rest'll come later.... Now, I must be ashore to tend the governor."

Arndell pointed to a horn beaker.

"A deep draught mid-afternoon. Earlier if the shivers take you again. I'll be back before dark."

Chapter 65

The voice of Arthur Phillip had now regained much of its former resonance. He was sitting up in bed and talking animatedly with Turnbull McQuaid when John White stepped into the sleeping quarters of the governor's marquee. At once the ship's chandler leapt to his feet and bowed deeply to White.

"I'm Turnbull McQuaid," he said.

White's nod was curt and he ignored McQuaid's proffered hand.

"I'd come to enquire about the governor's health," McQuaid went on.

"And you've made the enquiry?" White said icily.

"Well, yes."

"Then leave, please. My patient's in no condition to receive casual visitors."

In an instant McQuaid's obsequiousness had evaporated.

"Except, of course, for the convict who's here every couple of hours. You'd be well advised, Dr White....."

"When I require your advice, I'll ask for it. Now, if you please, go."

Face crimson, McQuaid swung on his heel and left without further word.

Silent throughout the exchange, Arthur Phillip, smiling wanly, said, "Thank you, John. I'd already grown bored with that man's planning. Better, though, if you'd dealt with him not quite so brusquely."

"Filthy pervert. - I'll deal with him as I think best."

"You will not, John White. So long as his plans're in line with mine, I'm prepared to go along with him."

"With a sodomite?"

"With anybody who can help establish us quickly in New South Wales. - No, don't shake your head like that, John. I need every ounce of co-operation I can lay hands on."

"And how, precisely d'you imagine a sodomite can assist the colony, sir?"

"Our felling axes, our saws, shovels, spades and the rest of the tools are poor, they're worn out and useless in weeks. That McQuaid's in an unrivalled position to lay hands on replacements - good quality replacements - shipped out quickly. So we can - and we will - endure the man."

"I'm by no means convinced, sir."

"Short shipments, in many instances no shipments at all. You yourself're only too well aware of dire shortages of medicines. The sick in your hospital have no blankets. There's no clothing for the convicts so they go on wearing lice-ridden rags fit only for the furnace. Most of the wretches - and some marines as well - no longer have any footwear. They stumble around on feet bound in strips of canvas."

Looking suddenly exhausted, Phillip pressed a hand to his temple.

"Better lie down again, sir," John White said, making to settle Arthur Phillip back in his cot.

Phillip thrust White's hand aside.

"We've no paint, no musket balls, no reap hooks, no wheelbarrows. The list's almost endless."

White threw up both hands in a gesture of hopelessness.

"And if you don't lie back back at once, we could soon be short of a governor."

Phillip sat bolt upright.

"Not before I've seen the colony firmly on its feet. Those shortages. D'you imagine the government'll supply? If they do, it'll be too little and far too late. But McQuaid'll have no difficulty laying his hands on everything. And he won't be looking at all those sea miles to London for supplies. His influence and standing at the Cape are solid gold - damn his dirty hide."

A look of incredulity had spread across White's face.

"I never imagined you could sink so low, Arthur Phillip."

"Better for Arthur Phillip to sink rather than the colony. Give what I've said a lot of thought, John.... And leave me to rest for half an hour."

The path to the hospital tents on the west side of the cove took John White past a collection of convicts' tents close to the shore. On nearby rocks, some convict women lay sprawled in the hot sunshine.

"Come and join us, sir."

"Payment in pounds of tea very welcome."

"Your breeches too tight, m'lord. They're causing a lady much distress."

"Try my bed, not hers. She crawls with Newgate bugs and lice."

A faint smile played around White's mouth as, eyes focussed straight ahead, he strode on.

Breathless, Andrew Miller, Commissary of Stores and Provisions, caught up with the surgeon and fell into step.

"I'd have 'em flogged, sir."

White turned his head briefly to glance at the women.

"Why?"

"For the insults, Dr White."

"They could be regarded as flattery," White said, smiling faintly.

"Flattery, sir?"

White quickened pace.

"A score of women lusting after me. Temptation."

Miller gave an uneasy laugh.

"Not exactly your kind of woman, sir."

"Oh? And what d'you imagine would be my kind of woman, Miller?"

"Well, I'd imagine none of that lot would be exactly welcome in a London drawing-room."

White's smile was wry.

"While I would be, of course?"

"Yes."

White paused. His burly frame towered over the slightly-built and clerkish Miller.

"Let me tell you something, Miller. One of those women could well be the innocent bastard daughter of the prime minister, flung aboard the convict transport at Plymouth to get her out of the way for good. Another woman's the result of a carefree dalliance of King George, for years an acute embarrassment to his majesty. Somewhere in the settlement there's the wife of a Bow Street magistrate convicted, like the other two, on some trumped-up charge so he could be rid of her in favour of some London drawing-room harlot."

Miller was persistent.

"But there must be some...."

"Maybe, maybe," White said testily. "But innocent or guilty I would never countenance flogging a woman. In any case I'm by no means averse to flattery, whatever its origins."

By this time, the pair had come to the huddle of hospital tents but, before going inside, John White paused to glance across the cove. He pointed to the Prince of Wales, her forward mooring rope fast to the base of a sturdy gum tree, which reared up almost at the water's edge. Alongside her, the storeship Borrowdale was similarly moored.

"Those two ships typify our separate interests," White said. "The Prince of Wales and her forty-nine female convicts, the Borrowdale crammed with ropes and canvas and sacks of this and that. Did you ever go aboard a convict transport?"

Miller's lips curled.

"I did not."

White sneered.

"Your education's been sorely neglected. You had a cabin aboard the Sirius?"

"Shared with Zecharia Clarke, my assistant."

"How much headroom?"

"About five feet."

"But you were able to escape?"

"Escape, Dr White?"

"To the deck and so forth."

"Of course."

"Then you'll never be able to imagine sharing with forty-eight others, headroom of four and a half feet, little or no escape for weeks on end, hungry, soaked, chilled to the marrow, paddling around in vomit and foul water and worse. And why? For picking a pocket for sixpence,

selling pardons as good as many a mealy-mouthed priest
supplies. Or for being the unwelcome bastard of some
London drawing-room. Learning anything, Miller?"

"I - I think so."

"So you'll no longer equate human beings with sacks
of flour, never again believe a flogging's a cure-all?"

Grudgingly Miller nodded agreement.

John White lifted the flap of a hospital tent and
beckoned Miller to follow.

"Another lesson," White said softly.

The stores commissary stepped inside and at once
rammed a handkerchief to his nose and mouth.

"God, the stench," he muttered.

"And this tent wasn't here a week ago," White said.

The sick, men and women alike, lay on palliasses
filled with rushes and, so close to each other, that it was
almost impossible to move without treading on some
outstretched, fevered limb. The air was filled with
mutterings and groans and curses.

Miller drew aside his handkerchief for a moment to
whisper urgently to John White, "Surely their bedding in
the 'tween deck's preferable to this."

White flung a look of disdain at the commissary.

"I had a feeling somehow the lesson hadn't quite
struck home. Palliasses and blankets from the convict
transports? Sodden with urine and salt water, alive with
fleas and bugs and lice? Tck, tck, tck - do have some
regard for our new land of promise and hope."

White picked his way carefully over recumbent
bodies back to the opening and, as he emerged into the
brilliant sunshine of the cove, he said to Miller closely
following, "Only wish to God I could give 'em blankets,

linen sheets and real food. Sugar, currants, spices, barley."

Outside the tent Turnbull McQuaid was hovering.

"Dr White," he said stepping forward and giving a faint bow. "I've come to apologise for my intrusion this morning."

White grunted.

"Yes?"

"I believe I heard you mention currants, spices, barley."

"Yes, yes," White said, then glanced away to sniff the air.

"Bread?" he said suddenly. "Baking bread?"

Beside a tent close to the water's edge, a man was lifting loaves of bread from a makeshift oven set in a rocky crevice.

"For whom?" White said

The baker pointed to some tents.

"The guards, sir."

"And the hospital?"

"Captain Bellamy ordered...."

"And the Surgeon-in-chief also orders." White turned to Miller, "See to it, will you?" he said, then strolled back to McQuaid. "You were saying?"

"That I might be able to help with delicacies for your hospital. May we discuss further over a bottle of wine, Dr White?"

Chapter 66

Unnoticed by the marines guard, Jonathan crept into the marquee. Margaret was reading by the light of a silver candelabra. She dropped her book and, startled, leapt to her feet.

"My love, you," she said.

Jonathan pointed anxiously towards the arras curtaining off one end of the marquee.

"McQuaid?" he whispered.

Margaret took his face between her hands and kissed him.

"No need for whispers. He's gone with the governor."

"Expedition?"

Margaret nodded.

"Leaving all this -" Jonathan's finger ranged the opulent furnishings - "to sleep on rough earth under the stars?"

"More than worthwhile, he thinks. Prospects of vast untapped resources of gold, silver, diamonds. An obsession with him. The faintest hint of rich finds and he'll be back in London, arranging to buy huge tracts of this awful territory."

Jonathan shook his head.

"Arthur Phillip would never agree...."

"Arthur Phillip's the governor, not the owner. London makes the decisions. Turnbull has friends in high places, and he can buy more, many more. He's absolutely confident. 'Go on pretending to share my bed and you'll share in my vast new empire' he's always telling me."

"When's he planning to leave for England?"

"If he has enough information - when the Friendship sails."

"And you'd stay, of course, darling?"

Margaret bit her lip.

"I - I just don't know. The only real hope for us is escape," she said.

"Impossible, my love, utterly impossible."

"But everything looks impossible. Here it'd be hell if I manage to stay on my own and hell if I have to sail in the Friendship with Turnbull. Imagine a six months' voyage, the only woman aboard, target for every seaman, with no interest in Turnbull himself. I'd go mad."

Jonathan took her in his arms.

"If I thought, my love," he murmured into her hair,"we'd the faintest hope of survival - but it's savage, raw, brutal out here. No food, very little water. If starvation didn't kill us, the Indians would."

"They didn't kill you."

"That was before the drunken oaf Bellamy murdered the Indian girl. Now as soon as it's dark there's spearing, clubbing and garrotting even deep inside the settlement. What earthly chance would we stand outside?"

Wriggling free of his embrace, Margaret seized Jonathan's wrists.

"I cannot, I will not go on. Please....."

"I'll find some way, somehow. When's the Friendship sailing?"

"In a week or two, Turnbull thinks. That's why he pressed the governor for more and more exploration before she leaves."

"My darling, decide you want to stay, decide you're going to stay."

"On my own, in this marquee? Marines officers, free settlers pursuing? Oh, no. Worse than aboard Friendship."

"Thomas Arndell would take care of you."

"No, no. In any case, Turnbull would never agree to leaving me. I'm - I'm a business asset."

Jonathan' brow furrowed.

"I wonder - I wonder if Arndell could persuade Francis Walton? A plan - but we're wasting precious moments, darling," Jonathan said, as he took Margaret's hand and led her into the bedchamber.

"Mrs McQuaid!"

The voice, a man's, was high with urgency.

Beneath the silk coverlet, Margaret nestled closer to Jonathan.

Again - but greater urgency, "Mrs McQuaid!"

"Answer," Jonathan breathed into Margaret's ear.

"Who is it?" she called.

"Captain Bellamy."

"What d'you want?"

"Permission to enter your marquee."

"No."

"It's important, Mrs McQuaid."

"Go away."

"I'm sorry. Instructions from the Deputy Governor, Major Ross. Escaped convict."

"I'm in my bedchamber and far from well, captain. No escaped convicts here, I assure you."

"May I search the rest of the marquee?"

"If you respect my privacy and damage nothing - yes."

"I promise."

It was clear that Bellamy was already inside the marquee.

There was a creaking sound and a crash as the lid of an oak kist was lifted then carelessly dropped. A series of heavy thuds followed as if Bellamy and his party were systematically beating the arras-lined walls in search of their quarry.

"You'll be held personally responsible for any damage, Captain Bellamy."

"Extremely careful, Mrs McQuaid."

"And finding nothing?"

"Nothing so far."

"Offer brandy," Jonathan whispered to Margaret.

"But we want rid of him, love."

Jonathan was insistent.

"Brandy the quickest way," he said. "The sooner they're drunk the sooner they'll abandon the search. It's me they're hunting for, of course. But why Bellamy himself, I wonder, not just an ordinary marine?"

"Captain Bellamy," Margaret called.

The sound of a loud gulp.

"Y-yes."

"My brandy to your liking?"

"Very much so."

"Searching for missing convicts highly rewarding then?"

A tipsy guffaw.

"Yes, yes."

"How many convicts did you say?"

"Er - one."

"One, Captain Bellamy? Seven hundred convicts in the settlement and you're spending your valuable time looking for just one?"

"A dangerous one, Major Ross says. Tried to poison the governor."

Jonathan squeezed Margaret.

"I told you. Me."

"How did this - this convict cook get so close to the governor?"

"Not a cook, a self-styled apothecary, Mrs McQuaid."

Margaret snuggled closer to Jonathan.

"Sounds extremely dangerous. When - er - when d'you plan to finish the search of my home? I wish to dress and some of my garments are in the large kist."

Bellamy's speech was now heavily slurred.

"At - at once. At once."

"Please leave time for a final goblet, captain."

"Th-thank -hic, hic - you."

Moonlight flooded into the marquee as Margaret raised the flap. A marine guard lay in a drunken stupor across the entrance.

Jonathan embraced and kissed Margaret.

"As soon as I can see Arndell - a plan."

Stepping over the drunken marine, he sped across the open ground to his tent.

It was still moonlight, when two marines brandishing cutlasses, followed by a convict overseer grasping a whip, burst in.

"Up, up."

A wired thong snaked across Jonathan's face.

As he stumbled to his feet, the flat of a cutlass sent him sprawling out of the tent.

"Why, why?"

Barefoot, shirtless, he blundered into a line of convicts. Once more the whip snaked, this time over his naked shoulders.

"On your feet."

Marshalled into single file, Jonathan and the other convicts were driven to the smithy at the water's edge. There they were swiftly manacled.

"Tell - tell Governor Phillip....." Jonathan gasped to a marine standing by.

Laughing, the man spat in his face.

"Hear that?" he called to another marine. "Phillip's favourite con won't be dining with him this evening." He swung round and drove a fist into the pit of Jonathan's stomach.

"You open your mouth too much, scarface."

As each convict was dragged away from the anvil, a spade was thrust into his hands and together they were marched over a hill to a low-lying swamp south of the settlement cove.

Under constant lashing daily from dawn to dusk, they were forced to dig out chunks of wet clay and stumble up the hill with the clay to a rocky outcrop.

Using lengths of tree trunk as pestles and depressions in the rock for mortars, there they pummelled the clay. With water from a nearby pool, they then puddled the sticky yellow mass with their bare feet into a condition suitable for brickmaking.

Jonathan's nearest companion in the digging party was a tall, ascetic-looking man, more suited to wielding a quill pen than a clumsy spade. Shoeless like the rest, he found it increasingly difficult to force the spade into the heavy clay with rag-bound feet. At length, in desperation, he seized the shaft of his spade with both hands to lunge at the ground. At the same he ducked to avoid the overseer's whip. The spade drove deep into his ankle. He collapsed, screaming.

Pitching aside his own spade Jonathan grabbed the man and hauled him upright. The blade had sliced through flesh, tendon and bone and the foot hung by a sliver of skin bleeding and useless.

Jonathan glanced anxiously at the overseer and the marine on guard.

"Look, his foot, almost sliced off. Hospital?"

The overseer smirked.

"Cuts down output."

The marine gave a cursory glance at the blood-drenched foot and spat.

"Horrible. Suppose he'll be moaning and groaning the rest of the day, putting the rest of 'em off. Yes, on your way with him, scarface."

The injured man uttered a piercing shriek as Jonathan, one hand grasping the injured foot, gently slung him over his shoulder.

The hospital guard regarded Jonathan and his burden with deep suspicion.

"Dodging?"

Jonathan pointed to the blood from the injured convict which, seeping through a makeshift bandage, had drenched his own breeches. The guard dragged aside the hospital-tent flap. The atmosphere was foetid, foul. Motioning Jonathan to follow, the man pointed to a vacant space on the bare earth.

"Drop him there."

The marine, hand clamped over nose and mouth, at once dived for the exit.

Jonathan laid the man gently on the hard ground and, straightening up, came face to face with John White, the chief surgeon. White peered closely at Jonathan, face almost unrecognisable under its coating of yellow clay.

"The convict apothecary?"

"Yes, sir."

"What brings you here?"

"Clay puddling."

"Come outside."

Jonathan pointed to the injured man, prone and quiet on the ground.

"And leave him in that state?"

White dropped to his knees beside the man to examine more closely the almost severed foot. He shook his head.

"I'll have it removed," he said, summoning an orderly.

"Yes, sir?"

"Laudanum, as much as you can lay hands on. Quickly.""

"Yes, sir."

Together Jonathan and White strolled to the rocky edge of the cove.

"Why did you leave Dr Arndell's tent?"

"I wasn't exactly a volunteer."

Head whimsically to one side, White said, "Not many friends in the settlement at the moment. The governor away, Dr Arndell with him, Major Ross riding high." He smiled wryly.

"You seem to have - er - perturbed the major somewhat."

"Perturbed, sir?"

"Your medicines for Governor Phillip far too efficacious. The governor makes no secret of it. Tck, tck, tck, a convicted rogue with such influence, such ability."

White glanced about him. There was nobody else in sight. "I shouldn't be saying this, least of all to a convict, but Major Ross wouldn't be the first deputy governor to wish his superior permanently out of the way."

Smiling ruefully, Jonathan rubbed the caked mud from his forearms.

"So that was the reason for the brickfields. Not as swift as hanging but just as final."

White laughed.

"I can arrange work in the hospital. Share a tent and labour with the grave-digger."

Jonathan looked aghast.

"Grave-digger?"

"There's little else for you to do, little else anybody can do. No blankets, not enough palliasses, very little medicine."

White pointed to the collection of hospital tents, "Charnel houses, no more, no less. But they die in peace…. Interested?"

Jonathan contemplated the caked mud clinging determinedly to the hairs on his forearm.

"I could wash?"

"Soap and water in plenty."

"Thank you, Dr White, I'll do it."

White nodded approvingly.

"One thing. Except for burials, when you and the other convict orderly are working together, you must keep within the vicinity of the hospital. That's my province exclusively. Outside those limits, I warn you, expect no quarter from Ross or Bellamy or anybody else."

"You mean I can't move.....?"

"Not one single inch while Major Ross's in charge," White said. "But you'll find distinct advantages over clay-puddling. No manacles and you'll feed as well as the stores allow."

A touch on the shoulder roused Jonathan and, as he scrambled to his feet, a hand clamped firmly over his mouth.

"Follow me," Arndell said in a harsh whisper.

The other orderly had not stirred. Jonathan crept out and joined Arndell in the deep shadow cast by the hospital tent.

"John White, he's told me," Arndell said softly.

"When did you come back?"

"Two days ago. I'd've been here sooner but I went aboard the Friendship and had to stay. Walton's desperately sick with scurvy and bouts of slaver's affliction. I've tended him night and day. He's frantic to set sail."

"And will he?"

"Possibly."

"And McQuaid?"

Arndell slowly shook his head.

"I've had no contact. He stuck to Phillip like a shadow all the time and I've seen nothing of him since we came back."

Jonathan eyed Arndell with anxiety.

"Can you find out?"

"If he's confided in Walton, yes."

"When's the Friendship due to sail?"

"Tuesday or Wednesday next week. The sheds are almost ready for the rest of the stores from her. It might've been sooner but Arthur Phillip's soft-hearted. Insists no work for the convicts from mid-day Saturday 'til early Monday morning. Doesn't much please Walton now he's feeling slightly better. He's desperate to put ten thousand miles between himself and Sydney Cove."

Arndell flinched at the severity of Jonathan's sudden seizure of his forearm.

"So - so what about Margaret?"

Arndell was silent.

"Did - you - hear - me? Margaret?" Jonathan said.

"I'm - I'm sorry. I don't honestly know."

"Surely....."

"Well, three possibilities...." Arndell began.

Jonathan's grip remained vice-like.

"Go on, go on, for God's sake, I've got to know."

Arndell frowning, slowly shook his head.

"Three possibilities, I said? All of 'em sheer madness even to contemplate."

"What possibilities, what madness?"

"Plans for poisoning Walton, poisoning McQuaid, sinking the Friendship."

Chapter 67

Features pallid and drawn, in spite of many weeks in the sunshine of the Pacific, Francis Walton, from his stance on a hatch coaming, watched in silence as his crew hauled aboard water casks, then rolled them across the deck of the Friendship.

Arndell was also watching.

"No convicts, no roistering marines, not a single sheep to water this time, Francis," he said, smiling.

Walton put a hand to his forehead and drew it away to stare for a moment at his moistened palm.

"No, thank God," he said.

"And a swifter passage?"

"Doubtful," Walton said.

He stepped down from the coaming and stumbled. Then, a hand to his forehead once more, he made his slow and laboured way below.

Arndell followed shortly. He found the ship's master sprawled in the cuddy, eyes tight shut, beads of sweat on his brow.

"Francis."

Walton's response was a groan.

"An electuary, I think," Arndell said, going to the cuddy locker.

Walton opened one eye and gave him a watery smile.

"Strange sort of man, aren't you? I've always been the one to scorn your pills and potions, yet you seem to be treating me all right."

Arndell's smile was wry.

"Not entirely without motive, Francis."

The surgeon put a glass phial to Walton's lips and held it there until the last drop of sluggish fluid had disappeared.

The ship's master licked his lips appreciatively.

"Pleasant enough. What's your motive?"

"McQuaid determined to sail with you?"

"He owns the Friendship."

"You don't sound over-enthusiastic," Arndell said, as he mopped Walton's brow with muslin.

"What exactly are you driving at?"

"I want you to take McQuaid - and leave his wife here."

Walton's eyes opened wide.

"So you and that convict woman....?

Arndell shook his head.

"No, not me, Francis…. Will you?"

Walton's brow knitted briefly, his head slumped forward and at once he was in a deep sleep.

"Damn."

Arndell stumped out of the cuddy and went on deck.

A marine confronted him.

"Dr White wants you. There's a boat waiting."

Arndell raised the flap of McQuaid's marquee and, removing his tricorne hat, he stepped inside. Margaret greeted him with both hands.

"Dr White's in there with Turnbull waiting for you," she said, pointing towards the bedchamber.

Deep in blankets, McQuaid lay in his fourposter. White, standing on the far side, nodded curtly in Arndell's direction.

"Medicaments handy?" White said.

"For what, Dr White?"

"A severe chill."

"Yes, of course, but surely...?"

"My own stocks? I don't know. I've never seen such chaos, moving everything from store tent to storehouse. I can't lay my hands on a single ingredient."

White jabbed a finger towards McQuaid. His voice dropped to a confidential whisper, "Urgent treatment essential."

A smile flickered across Thomas Arndell's face. White gave no indication that he was conscious of Arndell's reaction.

"Leave everything to me, sir."

"After discussion," White said peremptorily, and he beckoned Arndell to follow him through the curtain.

Margaret was waiting.

"Will he be well enough to sail?" she said.

"Dr Arndell and I are to discuss the possibilities," White said and, as he and Arndell walked out of the marquee, the latter glanced back to give Margaret a covert wink.

The two surgeons strolled along the east side of the cove, now almost cleared of trees.

"McQuaid's an idiot. Never his style, he ought to have known, sleeping out of doors under a single blanket," White said.

"Hence the chill, of course."

White nodded.

"Frantic, Arthur Phillip told me, to survey his potential dominions. Back in London by Christmas, he'll be trying outright bids for Port Jackson, Sydney Cove and, who knows, the rest of New South Wales."

"Bids to the government?" Arndell said.

"Not as such. But people who can influence the government."

"Are there really statesmen willing to bargain with a ship's chandler?" Arndell asked ingenuously.

"Find me a statesman who hasn't his price. McQuaid'll know of plenty of skeletons in cupboards." As White's shoe caught a flat stone an army of insects, deprived of their shelter, darted frantically hither and thither. He laughed. "McQuaid must be aware of many a stone like that just begging to be turned over."

"You surprise me, Dr White."

"Don't for one moment imagine McQuaid undertook that hellish voyage in the stinking barrel Friendship without good reason. A mystery to me how it kept afloat."

White paused and, shading his eyes with one hand, he pointed with the other across the shimmering waters of the cove to the Friendship, alone at the moorings now that the Scarborough had sailed.

"Extraordinary, McQuaid managing to persuade that lovely wife of his to accompany him."

Arndell snatched a sideways glance at John White. It was at once evident that the chief surgeon knew nothing of Margaret Dunne, the convict, and her strange marriage to Turnbull McQuaid.

"A curious business, yes," Arndell said, as they moved on towards the mouth of the cove. "A beautiful woman like that."

"It'd struck you as well?"

Arndell laughed.

"Lovely women always strike me."

"I can't understand how McQuaid appealed to her. Not particularly masculine. In fact a sodomite, Phillip says. And old enough to be her father...."

"But wealthy enough to satisfy her every whim," Arndell said swiftly. "Now, could we discuss treatment for McQuaid?"

"Indeed. Simple remedies to promote sweating."

"If he's bent on sailing with the Friendship, wouldn't it be wiser to get him aboard right away?"

John White glanced back at the moored convict ship.

"I'm not sure he'll be well enough to sail in that."

There was thinly-veiled anxiety in Arndell's tone.

"Not well enough?"

"Damp and rotting timbers, open invitation to the rheums and the cramps and then God-knows-what hellish ills a hundred Newgate convicts left on board."

Arndell's response was swift.

"But, ever since dropping anchor, the crew's been busy, careening and scraping the hull. Every nook and cranny scrubbed and sulphured, all the hatches wide open to the broiling sun day after day. I know what I'd prefer, sir, to a leaky marquee with hard clay floor - even if it is covered in sumptuous carpets. And Mrs McQuaid's a dedicated nurse."

Thoughtful for a moment, White nodded.

"Well, yes, you could be right, Arndell," he said in grudging tones.

"So when shall we move him, sir?"

The pair had now reached the mouth of the cove and, turning to stroll back to the settlement, White said,"Oh, right away, I suppose."

Arndell made no effort to conceal the look of relief on his face.

"What medicaments am I to give him, sir?"

"I'm a great believer in scabious powder. But elecampane, candied or in decoction, has its virtues. No reason for not administering both."

"Yes, sir."

"Massive doses the moment he's tucked up in his bunk aboard the ship, so he'll never miss the luxuries of the four-poster," White said, smiling.

They strolled in silence until they came to McQuaid's marquee.

"I think I can leave Mcquaid in your hands now, Arndell. Urgent business with the governor," White said, and he strode off swiftly in the direction of Arthur Phillip's canvas house.

*   *   *   *   *

Margaret nodded towards the bedchamber.

"Fast asleep," she whispered.

"Wine?" Arndell said.

"Half a bottle."

Arndell's smile was broad.

"Well done…. Now the plan. John White's happy to be rid of the problem. Turnbull goes aboard and is treated by me."

"When?"

"Today. Now. And you with him."

Margaret seized Arndell's hand.

"No, no. Please."

"But you must. All part of the plan. Turnbull in his bunk right away, then medicine as odious and thirstmaking as I know. Doses every hour washed down by a surfeit of his favourite wine. I'll tend him two or three times a day. You'll be with him until the last moment, when I snatch you away and ashore."

"And Francis Walton?" Margaret said, eyes wide with anxiety.

"Oh, I've bought Walton."

"Bought?"

"I'm treating Francis as well as McQuaid. Slaver's curse. Those fits of shivering and sweating'll not let him anywhere near the helm, never mind get his hands on it - until I step up the treatment."

"But however did he manage the voyage all the way from Plymouth?"

Arndell laughed.

"No need of a pills-and-potions man then. He made up electuaries from his own stocks of Peruvian bark. He has none left now. But I have plenty. Walton'll make sure your husband stays aboard until it's too late, I promise. And I'll've seen you safely, yes, safely ashore."

"No, no, Thomas," Margaret said. "Turnbull's the ship's owner. He'd order FrancisWalton to turn back for me."

Arndell's shake of the head was confident.

"Nobody orders Walton to do anything, least of all turn about the ship for the settlement. Half his crewmen already lost to the convict women and the scurvy. If any more of them jump ship, he'll have only rats and cockroaches to trim the sails. Now, shall we break the good news to your husband?"

Margaret crept into the bedchamber.

"Turnbull," she said, gently shaking her husband. McQuaid grunted and stirred. "Dr Arndell would like to speak to you."

Arndell touched McQuaid's brow.

"Mr McQuaid, the Friendship's sailing in a day or two and Dr White wants you settled aboard comfortably as soon as possible."

McQuaid grunted again.

Margaret flung an anxious glance towards Arndell as McQuaid wormed more deeply into the blankets.

"Turnbull."

"Mr McQuaid, please. Francis Walton's anxious to set sail Wednesday or Thursday, sir. I have excellent stocks of medicine on the ship but very little on shore. Mrs McQuaid, of course, will be tending you."

Face flushed, brows close-knitted, McQuaid grunted yet again and, irritably flinging aside the blankets, he tumbled out of bed and surged to his feet. He swayed, thrust out a hand to Arndell for support and the surgeon steered him gently to a chair.

Within two hours, McQuaid was settled in his bunk aboard Friendship. The flavour of his new medicine had been little to his liking. He grabbed the proffered wine goblet, drained its contents at a gulp and thrust it back into Margaret's hand.

""More," he said. "A lot more."

Chapter 68

Panting, Arndell scrambled to the wharf and moored the boat to a tree stump serving as a bollard. Without pausing for breath, he began to run. He skirted the head of the cove and waded knee-deep, sometimes waist-deep, across the stream then scrambled up the rocks. Idling in the sun, a group of women convicts cheered and jeered as he stumbled past.

Outside the orderly-tent, Jonathan sat cross-legged, naked to the waist, battling with needle and thread to repair a torn shirt. At the sight of Arndell, he leapt to his feet.

There was deep anxiety in his tone.

"Margaret?"

The pair, in sharp contrast, faced each other, Jonathan barrel-chested and richly bronzed, towering far above the figure of the slight and pale Arndell. Arndell, struggling frantically for breath, glanced quickly about him.

"The - the other convict?"

Jonathan pointed in the direction of a group of gum trees beyond the hospital tents and to the wisps of lazily spiralling smoke.

"Busy brewing porter," he said, smiling. "The only medicine we can lay our hands on. If we don't cure, we can at least ease. But Margaret...?"

Arndell nodded in the direction of Friendship lying at anchor in the cove.

"Tending McQuaid." Arndell put a hand to his heaving chest. "I - I'll have to sit down."

Jonathan dropped to the ground beside the surgeon.

"But she's not leaving?"

"That's why I'm here. I've come straight from Friendship. If the plan succeeds, Margaret gets ashore."

"And McQuaid?"

"To England. He's ill."

"Seriously?"

"A heavy chill. The plan's to make it worse."

"Not poison, surely."

"No, no. Scabious and elecampane every hour, followed by half a bottle of his favourite wine."

"Enough to floor an elephant. But Margaret's escape? How?"

"She's tending McQuaid. At the very last minute she'll give him huge doses of medicine and wine, then I'll get her ashore."

"With Walton's collaboration?"

"At a modest price. I stocked him up with Peruvian bark for his attacks of the shivers. Walton's sole interest is upping anchors and away."

Arndell struggled to his feet.

"Friendship, Borrowdale, Alexander and Prince of Wales, they'll all leave together in the morning, soon after first light, they hope. So, if you see all Friendship's sails hoisted at dawn and no rowing-boat over there -"Arndell pointed to his boat moored at the wharf "you'll know I'm on my way to bring Margaret ashore."

* * * * *

The Friendship strained on her anchor cables as the gentle southerly breeze fretted at her canvas.

Astir long before dawn, Jonathan saw the main topgallant being hoisted. He glanced in the direction of the wharf. Bobbing at its moorings, Arndell's rowing-boat was still there.

He plunged back into the tent and urgently shook the other hospital orderly who was still asleep.

"If the guard turns up, tell him it's the plague. Tell him to keep clear, that I've gone for help."

The man yawned.

"What?"

"Got to see Arndell," Jonathan whispered fiercely.

"You'll get shot or bayonetted."

Jonathan wasted neither time nor breath in reply. He dived at once for the gums which, like giant sentinels, still ringed much of the settlement. Darting, bounding, crawling, he was compelled to break cover only once, wading the stream, before flinging himself into Arndell's tent.

"Arndell?"

A groan escaped from a bundle of blankets on the floor in a corner. The stench of vomit lay heavy in the confined atmosphere of the tent.

"Arndell, what's happened? They're already setting sail."

One hand struggling to keep a blanket around his shoulders, the other pressing into the pit of his stomach, Arndell strove to sit up.

"I - er - I can't...."

The voice no more than a croak trailed into a faint whimper.

Jonathan lifted the surgeon and set him back firmly in his cot.

"What is it?"

Arndell, feeble, shook his head. Jonathan scanned an array of bottles and jars.

"Here, quick, columba root."

Arndell opened his mouth and Jonathan sluiced the entire contents of a bottle down the sick man's throat. Arndell gulped.

"I'm - I'm - sorry. Margaret.... I can't ....."

"Then, by God, I will."

Jonathan gently squeezed Arndell's shoulder, then hurled himself out of the tent and towards the waters of the cove.

"Halt!"

There was a crackle of musket fire.

Twenty yards of wharf lay between Jonathan and the rowing-boat. He stiffened, paused and glanced over his shoulder. Naked except for a blanket clutched about his shoulders, Arndell appeared, stumbling towards the armed guards.

"Let him go, let him go."

There were no more musket shots. Jonathan dragged the mooring rope free, leapt into the boat and seized a pair of oars.

Her forward anchor already weighed, Friendship was tugging at her stern cable. The southerly breeze freshened. The vessel's bows began slowly to swing in the direction of the mouth of Sydney Cove. The stern anchor jerked free of its sandy bed, Friendship shuddered and, following a series of lurches, she was rolling and under way.

Sitting up in his bunk, McQuaid was eating breakfast when the shudder of the vessel flung the tray across the cabin to crash on the floor.

"Margaret," he called.

Margaret, heavily cloaked, appeared in the doorway of McQuaid's cabin.

"Yes?"

"My breakfast," McQuaid said, pointing to the food scattered over the bunk and the floor. "Clean up and get me more." He peered closely at his wife in the dim light of the cabin. "The cloak? Why?"

Margaret turned to leave.

"I'll tell the cook," she said.

"I asked a question."

"Well?"

"Your cloak?"

"A chill breeze on deck."

"Deck?"

"An early morning stroll for a final glimpse of the settlement."

"A change of mind?"

"What d'you mean, Turnbull?"

"You told me, you've kept on telling me, you couldn't get away from the place soon enough."

"And it's true. Trying to convince myself the nightmare's almost over."

McQuaid flicked remnants of breakfast fish from the coverlet.

"Well, if you're now sufficiently convinced, I suggest you do as I say - clean up this cabin and get me more breakfast."

McQuaid was not slow to notice the look of anguish, which for a fleeting moment, seized Margaret's face as the Friendship began to roll.

"What's the matter?"

"I - I think we've set sail."

McQuaid clapped his hands.

"Celebrations then. To hell with breakfast. Get two goblets, two silver goblets."

"Y-yes, Turnbull."

Gathering the voluminous skirt about her Margaret hastened on deck and made her breathless way to the stern. In the wake of the former convict ship, a solitary figure bent over the oars of a rowing boat.

Arms frantically waving Margaret cried out, "Jonathan, Jonathan."

Clad in nothing more substantial than an embroidered silk nightgown and tasselled nightcap, Turnbull McQuaid emerged panting from the companionway.

"Stop her, Walton. Stop her."

Francis Walton remained intent upon the helm.

"Bloody women aboard ships. Stop her yourself."

McQuaid plunged past the ship's master and seized his wife by the hair. Walton spun round and hurled himself at the woman.

"Go, you damned blowse, go."

Margaret shrieked and toppled over the rail, head-first into the waters of Sydney Cove, leaving an open-mouthed McQuaid clutching a handful of auburn hair.

"Turn about, Walton. Turn about!" he roared.

Back now at the helm, Walton took both hands off the wheel and stepped aside.

"The ship's all yours, McQuaid. Full sail, a following wind, shoals to larboard and starboard.... Or explain to me how to turn about and I'll do it. Otherwise...."

McQuaid, teeth clenched, nostrils wide, stood stock-still. Walton's hands returned to Friendship's wheel.

"I order you, Walton."

Walton's hands were powerful hands. On countless occasions across five oceans, they had long grown accustomed to hauling his substantial frame from the foot of mainmasts to main topgallants and safely down again.

The thwack on McQuaid's thinly covered backside sent the shipowner careering across the deck. As the timbers of the companionway head brought him to a thudding halt, he screeched, "I'll have you...."

"Get yourself below."

"....hanged, hanged."

"Whatever you like, McQuaid, once we reach the Thames. Till then I'm in command of this ship.... Now, if you've no fancy for following that woman of yours - below with you!"

A wary eye on the stern of the other convict ship, no more than a cable's length ahead, Francis Walton, right hand firmly on the wheel, smiled and raised his left hand in brief farewell to the settlement at Sydney Cove.

* * * * *

The rowing boat, with its two occupants, would be beaching soon on a spit of sand close by the wharf of the new settlement.

But the brig Friendship, her canvas shuddering and filling as she cleared the waters of the cove to seek the Pacific Ocean, was destined never to make landfall again.

* * * * *

BIBLIOGRAPHY

Admiral Arthur Phillip. George Mackaness. Angus & Robertson, Sydney 1937

John and Nanbaree. Doris Chadwick. Nelson 1962

Journal of a First Fleet Surgeon. George B Worgan. Library of Australian History 1978

Sydney's First Four Years. Watkin Tench. Library of Australian History 1961

The British Sailor. Peter Kemp. Dent 1970

The British Seaman. Christopher Lloyd. Collins 1968

The Complete Herbal. Nicholas Culpeper.

The Convict Ships. Charles Bateson. Brown, Son & Ferguson 1959

The Timeless Land. Eleanor Dark. Collins 1941

Numerous history books including notably The Primitives and Historical Records of Australia.